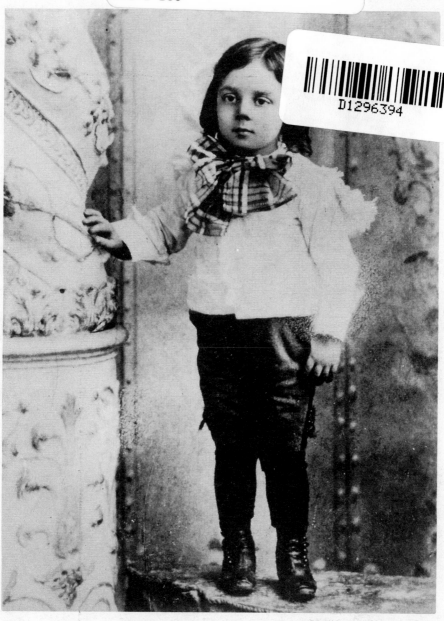

Buster Keaton, born 4 October, 1895.

In the same series

Projections 4½

In association with *Positif*

Film-makers on Film-making

Edited by John Boorman and Walter Donohue

faber and faber

LONDON · BOSTON

First published in 1995
by Faber and Faber Limited
3 Queen Square London WC1N 3AU

Printed in England by Clays Ltd, St Ives plc

A CIP record for this book
is available from the British Library

ISBN 0–571–17609–7

10 9 8 7 6 5 4 3 2 1

Contents

Acknowledgements

We wish to acknowledge the invaluable assistance of the stills library of the British Film Institute. Without the kindness and enthusiasm of its staff, we would not be able to achieve the high visual demands of our books. Thanks are also due to James Mackay and the staff at Basalisk Communications, to Mike Laye for the photographs from *The Last of England*, to Edmund C. Grainger of the Raymond Rohauer estate, and to the staff of Photoplay Productions.

Stills courtesy of BFI Stills, Posters and Design. Copyright for the stills are held by the following:

Warner Bros. (*Baby Doll, Bonnie and Clyde, The Huckersucker Proxy, McCabe and Mrs Miller, Mr Skeffington, Old Acquiantance, Other Men's Women, Rio Bravo, Springfield Rifle*); Universal (*The Beguiled, Foolish Wives, Ulzana's Raid*); Columbia (*The Big Heat, Close Encounters of the Third Kind, Mr Smith Goes to Washington, On the Waterfront, Taxi Driver*); Paramount (*The Desperate Hours, If ..., Vertigo*); MGM (*Greed, The Philadelphia Story*); United Artists (*The General, Stagecoach*); Cino del Duca (*Accattone*); Vicomte de Noalles (*L'Age d'Or*); Werner Herzog (*Aguirre, Wrath of God*); EOS/Marion Films (*L'Argent*); Goskino (*Battleship Potemkin*); Channel Four (*The Belly of an Architect*); Allied Artists (*The Big Combo*); Hal Roach (*Blockheads*); Riama/Pathé Consortium (*La Dolce Vita*); Pathé (*Les Enfants du Paradis*); Rank (*Hamlet, The Red Shoes*); Palomar (*The Heartbreak Kid*); RKO (*It's a Wonderful Life*); Sigma (*Le Jour se lève*); Basilisk Communications (*The Last of England*); Lion's Gate (*The Long Goodbye, Three Women, Vincent and Theo*); First National (*Long Pants*); Nero Film (*M*), Ealing (*The Man in the White Suit*); TCF (*My Darling Clementine*); GDF/Ultramar (*Odd Man Out*); AID (*The Raven*); Alfred Hitchcock Productions (*Rear Window*); Elias Querejeta (*The Spirit of the Beehive*); Pont/de Laurentiis (*La Strada*); Universalia (*La Terra Trema*); Aetos Film (*Teorema*); British Lion (*The Third Man*); RAI (*The Tree of Wooden Clogs*).

Fade In ...

John Boorman

Projections is an annual publication, so to protect that status we have called this extra centenary edition, 4½.

Since the purpose of *Projections* is to give a platform to film-makers to discuss the process, we were fascinated by *Positif*'s fortieth anniversary issue in which directors admired by the magazine were invited to write a piece about what *they* admired in cinema.

Michel Ciment follows with an account of *Positif*'s history, but I would add a word or two about this admirable magazine. It has maintained its passion for movies by the expedient of being written by a group of unpaid enthusiasts with no editor. They see only the films they want to see, nurture and defend the directors they love and thus avoid the film fatigue syndrome that afflicts so much film criticism.

The contributions in this collections are a result of the dialogue *Positif* has maintained with these film-makers over the years. They make a fascinating and penetrating picture of the messy and marvellous trade we ply.

Most of the contributions are stories; anecdotal, as you would expect from story-tellers. The only exception is Chris Marker's masterful analysis of *Vertigo*, but even his passion breaks through when he concludes that he could not possibly like anyone who dislike *Vertigo*.

The *Positif* Collection

Commissioned by the editors of *Positif*

Edited by Michel Ciment and Hubert Niogret
Translated by Yves Baignères

Michel Ciment

For Pleasure

A brief survey of forty positive years

The political, cultural and cinematic landscape has changed much in the forty years since the birth of *Positif*. So perhaps now is the moment to look back on the development of the magazine and to identify what it was that gave it its specific character and linked its successive generations of writers. Every Sunday for four decades, a circle of friends, film-buffs one and all, would meet at one of their houses to talk about contemporary cinema (or perhaps just talk!). They would discuss the content of coming issues, choose the cover, read submissions and vote on their inclusion. They would also choose the films to be analysed in depth and discuss future projects. Unlike most of the specialized press, the editorial board of *Positif* had the distinctive trait of having no editor-in-chief. Also, new contributors would always be welcomed. Often, at editorial meetings, writers who had contributed to the very first issues would find themselves sitting next to youngsters whose name had appeared only a year or so before.

Such successive waves of new writers have given the magazine its special sense of continuity and debate, two elements which make *Positif* the kind of publication one can genuinely describe as having a 'spirit' and a 'tone'. *Positif* is a true forum of opinion and, as such, receives contributions from like-minded readers who wish to join its ranks. These pieces interest us far more than the photocopied critical pieces sent out willy-nilly to the media by aspiring writers.

The fact that *Positif* was founded in 1952 in the provinces – in Lyon by Bernard Chardère, now a curator of the Lumière Institute – is extremely pertinent. A rejection of Parisian attitudes has always characterized the magazine, which goes some way to explaining why, even when it moved to Paris, the undisputed centre of cinema in France, it rarely ingratiated itself with the larger media powers or the adepts of 'cultural correctness'.

The original team from Lyon (Bernard Chardère, Jacques Demeure, Paul Louis Thirard and some other ephemeral contributors) was soon joined by Roger Tailleur, Michel Perez and Louis Seguin, patients at the next-door sanatorium of Saint-Hilaire-du-Touvet, who had founded their own magazine, *Sequences*. Coming to Paris (all except for Chardère), they were to meet Ado Kyrou, Robert Benayoun and Gerard Legrand, ex-editors of the surrealist

3

L'Age du Cinéma, who would bring another dimension to *Positif*. There were also men from the South: Marcel Oms (future host of the *Encounters* of Perpignan and editor of the *Cahiers de la Cinémathèque*), Raymond Borde, founder of the Cinémathèque of Toulouse, and Jean-Paul Torok. Finally, the militancy of Gerard Gozlan and Michele Firk, both Communists and already anti-Stalinist, reflected the left-wing sympathies shared by all the editors.

For the originality of *Positif* in the fifties, a decade culturally dominated by the left-wing, especially by the Communist Party and its allies, lay in its ability to express its love of cinema in all its forms (and Hollywood in particular), far away from Stalinist puritanism, while at the same time actively contributing to the political struggle. Those who haven't lived through that period cannot imagine the intense political rifts caused by the colonial wars, the still great moral influence of the Church and the role of state censorship. If one can accuse the magazine of having ignored important film-makers such as Hitchcock and Rossellini, its then editors would be justified in replying, as Sartre did in another context, but with more reason than him: 'We were wrong, but we were right to be wrong.' For the defence of Hitchcock and Rossellini was being conducted in other quarters in the name of 'grace' and other religious values, extolling 'miracles' or 'confessions'. It seemed more important to defend the values symbolized by those who often featured on our covers: the poetic and liberating Jean Vigo, a reference for a necessary renaissance of French cinema; Buñuel, the ironic examiner of bourgeois society and paragon of a total faithfulness to one's self; Kurosawa, the trail-blazer of a new Japanese cinema; Wajda, who expressed the first sign of unrest in the shameful regimes of the East; Antonioni, the creator of modernism, a modernism that would dominate the following decade; and, finally, Huston, the rebellious writer-director, who would upset the conventions of American cinema. For if *Positif* (along with *Cahiers du Cinéma*) represented twin poles of a love of Hollywood, *Positif* also favoured the American cinema which ran against the current, or at least didn't share the values of the Eisenhower years. Its gaze was drawn by dreams embodied by musicals (Minnelli, Donen), by the pessimism of *film noir*, by the radicalism of Aldrich or Welles, the liberalism of Brooks, the originality of Tashlin, Kubrick, and, lest we forget, by the anarchic follies of Tex Avery and Chuck Jones cartoons.

The internationalist vocation of the magazine, which would bloom in the sixties with the advent of so many new cinematic movements, has always been reflected by the number and quality of foreign contributors who brought their sympathetic but different sensibilities to the magazine: the Iranians, Gaffary and Hoveyda; the Italians, Fofi, Volta and Codelli; the Brazilian, Paranagua; the Czech, Kral; the Swede, Aghed; the Pole, Michalek; the Swiss, Buache; the Englishmen, Elsaesser and le Fanu and the Mexican, Perez-Turrent. The fact that some of these writers belonged to surrealist groups in their countries underlines again the real importance of that movement in relation to the magazine.

For, at *Positif*, cinema was not only never dissociated from politics, but was also seen in terms of painting, literature and other art forms. The auteur theory was therefore always coupled with a study of his collaborators, writers, designers, cameramen, composers. Without doubt, our constant interest in animation, for example, arose from a knowledge of art and cartoons. It is hardly surprising that three publishers known for their literary achievements – the *Editions de Minuit*, Eric Losfeld's *Terrain Vague* and *POL* – crossed *Positif*'s path. Numerous contributors have been, or still are, poets, novelists and essayists, from Frederic Vitoux, Jean-Philippe Domecq, Gerard Legrand and Emmanuel Carrere, to Jean-Loup Bourget, Petr KrÀl and Robert Benayoun.

The magazine was sometimes unjustly accused of underestimating French cinema. However, its international perspective does explain the magazine's comparative circumspection *vis-à-vis* the national product, and its desire to judge it in the light of that of other countries, without the all-too-common complacency, the red-cross spirit and buddiness all too often prevalent in the French press. For example, the *Nouvelle Vague* wasn't accepted whole and unconditionally as if it were a multi-talented, revolutionary phenomenon (and some careers were, indeed, brief). However, even though Godard remained *Positif*'s blind spot, there was praise for Truffaut's *Tirez sur le Pianiste*, Demy's *Lola*, and Rivette's *Paris Nous Appartient*. By contrast, the 'Left Bank' group, Marker, Resnais, Varda and Franju, were closer to the magazine's sensibilities. Also, those who could not profit from the prevailing group snobbery – directors such as Sautet, Deville, Cavalier and Pialat – also had to be supported.

Labels are reassuring. *Positif*, however, abhors all classifications and its freedom of expression has not enjoyed universal support. Either too theoretical or not enough, such are the accusations that have been levelled at it. How could these intellectuals revel in the labyrinth of *L'Anée Dernière à Marienbad*, the speculations of Raoul Ruiz and Peter Greenaway brainteasers, while at the same time defend Hammer horror films and Michael Powell's *Peeping Tom*, all unanimously rejected by 'serious' writers, as was Italian comedy, then in its golden age? These contributors, messengers for the FLN, signatories of the 121 Manifesto, could sing the praises of so-called 'opiums of the masses' such as Anthony Mann westerns or Blake Edwards comedies and not necessarily find qualities in the whole Third World cinema! Not to follow the prevailing wind, but rather to explore the future of cinema or rediscover buried treasures can be a hazardous thing. One runs the risk of being accused of élitism, or anachronism for having revived past pleasures.

The early sixties, however, were different. Other critics, up till then not so politically aware and not as curious about foreign cinema (apart from

5

Hollywood) as *Positif*, recognized the value of ideology, learnt the curiosity of true lovers of cinema and rallied to positions always held by the magazine. This marvellous decade saw the defence of what was innovatory in world cinema: the Polish renaissance with Polanski and Skolimowski; the Hungarian with Jancsó, Gall and Szabó; the Russian with Tarkovski, Ioselliani and Panfilov; the Italian with Bellocchio, Bertolucci and Mingozzi; the Brazilian with Rocha, Guerra and Diegues; the Czech with Forman, Passer and Chytilova. In their enthusiasm for discovery, *Positif* and *Cahiers* launched their weeks of new films. Unfortunately, the end of the decade and the beginning of the next saw *Cahiers* firmly stuck in a Maoist rut, revelling in the Cultural Revolution and regurgitating chunks of Peking information which sang the praises of the work camps. In spite of the gibes of the admirers of the Red Guards, *Positif* (while welcoming, though not surprised by the events of May 1968) provided shelter to those who always resist such zealous excesses. In this poisonous climate, as the Vietnam War fanned the flames of anti-Americanism, *Positif* refused to join in the backlash against American filmmakers. These were directors who expressly did not share the dominating values of their society and were renewing the forms and themes of Hollywood cinema: Altman, Hellman, Scorsese, Coppola, Rafelson, Schatzberg, Pollack, Malik, Woody Allen.

Calm always follows the storm. Although the subjects of conflict are less obvious, there is still a need to fight. But the context has changed. *Positif* was born at a time when a profound and intense love of cinema was being stimulated by the burgeoning enthusiasm of the Federation of Ciné-clubs. In every town, however small, it was possible to see regularly the classics of world cinema. Such cultural activity gave birth to innumerable magazines.

The ciné-clubs, irreplaceable cultural landmarks, have fallen by the wayside to be replaced by more spectacular if less culturally ambitious audiovisual organizations. Since television plays less and less of a role in showing exclusively English-language and French films, nothing has replaced the industry of the ciné-clubs. Theatrical distribution is in a sorry state. The few independents searching for originality fall prey to the dominance of certain exhibitors (for example, the Pathé-Gaumont alliance is a kind of monopoly unheard of in America) and find it impossible to balance their books by selling their films to television.

The vivacious hunger for the new, which still characterizes certain audiences, explains the success of the cinema festivals of which France has so many and which each year, for a short while, thanks to a retrospective, allow local audiences to discover less well-known works of the past and present. More than ever, *Positif* has fulfilled its duties in that field. The importance we have given to rediscovered films and historical research seems to us vital: any reflection of the present and future state of cinema cannot ignore an exploration of the past and its gifts.

The affirmation of cinematic curiosity, of artistic choice, of historical knowledge and critical analysis, seems to us born out of a polemical attitude in the face of promotional excesses and the ever-shrinking space given over to film criticism in the popular press.

Neither an academic publication nor a promotional magazine, *Positif* is blessed with a readership composed of film-makers, students, film-buffs and fans, pure and simple. Its 400th issue, now being published in English, also shows the confidence many directors have in us and the dialogue established in our columns between critics and creators. Painting, literature and music have known such collaborations, thus refuting the argument that the gap between creators and critics is unbridgeable. The best proof of this mutual esteem between critics and creators was the protest signed by fifty-five prestigious directors (including Woody Allen, Ingmar Bergman, Federico Fellini, Jean-Luc Godard and Stanley Kubrick) when the editorial independence of our magazine was threatened by the then editor. It attributed the international reputation of the magazine to 'the independence and integrity of its editorial board, to its quality of analysis, the seriousness of its research and information, the open-mindedness of its contributors'.

For the 400th issue, we asked our favourite film-makers to write a piece about an actor, or a film, or a director who has had a special significance for them, or who has evoked a strong response in them. Some played the game, others played variations on it, but whatever they did, we were delighted ...

To conclude, since it is a British publisher who is presenting this collection, I'd like to recall the relationship between the magazine and British cinema. Making a rare critical mistake, François Truffaut declared that the words 'cinema' and 'British' were contradictory and only awarded Hitchcock the label of director. To us – and often against the current – the opposite has always seemed true. A genuine creativity was evident on the other side of the Channel, in the form of realism (Karel Reisz's Free Cinema, Ken Loach, Stephen Frears, Mike Leigh), in the exploration of a fantastic cultural mythology (Hammer horrors), in the scrupulous adaptation of literary works (David Lean), in its use of the plastic arts (Peter Greenaway and his aesthetic extravagances), and, finally, in the daring and singular romanticism of true mavericks such as Michael Powell and John Boorman. *Positif* is proud to have helped disseminate the names of these unique talents.

Robert Altman

The actor as *auteur*

When I watch a film by Stephen Frears or Mike Leigh, I encounter the kind of cinema which interests me more than that which I usually see. Directors who use actors like painters use pigment or colour are rare. Most directors believe the most important element of a film is the script; that they must tell the actors what to do. Actors are not allowed to be *auteurs*. Directors are becoming increasingly known as *auteurs*: there are innumerable reports of conflicts arising between writers and directors as to who is the real author of a film. But it seems to me that the increasingly indefinable relationship between actor and director has been underestimated. For my part, I believe actors, notwithstanding the adulation they receive, aren't famous enough. What Robin Williams contributed to *Aladdin*, for example, could not have been the work of either a director, a writer or an animator. The creativity contained in his work was his alone. Actors receive praise and awards, but their achievements go unnoticed. Many actors – such as Robin Williams and Roberto Benigni – are genuine artists, true creators.

Prêt-à-Porter, the film I am currently preparing, has no clearly defined script as far as the atmosphere and the emotions the audience will find on screen are concerned. But I've chosen my actors according to their personalities and what they can bring to the work. I know that, mid-March, I shall be directing Tim Robbins and Julia Roberts, and I've sketched out the essentials of what I want their scenes to express. But the scenes that will end up on screen will be quite different from the ones I've imagined, because when the three of us meet on set, they will give me their ideas and the scenes will be created as we shoot them. The more confidence I have in an actor, the more I make him create. People tell me, 'It's wonderful what you managed to do with so-and-so.' But all I did with so-and-so was to insist that he or she invent. I am not the Creator, but a trainer shouting from the ringside, 'Throw him a left! Throw him a left!' The man who throws and receives the punches is the boxer, not me. It's something people don't talk enough about.

When I saw *Naked*, I asked myself who should be credited with the script. In such a film, the actor is forced to become a considerable artist, and the differences between creation and interpretation get very blurred. I have the impression that critics, people who think about cinema, tend to ignore this fact, even though they understand what it means intellectually. In a way, the actors write their parts. I talked to Tim Robbins on the phone about his part.

He was thinking not about turning up on set and reciting his lines, but about his character. He's playing a sports journalist, and he wants to arrive smoking a cigar. He's looking for the truth of the character. In our society, smoking a cigar is now considered an act of aggression: you know that most of the people around you would prefer you not to. If you then carry on smoking the cigar, they become hostile. Tim Robbins, therefore, will have to deal with Julia Roberts, who may refuse to share the set with someone smoking a cigar and detest him as a result. No one imagines this will be the case, but let's just suppose it is. Tim Robbins will then suggest leaving the room and stepping out on to the terrace. Suddenly, the scene someone has written, a scene I have visualized, changes direction solely because of the cigar and the attitude of the two characters towards it. The dialogue remains the same, as does the dramatic development, but suddenly we believe in the characters because their behaviour grew organically out of the actors. This has nothing to do with a scene in a play where the author indicates that a character is smoking a cigar.

Julia Roberts, meanwhile, is thinking about something else. Both actors will meet for the first time on my set. They have both been preparing for it and, in doing so, have manipulated each other in their heads. Both believe the other will go along with what he or she has planned, and have imagined the possible reactions. But when they find themselves face to face, they won't be able to control each other any more; they'll end up reacting just like their characters. This also happens in life. However much we prepare for a given situation, we always end up improvising.

I see this every time I make a film. Actors come to see me and talk about themselves. What they tell me contributes to the development of their scenes, which are re-written not by the writer but according to the actors' behaviour. You see this in the work of John Cassavetes and Mike Leigh. This is perhaps why actors ask to be in my films. They don't really know why they do this, but they've seen things happen on screen and want to participate in the process, to become creative, to enjoy a certain artistic freedom. Some actors can't live in such a situation, but most can.

Believing she'd suit the part because of the emotional charge of the text and the situation she's placed in, I cast Andie MacDowell as the mother in *Short Cuts*. But what Andie managed to do was way beyond what I had imagined. She plays a mother who fulfils her duty in every way, but is still in a state of chaos. In *Nashville*, Gwen Welles plays a waitress who tries to sing. Even today, I don't know whether Gwen can sing or not. I do know she spent months practising and taking lessons. She arrived on set and sang so badly that her character broke our hearts. She died last year, and I wouldn't be able to say whether she really couldn't sing or whether she knew instinctively that to sing badly was the right way to play the character.

Shelley Duvall's performance in *Three Women* is equally mysterious. Shelley herself wrote the short texts we hear in the film. They are so naive coming from an adult, they become moving; we think we're in the presence of a child. I still don't know whether the texts were her way of preparing the part intelligently or whether she genuinely thought they were good literature. I rather think she was following her intuition. I certainly wouldn't have been capable of writing such lines for her. When Elliott Gould arrived on the set of *M.A.S.H.*, he refused to act in the style established by the rest of the cast and everything had to change. Because everyone turned against him, he needed an ally and so befriended Donald Sutherland. I witnessed all this and let it happen. It went way beyond the limits of the script. The writer, Ring Lardner Jr., was terrified. I wasn't, because I had discovered a great truth. Elliott behaved the same way in *The Long Goodbye*. As for *California Split*, there wasn't even a story to start from. Perhaps this is what Mike Leigh and his actors are aiming for when they rehearse for so long. Creativity springs from the actors; they are more than just interpreters. If one sees qualities in my films, those qualities arise out of the chemistry of the ensemble. I depend on my actors. One of them starts a scene, another reacts, and before you know it, something's happened. The film's sent to the lab, you watch the rushes and see a wonderful scene. Who is the *auteur* of what we see on screen? All of us.

Altman's *auteurs*: Julie Christie ...

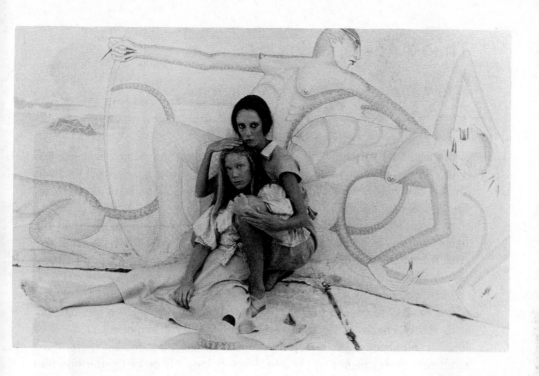

Opposite above: Nina Van Pallandt and Elliot Gould ...

Opposite: Paul Rhys and Tim Roth ...

Above: Sissy Spacek and Shelley Duvall.

Theo Angelopoulos

A few shots rescued from oblivion

When asked the question 'What are the directors or films which have marked you?', I've always mentioned, amongst others, Murnau, Mizoguchi, Orson Welles, Dreyer, Antonioni, *Ugetsy*, *Sunrise*, *The Magnificent Ambersons*, *Ordet*, *L'avventura*.

As I get older and refashion my personal history of cinema, I forget the names and the films. A few gestures, a few faces, words, a few shots are rescued from the oblivion of an ocean of innumerable works. They don't always belong to the directors and films mentioned above.

The cry 'I don't want to die!' in Michael Curtiz's *Angels With Dirty Faces*; Orson Welles's damaged face in *Touch of Evil*; the young Irish girl dancing with Henry Fonda in *My Darling Clementine*; Ingrid Bergman's face full of love in *Notorious*; Peter Lorre's monotone whistling in *M*; these short moments, shots cut out of the films they belong to, make up the one film which marked me, the film which still does.

Olivier Assayas

Andy Warhol

How can I pick my way through the tangled mass of favourite films and choose from the absurdly different works which have accompanied me ever since I started wanting to make films – the films which give me the energy and conviction to continue when I am most discouraged, or those which, quickly or slowly, have criss-crossed my work, my doubts and preoccupations?

I would have liked to talk about someone living, about a friend. I would have liked to place a wager on the present, and seized on an image, even if fleeting, rather than pay my respects to my elders, lay a wreath on some grave or other, or flick through a dictionary.

I shall try to do none of these things. Instead, I shall say a few words about a work that possesses the quality I believe to be more important than any other: the ability to seize the moment in all its fragility, movement and absurdity – an absurdity which enriches it, since once the moment has passed, this absurdity is immediately lost – the ability to create an eternal present, not fixed but animated by constant movement.

This could apply to any period when cinema was collectively alive, not only as cinema but as art. I don't mean this grandiloquently, but in the simplest sense of the term: a time when cinema, as an interpretation of the world, as an instrument for expressing a new perception, could contribute to the world and thereby transform it. This could apply to any avant-garde (there haven't been many), to any *Nouvelle Vague* (and there's only been one, in different places). It could apply to either Robert Bresson or Guy Debord.

But I'm also thinking of Andy Warhol, whose strange fate was to become both one of the most famous artists of his age and one of the least understood film-makers. The history and analysis of his work, which I believe to be the most important and essential in American cinema, needs to be rewritten. Clearly, this is not the place to do so, yet sooner or later we will have to recognize his true role as a pioneer of cinema.

He was an unmethodical and generous innovator who, in four or five years of frenzied, enthusiastic activity, motivated by nothing but the clarity and simplicity of desire, recreated for his own use the universe of cinema, and all its cosmology and logistical processes, in such a way that all the rules of cinema could be constantly reinvented.

He started in the limited field of experimental cinema, on 16 mm black and white, and in primitive silence. Step by step, and on his own terms, he remade and rediscovered the history of cinema's evolution. First came sound, then colour, and finally fiction, which I believe is the most fascinating part, the kernel of his work.

Warhol wasn't taken seriously, just as people had not taken Cocteau seriously. The group of misfits he assembled around him like a family were regarded as absurd as they copied and questioned, like a cabaret act, the rituals and manners of Hollywood.

Classical cinema was in its death throes. Asphyxiated by mannerisms, it was dying from having exploited artifice to the death, the artifice of genres, of 'stars'. Warhol seemed to be presenting an obscene caricature of all this, as if he'd bought at rock-bottom prices the Hollywood junk-bonds nobody wanted any more. It was as if he had appropriated Hollywood in order to subvert it, to push into the visibility of pornography what in the syntax of desire had until then been kept invisible.

All this was the most superficial aspect of Warhol's procedure. Everyone knows that, even though the media smoke-screen behind which he liked to hide communicated this image, in no way did his films speak to Hollywood and even less to the Hollywood melodramas whose pathos could only have horrified him.

Nevertheless this aspect was essential in the crucial influence he had over European cinema: from Fassbinder and his numerous acolytes in the underground cinema of the seventies to Almodóvar today, in a form which would then have been called 'sanitized'. (That said, it was Warhol himself who, after the famous attempt on his life in 1968, when he had lost interest in cinema – he had completed his journey anyway – 'franchised' his style to Paul Morrissey and others.)

The only really important aspect of this playful relationship with classical cinema is that – in part – it helped Warhol find a solution to the most difficult problem he faced during his reinvention of the form: the problem of fiction.

I am well aware that theoretical terminology – a terminology which becomes clumsy only if one expresses it, which he never did – immediately sounds wrong when applied to Warhol, in that it does not do justice to the grace and lightness with which he solved the problem.

His innovation was to invert the problem. Instead of appropriating the cheap pathos of traditional fiction and giving it to his actors to imitate, he situated it in reality. Because Warhol's aim was *physically* to film a moment, a *situation*, he affirmed that his actors, his 'superstars', should first become fictional characters in order for him not to direct but to film them as if they were in a documentary. The circumstances were indeed fictitious, but improvisation was legitimized by the fact that either the actors had assimilated the arbitrariness of dramatic invention, or Warhol had created it himself beforehand. Improvisation, therefore, became part of the act of filming.

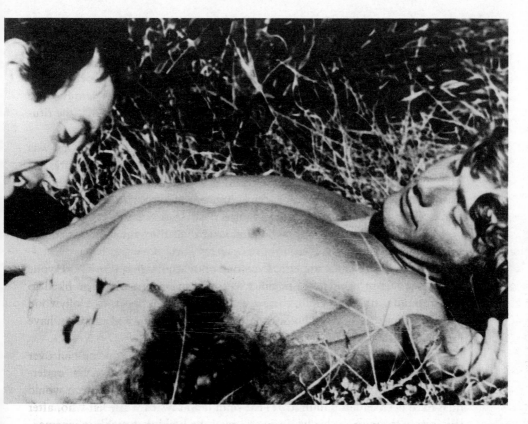

Warhol: *Lonesome Cowboys.*

And this cheap pathos of conventional cinema, begging audiences for their compassion and tears – and occasionally getting them – thus became real, became a Polaroid of the world, exhibiting its self-destruction and, being the accomplice of its objects, their true downfall. It revealed itself in all its crude veracity; and this crude veracity unmasked the spectator, revealed his indifference (the 'hypocritical reader' of Baudelaire's phrase), his cruelty, his complicity, his connivance in the process of destruction – during which he behaves as if he were *moved*. Such is the pulse of the world, the witness of life.

Pupi Avati

Memories

Summer 1990, by the sea, at Torvaianica

Midnight in this big house. His wife Franca went to bed early after dinner, leaving us alone by the swimming pool. And as she left, she handed him over to me, like a child, with an eloquent glance.

Ugo has been depressed for some time now, racked by the illogical anxiety he is prone to. There are all kinds of reasons for it, the strongest being the sudden awareness of advancing age. Everyone who approaches him knows that it's an idea he obstinately refuses either to accept or prepare himself for.

But already, all around him, there are the first signs of the land to which he, like all mortals, is making his way. These signs are more and more evident, more and more numerous. They're besieging him.

It's very late when I get to my car. I open the door and he suddenly tells me he wants to die. I turn round. He smiles a little awkwardly, a touch embarrassed perhaps by what he's just said. But I know it's true, I know that's what he wants. A street lamp illuminates the road, and rays of white light from the villa pierce through the hedge. I can still see Ugo's eyes that night, those lucid, frightened eyes. I pretend not to understand, ask him what he's talking about – hell, I shake his hand and hold it tightly – but he doesn't respond, he simply lets it happen. That's all.

I tell him he has an infinite number of things left to achieve in films, on television and – now he's returned to the stage with such success in France – in the theatre. He nods but I know he isn't listening. He manages a smile. And I get into the car.

Autumn 1972

I'd been living in Rome for four years and I was out of work, writing stories nobody liked. But I was different from the others who, like me, tramped in and out of producers' offices with their scripts under their arms; I had two independent films, made in Bologna, to my name. Two flops. So I was expiating this mistake in the capital, playing the uncomfortable role of someone who is looking not for the first, but the third opportunity of showing his talent.

During these four interminable years, all my moral, physical and economic resources had become exhausted. Most of all, I'd lost the ability to delude myself, an ability I had once possessed in abundance. It was when the temptation to surrender was at its strongest that divine providence intervened: Ugo Tognazzi, the most popular actor of the time, had by chance read one of my scripts and, without expecting any immediate reward, had decided to play the lead. Out of the many emotions I've experienced in my life, this was one of the strongest. Out of the many wonderful days, this was one of the most luminous. My wife wept in the corridor, incredulous, while my brother and I phoned relatives, friends, everyone, to announce the good news. And so, in the summer of 1973, we made this film with Ugo Tognazzi.

I could recreate every moment of the tension we felt in the days leading up to meeting the star, whom we had all seen on the screen since we were young, and who now, accompanied by a retinue of secretaries, make-up artists, hairdressers and press-attachés, was suddenly going to appear in a small village deep in the Emilian countryside. He would be staying on the top floor of a motel where we had improvised a kind of suite by knocking together several rooms. We cheerfully carried on working, pretending that it was quite normal to be waiting for Ugo Tognazzi. I convinced myself that I was there to direct him: to tell him what to do and say every day for thousands of shots; to give him precise instructions on how to move, open the door, frown, smile, drink, telephone, kneel, cry, scream with rage. And then after each take, amidst an expectant silence, I'd cross over to him and give him my opinion – I, who had been used to directing friends, relatives, the local eccentrics.

Late that Saturday afternoon his shiny black sports car pulled up in the village square and everything – nature, men, objects – went silent. The door of the car slowly opened and his face appeared. The hotelier started the applause and Ugo, maybe a little embarrassed, smiled.

I knew I owed everything to this man who, refusing other projects, had come all this way to be in my film. I knew that, without him, I would never have been able to escape from my nightmare.

Aware of this, I went up to him and embraced him, and our relationship developed with the same certainty throughout the film. It was a mixture of love, psychological dependence, and a return to childhood. At the end of each take, my 'Cut!' resounded like an expression of gratitude. Everything he did amazed me; I found myself agreeing with his every suggestion even before he'd finished making it. I don't know whether one can really love an actor, to feel one's need of him and fear him at the same time. Most of all, to be afraid of disappointing him. This was how I 'directed' Tognazzi in this film, in a state of perpetual and ecstatic admiration.

But it was thanks to this film that I was able to begin my career and work steadily, finding new possibilities year after year.

Fifteen years passed after our first collaboration, and whenever I thought about the film, I felt uncomfortable, frustrated. I had had at my disposal one of the greatest talents of our cinema and I hadn't managed to make a film of which either he or I could be really proud.

So by the time I had established myself as a director, and my beginner's fears had gone, I felt ready to attempt a new experience. The circumstances were by now totally different: a whole new generation of brilliant actors were beginning to take the places once reserved for Sordi, Gassman, Manfredi and Tognazzi.

Ugo too had sensed this change and knew he was in danger of being pushed aside.

So, developing an idea of my brother's, I decided to call him and offer him a film, telling him we'd write it specially for him. The film would be a kind of tribute, with a quiet, understated *mise-en-scène* that would tell in the most moving way possible the story of the hero, a manager of a football team at the bottom of the league, a man incapable of adapting himself to 'new ideas' who tries to survive despite the fraud and subterfuges which, in a way, had served to tranquillize an Italy that was now destined to disappear for ever.

Even in that very first conversation, it was moving to hear how enthusiastic, how immediately excited and curious he was. I knew I'd made him happy. In a sense, I was trying to return the immense favour he had granted me some fifteen years before. We made the film and, without any doubt, Ugo put the best of himself into it. I believe that *Ultimo minuto*, although not significant in my personal filmography, certainly was in Ugo's. I know that, for some years beforehand, Ugo hadn't been as convincing or as personally involved in a part as he was in this one. He dug deep into his most intimate and painful experiences, he put so much of himself into the role.

We all knew, Franca and his children included, that he needed this film, that it had come at the right time, that the success which awaited him would chase away the anxieties that were beginning to haunt him. All the screenings we arranged, an infinite number, which Ugo always attended even if we weren't expecting him. This confirmation that he felt the film to be his gave me immense pleasure and made us even more confident of success.

Alas, the box-office receipts were very disappointing. Cannes refused to take the film and, even though Ugo's performance was universally praised by the critics, he didn't receive a single award. The success I had promised him, which would have vindicated him and put him back in the saddle, didn't happen.

But the film did deepen our friendship and make Ugo one of the people I consider most special in my life. His personality, his truth, seemed covered by a hard, jagged shell that protected him from the assaults of the outside world. But if you knew how to wait, this shell would open, suddenly and at the most unexpected moments, and you would have to be ready to accept his intimacy, his trust, his capacity for confiding in you his most private, painful and terrible experiences as well as his most blessed ones, experiences he could both cry and laugh about.

Ugo confessed to me things that had probably never been told in the confessional, because suddenly – and I don't know to what I owe this strange circumstance – he decided he could trust me, that he could open up in front of me without fear of betrayal. So he spoke to me about his work in a totally new perspective, about his family, his fears, about so many things which I shan't describe here and which I shall never repeat, but which stay with me and make him, for me, even more noble. Because he was profoundly human. There were occasions, when others hadn't immediately recognized his need to confide in them, when he'd suddenly feel too exposed, too removed from the 'character' behind which he usually hid. He'd instantly withdraw into himself, his claws would come out, and his nostrils would flare with the anger of an old peasant. It was as if he were about to attack and reconquer the territory he'd lost. He would thus avenge all he had offered of himself, all that was precious, special and misunderstood. There are plenty of descriptions of his fraternal relationships with various *auteurs* (from Ferreri to Monicelli, from Scola to Bertolucci) but those that describe his negative relationships, the arguments, misunderstandings and disappointments, would be just as rewarding.

He was a creator of spaces and occasions into which he would welcome friends and relations. Invitations to dinner were a way of avoiding the solitude, the great emptiness that silence could create and that he'd never learnt to fill. And the food he'd cook, the way he'd serve it so affectionately to his friends, became a kind of blackmail, a demand.

But towards the end, the evenings, the vast salons, the long tables, the swimming pools, the tennis courts and the armchairs were empty. And he was perhaps there, waiting. He was perhaps the first Italian actor to understand, in a clear and definitive manner, what playing a part on screen consisted of. He rejected the kind of seductiveness which brings an actor in front of the camera through a series of glimpses and deliberate emphases, and instead waited for the camera itself to find, in the tiniest changes of expression, the movements of his soul, the deepest and most mysterious emotional truths. There was no complacency in Tognazzi. He was the first to make me understand that the truth of what one says, of the emotions one feels, must emerge in spite of us; that this truth is already present in the situations we are in, and that we must simply let it live and breathe without imposing any conditions on it.

On set, he knew how to communicate without artifice the simplicity and naturalness that were his gifts from God. This was far removed from 'technique'. In how many films did Ugo succeed in being 'true' in situations which were clearly the opposite? But he swims impassively against the current, without seeming to worry about what is going on around him. He had such courage! How confidently he would take risks, go against the current, throw himself into hopeless projects, against all advice and without any of the guarantees other actors of the time would more prudently have demanded.

Ugo is there in all the adventurous Italian cinema of those years. He was the standard-bearer. Even at the end, although hardly young, he still managed to be beautiful. Many people would tell him this and he'd joke about it. His face had the glow of someone who had been very much loved; a particular luminosity, difficult to describe. And with his moustache, which from now on he always wore with pride, he looked a lot like my father. Or was it me who wanted him to look like my father?

I started up the car, manoeuvred. He's there shutting the wooden gates. I drive up to him: 'You didn't mean it seriously, what you said?' He looks at me. He waits a moment and then nods. Yes.

I speed away.

I don't think I saw him again. I think that was the last time.

John Boorman

Lee Marvin

Lee Marvin.

Movie stars look smaller in the flesh than on screen. Lee Marvin was even bigger off than on.

We first met in London in 1966, in a Soho restaurant. A Gulliver, he towered above us. His movements were careful and surprisingly gentle, as though he were afraid a sudden jerk of his hand might inadvertently crush the passing skull of an Italian waiter.

The impression of size came partly from the huge head. The conflicts and contradictions that made up the man were chiselled into the red granite of that face: the hard jaw, the big sensual mouth, the prize-fighter's nose, the fine white hair; and, peering out from two deep holes chipped out of the rock, those two ironic eyes that seemed to say, 'How did I get trapped inside this hulk?'

Judd Bernard was a press agent who wanted to be a producer. He had an option on a script that he had sent to me and Lee. Judd was in a state of high excitement. Lee had just won the Academy Award for *Cat Ballou*. He was in London shooting *The Professionals*. He was hot. And here he was at the table.

Judd talked about Lee's films, his TV series *M-Squad*. He knew all the dirt and gossip, and he heaped flattery on Lee. He was funny and steeped in movie lore, but he couldn't stop. He was like a jazz musician improvising a solo. He couldn't get off it. He didn't really want to get off it because, as long as he kept talking, Lee was under his spell, captive.

Lee and I sat there, taking each other in. Finally, a waiter put a menu in front of Judd's face. It came down like a curtain on his act. Lee said to me, 'So what do you make of this script?' Judd winced. It was the direct question he wanted to avoid. He had told me to enthuse about the character, to describe juicy scenes I would add. Judd knew it was a lousy script, but he was a salesman. 'Don't talk about the product, talk about what it can bring: admiration, happiness, money,' he advised me. Lee looked at me with those eyes that saw through everything, and I found myself saying, 'It's bad.' It was a sword through Judd's heart. He blustered. Lee cut across him, 'I agree. So why are you here?' I mumbled something to the effect that I would like to explore this character, make a movie about a man you knew nothing about, except by gestures and movements. Anyway, I was very vague. I was hardly clear about what I meant myself.

Afterwards, Judd was disgusted with me: 'You threw it away.' He went off to LA the next day. An hour after he left, Lee called me: 'You want to talk about this thing?' We spent three evenings doing that. Lee spoke a lot about violence, the violence he had perpetrated during the war, the violence done to him (he was shot by the Japanese). He was fascinated by the capacity for violence in himself that the war had forced him to explore. Violence enthralled him, yet deeply shamed him. By extension, he believed America was founded in violence, genocide, and that it was a nation condemned to project its violent past into its future.

His conversation was allusive and cryptic. You had to find your way through it like a minefield. If you made a false move he would blow you away with a scathing remark or a sarcastic put-down. The thick skin was acquired as protective covering by the seventeen-year-old Marine to conceal a nascent artistic temperament. It had callused into his acting persona. As we talked, I began to realize that the film which was forming in my mind was an exploration of Marvin and his relationship to violence, the impulse to act and the self-disgust that followed.

One night we had been drinking. It was late, late enough and drunk enough for the deepest commitments and silliest promises to be made. Lee said, 'I'll do this flick with you, kid. One condition.' And he threw the script out of the window. It fell three floors and flopped open on to the wet street where the draught from passing cars made it flutter like a dying bird. It was a perfect Lee Marvin gesture. It said: ignore the conventions, be daring, throw away the rule book, and I'll go all the way with you.

I called Judd and said that Lee had agreed to make the picture. Judd spoke to Lee's agent, who told him that when Lee got drunk he always agreed to do everybody's picture. Forget it.

A week later, Lee returned to LA. A call came from an astonished Judd. Marvin was telling everyone that this was his next picture. I should get out to LA right away.

Lee called a meeting with the head of MGM and the producers. The MGM moguls were delighted to have a Lee Marvin picture, but they had no idea what it was. Lee made a brief speech: 'I have script approval?' Yes. 'I have cast and crew approval?' Yes. 'I defer them to John.' He turned on his heel and left. All eyes fell on me, a young, unknown British director. I felt somewhat embarrassed and certainly undeserving, but I saw in those eyes something I did not recognize.

Later I saw that look lavished on others. It was more than deference, it was awe. Power had shifted. The power to get a movie made. It had passed to me.

Lee knew better than I that our bold plans for *Point Blank* would be eroded and emasculated by the studio and producers unless I was empowered. He did not just do it, he did it with a characteristic gesture.

I brought two friends over, Alex Jacobs and Bill Stair. We locked ourselves in a room and wrote the script in three weeks. I would drop by Lee's Malibu house every other day and describe the scenes we had written. Lee would listen carefully, then search for the gesture that would express through his character the intentions of the scene.

Walker (Lee Marvin) bursts into his wife's apartment intent on killing the friend who betrayed him. He expects to find him in his wife's bed. The bed is empty, but the twisted sheets suggest a sexual aftermath. He shoots the bed with the massive Smith and Wesson .44 Magnum. (Lee chose it long before Clint.)

Lee's idea was to exaggerate the recoil so that it appeared to drive his arm back, suggesting that the gun was an externalization of his own violence which he could not wholly control. I had the walls covered in antique mirrors so that, in the silence after firing the gun, he could catch a glimpse of his reflection. He is startled by the fractured image of himself, his true opponent. It was Lee's idea that he should find himself alone in the room save for his mirror image. It was mine to fracture the reflection.

We continued the sexual metaphor as the scene developed. He slumps down into a sofa, the gun hangs limp from his hand, the spent bullets drop on to the marble table in slow motion, dancing on the cold, hard surface. It was our ambitious aim that Walker's cold, hard face would be impenetrable, but that these gestures, these visual metaphors would externalize his feelings. The film followed the pattern of our conversations in London, he defending, I probing the defences – the implacable face and the revealing image.

The scripted scene that followed required Walker to ask his estranged wife a series of questions about the whereabouts of Reese, her lover, his friend.

When I rehearsed the scene, Lee could not say his lines. Sharon Acker, playing his wife, waited for the questions, and when they failed to come, she answered them anyway.

Lee was signalling to me that we had taken the character into such a deathly void that he could not interrogate. I quickly rewrote her responses so that they made sense without the questions. As we shot the scene, she hears the questions in her head and answers them. Walker listens, his face drained and ravaged.

One of the many things Lee taught me was that an actor's duty is to defend his character against the script and, if necessary, the director. We had talked a lot during rehearsals, but on the first day of shooting Lee said, 'I'm on my side of the camera, you're on yours. Stay there.' And it was true that we hardly spoke after that, but our understanding was complete. We had an instructive understanding of each other's mind that jumped over language. Although we remained friends until his death, wherever we met we had little to say to each other. It was always more comfortable to have others around who could do the talking, a Judd Bernard, so that we could simply take each other in without words.

I also learnt from Lee the importance of economy. Lee was always searching for a way of expressing the idea or emotion in a sharper, simpler, clearer way. These lessons were put to the test in our next film together, *Hell in the Pacific*, which had almost no dialogue since it was about the relationship of two men who could not speak each other's language. Lee and I shared an admiration for the silent era of cinema and in this film we had to relearn film-making from its beginnings.

Towards the end of the shooting schedule on *Point Blank* we found ourselves in Alcatraz. I was exhausted. I had a panic attack. I could not think of where to put the camera, what the first set-up should be. Lee was suddenly at my side. He said, 'Are you in trouble?' I didn't reply. 'Leave it to me!' he said. Moments later I heard him roaring and yelling. The production manager ran over to me saying, 'Have you seen the state Lee's in? He's falling-over drunk. There's no way you can shoot on him. We're getting black coffee, walk him around, try to sober him up.'

With the pressure off, I worked out the sequence of shots in ten minutes. I went over to Lee and told him I had figured it out. He made a sudden and total recovery.

William Hurt said that he knew nothing about film acting until he worked with Lee. I certainly didn't. He was admired more by actors and directors than by critics. He had a powerful mind and almost uncanny perception. He was one of the few truly great men I ever knew. When he died, there was a huge hole in the fabric of the world.

Catherine Breillat

One day I saw *Baby Doll* ...

One day I went into the Action Christine cinema at two o'clock in the afternoon and came out at midnight. I was transported, determined to write *36 fillette* as if the film I had just seen had given me the password.

I'd seen all Kazan's films before, except this one. And I haven't seen it since.

I haven't stopped liking it, but I'd *forgotten* it. I used to say it was the only film where the girl is both sublime and stupid, haughty and banal, candid and calculating; where her seducer seduces her by what is repellent in him. He hasn't the beauty of the Devil, far from it. Swarthy, vulgar, with his piggish but piercing eyes, he is the Devil in person. He embodies pure temptation. Not for the Absolute. But for the Fall.

An ordinary Prince Charming would have confused the dialectic: shame is

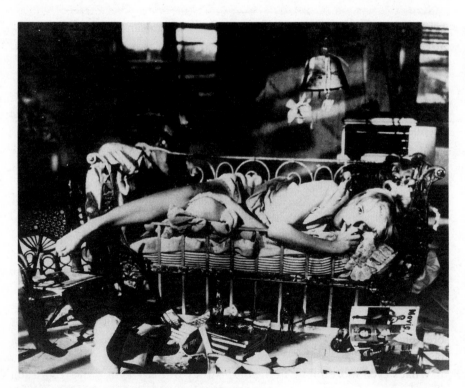

Carroll Baker as the woman-child Baby-Doll.

28

what drives the girl towards Man as much as attraction. She is also sufficiently egocentric to realize that beauty must be her domain. Beauty is her prerogative, the tribute she pays to the Beast. Opposites attract.

And if one can overcome the taboo, the Beast becomes a prince.

The relationship between *Baby Doll* and *36 fillette* (to which I almost gave the subtitle *How Young Girls Ask to be Murdered*) was very precise, I remember. The dialectic was the same – with the exception that the film contained memories I transformed for my own ends, and that the way I used them was *pure invention*.

Like the road one travels down is not the voyage.

When *Positif* asked me to write for their 400th issue, I didn't hesitate for a second. I wanted to write about *Baby Doll* as an excuse to see the film again. And also to know.

Memory is an unreliable yardstick. I'd forgotten not the main lines, but the details of the film! Everything in it melts together. It's supremely intelligent. Perfect. I watched the tape four times, just as I had watched the film four times in the cinema.

Kazan is one of my favourite directors. I love all his films. But none as much as *Baby Doll*. I never tire of it.

East of Eden and *Rebel Without a Cause* are films emblematic of adolescence. They are simple, like boys are simple: no longer whole, not knowing where they are, but knowing what they don't want. They have a problem with existence.

Girls are not the same. Their beauty gives them an advantage over the world. But a contradiction exists within them nonetheless, for the realization of their power leads to their fall, what attracts them is that which enslaves them.

At times pure and icy, at other times a stupid goose, Baby Doll shares the common denominator of all her peers: beauty is ephemeral. A moment of grace.

A girl exists only in order to stop existing. She is a being who commits suicide, who passes from a future where everything is possible to probable banality once her destiny has been sealed.

What makes the moment particularly acute is the imminence of what is about to happen. In fact, the girl has nothing special about her apart from the transitory state she is in; like Carroll Baker on the see-saw with Eli Wallach, she is balancing on the dividing line between fire and ice. Innocence and murder. The moment burns so brightly one wants to be her, to be him; one stands breathless between the two. It's the moment when the girl, the *object of desire*, becomes the *desirer*. The moment when she loses.

What's even more subtle in the dramaturgy of *Baby Doll* is the realization that the magnificence of young girls lies in the fact that everything is possible for them, that what will happen is *already happening*. The die has been cast; it always has been.

The pure, graceful woman-child is also a horrible little creature, prosaic and basely calculating, who by using her beauty as capital has already negotiated her establishment: she marries Archie Lee (Karl Malden) only if they can live in the biggest house in the county with *five complete sets of furniture*.

Her ambition aims solely at sofas and chairs to sit on. She is worthless, ignorant, lazy; she doesn't know anything apart from how to knot blue ribbons in her hair. 'Baby blue' like her eyes.

The day Archie Lee asked her dying father for her hand and promised to wait *until she was ready* before consummating their marriage, he didn't just put the cart before the horse, he *bought a ticket to hell*.

She's very good at giving him a hard time, she is merciless. With his balding head, Archie Lee is hardly a young girl's dream. And he knows he only bought her. Bought her out of cowardice. His own cowardice, and hers for accepting.

But it's a fool's market. Because he bought it all – the wife and the furniture – on credit and he can't pay. Like the furniture, she will never be his. Obstinate like a child, she prefers to find refuge in her crib with the sides down – her first splendid appearance in the film – curled up like a kitten. She absently sucks her thumb while she sleeps. One is dumbfounded by such grace and innocence, reduced, like her husband, to glimpses through the hole he secretly drills through the wall. Even the dog doesn't stir.

But she is watching him too. With unfailing instinct, she wakes up and catches the voyeur in all his misery.

When one has become the whipping-boy, there is little hope for change. The countdown has begun (it is the fifth of the month, Baby Doll will be twenty on the seventh). If Archie thinks his suffering will end, he is cruelly mistaken.

A young girl doesn't respect a man who respects her; she despises him.

Weakness and surrender, these are the rules for a young girl. She is not to be seduced but to be mastered. She doesn't want romance, but violence.

The man of the hour is Silva Vacarro (Eli Wallach), with his cowboy boots and whip, the sworn enemy, the man who is ruining Archie and all the old cotton-growers like him: the man, therefore, who gives Baby Doll every reason to break her promise. But Archie's ruin runs deeper than that; it is within him. Because he is the end of a line and Vacarro is the new breed. That is the difference.

Vacarro has no social standing, no manners. He cannot rely on the law, for whom he is neither black nor white. He relies on his own power; he is a conqueror. Whatever one may reproach him for not being, he is seductive precisely because he lacks delicacy, because he doesn't mince words, because he is crude and brutal like desire. Because it amuses him to play cat and mouse with his neighbour's wife.

She doesn't stand a chance. And she loves that. Carroll Baker is the kind of woman (all women) that the eyes of men illuminate. She becomes more and more beautiful as his gaze caresses her. The face becomes transparent, the lips become fuller. She becomes daring, cheeky; she looks away, flirts without seeming to, dimples appear, giggles puncture the moments of greatest tension. It's simple: the second the two set eyes on each other, the space between them becomes electric. The slightest gesture gives them goosebumps. Desire is tangible.

At the heart of the film lies one long scene of seduction-repulsion during which it's impossible for us to draw breath: starting from the magnificent promiscuity of the see-saw, moving on to the endless preparation of the lemonade in the kitchen, where the ban on crossing the threshold is already a first surrender (the expression is an acknowledgement, the acknowledgement is a command; the proof lies in the interminable time Baby Doll spends *not making the lemonade* so that Vacarro will lose patience and cross the line), and which ends in a game of hide-and-seek.

It's already been established that Baby Doll has never been to the attic, that there are rooms in the house she has never visited. The metaphor couldn't be clearer: she is the house; young girls are frightened of themselves. The attic is also where she goes because *she wants to be caught*. And if he doesn't hurry, it's because he wants her to realize he knows exactly what she wants. The tension is delicious.

When she's hanging on to the beam, her fear of falling is as visible as her desire, if not to fall, at least for the torture to continue indefinitely. But then he makes her sign the paper accusing her husband of setting fire to the workshop. Then, having held up a handkerchief on the end of a pole for her to dry her tears, he cruelly goes.

He leaves her. He leaves her, free in her gestures and in her body.

So, abandoning her pride, she decides to go to him whatever the cost. Baby Doll catches up with her conqueror on the stairs, and it is she who humbly asks him to join her in her child's crib. If he lowers the sides and curls up, he can sleep there. Since the five sets of furniture have gone, she offers him the only bed in the house.

And after they've made love, she offers to cradle him as he sleeps. Like a soft and gentle woman. Almost maternal.

When the husband returns, he bears the brunt of this flagrant transformation. She is in her slip. Her attitude is unmistakable: she has the impudence, the effrontery of a woman. She is a woman. And she exists only through the man who made her so. Royally.

She spits out her disdain and hate for his having not been the one to conquer her and lead her by the whip.

In other words: in love, the respect of a man is the worst humiliation a girl could experience.

But love doesn't rest on its laurels for long. Its victories are mere flashes in the pan.

Already, life is imposing its law on a woman who is no longer a girl. She says so herself, with sudden nostalgia and resignation: 'There's nothing to do but wait for tomorrow, and see whether we've been forgotten or not.'

For me, that's unforgettable.

Jean-Claude Brisseau

Psycho

The virtuosity of the *mise-en-scène* of *Psycho* has always fascinated me. That's why I've seen the film perhaps fifty, sixty times. Recently, I managed to get hold of an early draft of the script and realized that some of Hitchcock's pronouncements about the film were, in part, inaccurate. For example, during his conversations with Truffaut, Hitchcock says he is proud to have made a film without a major character. It's true that the film is a little abstract, and that it's the camera-work which makes audiences scream the world over. But Hitchcock only realized this while editing the film, when he was attempting to solve a problem of plot construction after Janet Leigh's disappearance.

When one sees the finished film, it's easy to say that because the murder in the shower is so powerful, the characters do not need to be developed much afterwards in order for us to be frightened.

But, reading the script, one sees that the director tried everything to dramatize the detective Arbogast's character and to increase identification with the Vera Miles-John Gavin couple.

The sequence where Arbogast looks for the Bates motel was much longer. Initially, he goes backwards and forwards along the road in front of the motel without seeing it, and ends up by spotting it during a traffic jam.

There was more on the Gavin and Miles characters. One wondered where they were going to sleep, whether they were going to spend the night in the motel ... In the scene where Vera Miles visits Anthony Perkins's room, we were also to see her sickened by discovering a porn magazine.

All of this appeared in the script but was cut during the editing because it didn't work.

After parting from Janet Leigh and Anthony Perkins, the situation is so powerful that the audience is no longer interested in the characters who then appear.

One reason why Hitchcock cut so much from the second part may have been to avoid giving the audience time to think. Actually, he risks turning it into a whodunit where one of the two possible suspects has been dead for fifteen years.

But the entire last section of the film with Vera Miles in the house works because a defenceless girl is walking around in a place where a mysterious, psychopathic murderess is on the loose.

If one already knows who the killer is, since Perkins is held up in the other

Psycho: Vera Miles, defenceless in the house.

building by Gavin, the suspense melts away, and fear only returns when the girl walks down the stairs into the basement.

It was to dramatize this finale that Hitchcock invented the famous crane shot showing Perkins fetching his mother from her room and taking her downstairs. People have spoken about metaphysics here, but it's really a matter of logic and dramatic construction. To prevent the audience from suspecting anything, the director had to show Perkins and his mother in the same shot. But where to put the camera?

He couldn't put it at the bottom of the stairs, nor opposite the door of the room, because her face would have been too visible. Nor could the camera focus on Perkins's back: the audience would have guessed that Hitchcock was trying to hide the mother's face. The only solution, therefore, was to raise the camera as soon as Perkins walks up the stairs, so that the audience isn't surprised by the high angle on to the landing at the end of the shot.

By examining these 'practical' matters (which critics too often ignore), one understands much better the extraordinary achievement of a *mise-en-scène* which for me had long remained a mystery.

Within a relatively tight schedule, Hitchcock spent between ten to fifteen days shooting the shower scene, Arbogast's murder and the famous crane shot of Perkins and his mother – which amount to two minutes' screen time. Hitchcock still had about one hour and forty-five minutes of the film left to shoot (about six hundred shots with sixty changes of set). Which means he must have worked at an unbelievable rate afterwards.

Watching the film, you can easily spot the bad lighting continuity, the occasional blurs, and the unthinkable shot, for a traditional Hollywood movie, where you can see the hair on Janet Leigh's arms. But none of that matters. Hitchcock's aim with *Psycho* was to frighten the audience and he was brilliantly successful.

That said, I think *Psycho*, like all great films, defies analysis.

Even when you think you've said everything there is to say about the *mise-en-scène*, there remains an area of mystery.

Alain Cavalier

Carne

What I like best is going to see someone's first film. I try to divine the future pitfalls and the present splendours. All the future *oeuvre* is there. I remember the sleepless night before my own first day of shooting, the hurried breakfast before deciding on the first camera position.

In recent years, I've been struck by one particular first film. For simplicity's sake, let's say it's about horse-meat and an impossible love-affair. A film where, for once in our domain, the physical takes precedence over the metaphysical. A blood-drenched film, sturdy and flexible, like the child which emerges from its mother's womb at the start of the story. I felt a terrible tenderness, never before experienced, coming from the screen, a tenderness for the stammering human race.

I got hold of a video of the film and, frame by frame, studied the progression from shot to shot. These transitions bore the stamp of a film-maker of the first rank.

The film was *Carne*. It only came out in a few cinemas; few people have seen it. It was by Gaspar Noé who – lucky chap – passed through Buenos Aires and New York before filming in Paris.

Claude Chabrol

B.A., or a dialectic of survival

The man was big, without an ounce of fat. A strong chin, lively eyes and an epic laugh. The hand which gripped yours, with the apparent intention of crushing it, was unexpectedly soft and silky. He drank Coca-Cola during meals and always apologized for it: 'I know it's stupid but I can't help it: I'm American.' His films resembled him: lean, extrovert, punchy, framed in concrete and edited with a trowel. Enough to wake up any sleeping film-buff.

Robert Aldrich was one of the rare film-makers who reconciled for once the views of those fraternal enemies *Positif* and *Cahiers*. True, the worth of *Apache, Vera Cruz* and the sublime *Kiss Me Deadly* (aptly retitled *In Fourth Gear* in French) could hardly be contested. I can hardly remember any doubts being expressed on either side, although I myself may have dismissed them with a shrug.

The important thing is that his key theme is clear from his first films onwards, as clear as the characteristics of his style – the style which his theme, of course, justifies. And because this theme hasn't been recognized, a misunderstanding – several misunderstandings — have arisen between Aldrich and his admirers.

Yet the theme is very simple, if discomfiting: man's adventures are born out of his antagonistic relationship with the society, environment, world – call it what you will – he belongs to. The adventure of man is therefore a dialectic.

The strength of these three films, and most of those that followed, arises out of the formidable (and, in the case of *Kiss Me Deadly*, apocalyptic) rigour with which he develops this theme. He is fully aware of its implications: a totally individual morality, whose only justification is survival (plus its eventual corollary, happiness), and an acceptance of the self. The enemy has many faces and they are interchangeable. The hero exists only in so far as he stays alive. Victory is never certain.

We are far away from the Hollywood myth here, and Aldrich knows it. He only managed to make these films with the help of independent producers. Nothing is more pressing than the need to assert one's independence. But, lucid even in his greatest excesses, Aldrich alternated between his personal films and outside commissions. He made *The Big Knife* and *Attack!* for himself. And for others, he made *Autumn Leaves* and *The Garment Jungle*. Bang! Hollywood doesn't like such open defiance (compare Coppola and Zoetrope more recently); *The Big Knife* sticks in its throat. *Attack!* is the only war film the US Army refuses to participate in. Aldrich is fired midway through *The Garment Jungle* and replaced by Vincent Sherman.

And it doesn't stop there. *The Big Knife* and *Attack!* are adapted from stage-plays, and Aldrich makes no attempt to hide their theatricality. On the contrary, he underlines it, contrasting it with the fluid narrative he rejects because he wants a dialectic in both his staging and his editing. Theatricality is the very stuff of dialectic. Brecht was hardly the best novelist of the century. But the admirers of Aldrich's first three films were not prepared for this unpredictability in their director. Some even started sulking.

It was all going wrong! But this was to be expected, given his attachment to his key theme.

There followed a period which, for Robert Aldrich, I'd call a little sad: four years during which, shooting here and there, he never managed to make a truly finished film. Working as ever with independent producers, he saw them cut his films to ribbons. Probably the only interest the situation had for him was to work in various European countries and to realize that the limitations of their film industry, although different from Hollywood's, were just as ridiculous.

Bravura wasn't enough, wiliness was called for. And, returning to Hollywood, Aldrich began to be wily. He pretended to play the game. Between two films of an unalloyed physical brutality intensified by a theatricality that exploded from the screen, Aldrich made *Four for Texas*, a fake Western with the Sinatra 'rat pack', in which he unblinkingly inserted a number from the Three Stooges. As far as he was concerned, he hit the jackpot with *The Dirty Dozen*, a huge hit which gave him back his freedom but also compounded the misunderstanding. The film was so well-made and so violent that it was taken as an apologia for brutality when it was really the opposite: a virulently anti-militarist tract (peace-time murderers make the best soldiers and vice versa). Dialectic and wiliness: the new Aldrich had arrived.

What followed was rich with irony. The next twelve films, pure jewels, made either within or outside the system – unforgettable, iconoclastic works of admirable energy and daring – were received by his old admirers (apart from, perhaps, *Positif*) with a shocked expression. Of course it's difficult to accept, out of the blue, red Indians toying with skulls, pathetic old lesbian alcoholics, mocking Japanese officers, cops in silk stockings and suspenders, neuropathic soldiers indulging in nuclear blackmail, and violent female wrestlers.

But it's part and parcel of the Aldrich dialectic that this world, alas, is not made for weaklings. It's either him or us. Here are the titles of his last twelve films, his own 'dirty dozen':

The Legend of Lylah Clare
The Killing of Sister George
Too Late the Hero
The Grissom Gang
Ulzana's Raid
The Emperor of the North
The Longest Yard
Hustle
Twilight's Last Gleaming
The Choirboys
The Frisco Kid
All the Marbles

Ulzana's Raid: Bruce Davison and Burt Lancaster.

Joel and Ethan Coen

Our Favourite Actor

Our favourite actor of all time would have to be Harry Bugin. Harry had a small part in our gangster movie *Miller's Crossing*, but unfortunately his two scenes were cut in the course of getting the movie down to length. Harry not only did good work, he was gracious when we informed him that we'd had to lose his scenes: 'No problem, fellas. Just remember me on the next one.'

We were happy to do so. We asked Harry to play Pete, the impassive elevator operator in *Barton Fink*. Though most of his work remains in that picture, one of Harry's scenes there was deleted too. It occurs towards the end of the movie, when two police detectives return to Barton's hotel to arrest him. They are interrupted by the reappearance of the John Goodman character. As written and shot, Goodman, who enters the hotel hallway from a smoking elevator, is immediately preceded by Pete, who staggers out, hands pressed to either side of his head as if oppressed by a splitting headache, lurches down the hall towards the two goggling detectives, and then tumbles forward, whereupon his head topples off and rolls inertially forward. Harry performed the gag well (he did the initial entrance and staggering before a stunt man stepped in to do a dead fall and release the fake head), but we ended up cutting the scene. In the sequence in question, doom so palpably impended that we felt that Harry's appearance as harbinger was superfluous. Again, Harry was gracious about some of his work ending up on the cutting-room floor – but again, that is not why Harry Bugin is our favourite actor.

We are ashamed to admit in print here something that we never told Harry. Although he was clearly right for the part in *Barton Fink*, we had at one point come close to offering it to someone else. We had met an actor called Robert Beecher for another role in the movie, and it evolved in conversation that Robert had just had a false head made for a small part he'd done in *Dick Tracy*. Stumbling across an actor who already had an artificial head seemed almost unbelievably fortuitous, and we were tempted to save ourselves the expense of head-making by offering him Harry's part. When we learned, however, that the false Robert Beecher head was, in fact, still owned by Walt Disney Pictures, who snippily informed us that though they still had the head they were not interested in renting it out (company policy?), the bubble of temptation burst and we went back to the name at the top of our list: Bugin. (Robert Beecher ended up playing, and very nicely, the part we had met him for: referee in the wrestling dailies.)

And so Harry Bugin came out to California to have a cast of his face prepared. This entails an actor sitting in a make-up chair while goop is poured over his head and left to set. The actor spends two hours deprived of his sensorium, face held perfectly immobile, drawing breath through two straws stuck into his nostrils. We dropped by to chat with Harry about his facial expression just before the pouring of the goop. He said, 'Fellas, the guy has just had his head sliced off; I figure he would look like this.' We waited for Harry to do something. And waited. At length Ethan cleared his throat and murmured, 'Yes, Harry. Very nice,' and the goop was poured.

Again Harry bore up with good grace, but again, this isn't what makes him our favourite actor. The point of this story is not just that Harry Bugin is no eye-popping ham. Yes, his slightly slack-jawed, eyes-focused-bemusedly-on-the-middle-distance stare (which we are still in a position to appreciate, since the *faux* Bugin head now sits in our office bookcase) had a delicacy that nicely balanced the shocking nature of the scene. But the main point is that Harry Bugin is interested only in the inner truth of his character. He does not raise small, literal-minded questions along the lines of: 'How is it my character manages to stagger around after his head has been severed? How come it's still sitting on his neck if it *has* been severed? And even if my guy could hold it there, why would he want to?' No; only, 'Fellas, the guy has just had his head sliced off; I figure he would look like this.'

And yet still, this is not why Harry Bugin is our favourite actor.

Last year, we asked Harry to play Aloysius, the malevolent door-scraper, in our movie *The Hudsucker Proxy*. Harry understood immediately that an evil door-scraper would, in the nature of things, have a shaved head, and was amenable to shaving his: 'Sure, fellas. It grows back.' He even seemed to welcome the opportunity to act with his entire head, no longer constrained to communicate his character's emotions through the surface area of the face alone.

But any actor can shave his head. As shooting drew near, we were still groping for a means of ending the climactic fist-fight in the Hudsucker Building's clock room. The script called for our great clock to be stopped twice, once by a broom shoved into the gears, which was well and good, and a second time by something else – not just anything, clearly, but a capper that would keep the audience from resenting our repeating the gag of the stopped clock. The nature of this was a puzzle of daunting specificity. The object had to be of just the right size to be stuffed into our great clock gear, and had to be of such consistency as plausibly to offer temporary – but only temporary – resistance before being ground away. Mere days before the scene was scheduled to be shot, co-producer Graham Place had a leaping insight: Harry's character might have his dentures knocked out in the course of the fist-fight. This would leave an ideal gear-stopper at hand, and would incidentally let us punctuate the fist-fight with the classic Chattering Teeth Gag. Dentures were clearly the one perfect – the only perfect – the only *conceivable* – solution. There remained only one question, and on it rode all our hopes for satisfactorily resolving the very climax of our movie: Did Harry Bugin wear dentures?

'Sure, fellas. Full uppers and lowers.'

And that's why Harry Bugin is our favourite actor.

Harry Bugin as the malevolent door-scraper.

Luigi Comencini

Eduardo

My film *Tutti a casa* (*Everybody Go Home*) is set on 8 September 1943, the darkest day of the war, when the Italian Army casually changed sides from the Germans to the Anglo-Americans. After a dramatic journey, the two main characters, played by Alberto Sordi and Serge Reggiani, arrive, hungry and exhausted, at one of their homes. They hesitate before knocking because, as the man whose home it is remarks, 'My father has a heart condition. Great joy can be as harmful to him as great sadness.' His friend, therefore, knocks at the door and prepares the way. Unfortunately, his clumsiness and the tone of his voice convince the old man he has come to announce his son's death and he ends up almost having an attack. The old man was played by Eduardo de Filippo.

We discover that the old man is a devotee of the New Republic and a loyal admirer of Mussolini. He still dreams of a heroic son, a conqueror: 'Let him enlist at once. The war isn't over. The Germans have a secret weapon!' Eduardo plays the kind of character, ingenuous and pathetic, who though he appears for only a few minutes, leaves an indelible mark on a film. I had wanted him to play Sordi's father from the very start. Sordi has such an aggressive screen presence it's almost impossible to imagine him having a father. So I needed an actor whose exterior aspect was modest and resigned, but who also had a great interior strength which would enable him to express in just a few lines the tragedy of a father crushed by destiny. Eduardo had already said no to Dino de Laurentiis: he very rarely acted in films, especially if they weren't his own. But I eventually succeeded in persuading him. To make Eduardo believable I situated Sordi's family in Latina, midway between Naples and Rome (Sordi was from Rome and Eduardo from Naples; with all the dialects, casting isn't easy in Italy).

When I came to Rome in 1947, *Filumena* was playing at the Eliseo Theatre. Written, directed and played by Eduardo, it became one of his key works. I went to see it two nights running. I'd never seen anything like it in the theatre: the apparent simplicity of the acting and the direction produced an expressive force that effortlessly captured the attention, the laughter and the emotions of the audience. It was all so new, so original. I was profoundly struck by it.

Then came *Napoli Millionaria* (*Side Street Story*) and all the other plays. But what was he, Eduardo? He was an *auteur*, an actor who wrote his own lines, who translated Neapolitan into Italian and vice versa. He was an actor, but what an actor! Singular, omniscient, directing both himself and others.

His theatre constantly feasted on new subjects and we, the audience, watched open-mouthed the tricks of a magician. Naples sprang to life before our eyes, a Naples quite different from the folkloric Naples which had existed in the theatre until then.

Eduardo's plays have been performed practically all over the world, and always successfully. When he visited these theatres, where they were performing his work in so many different languages, all he'd do was rub out everything which overtly recalled Naples. For the more Naples he took out, the more there was there ...

Eduardo was born in the theatre. From childhood, he was educated in the great school of Neapolitan popular theatre. But he devoted his life to making Neapolitan a universal language. When he died, he was working on a translation of *A Midsummer Night's Dream* into old Neapolitan.

Tall and thin, he always looked dreamy. He felt himself an outsider everywhere and always. He looked at things, people, with a detached, puzzled gaze. He'd look at you and you'd never be sure whether he'd seen you. His slow movements made him seem tired, unsure of himself. In fact, Eduardo exuded great authority. His words fell like stones in a lake. His long, bony hands moved in the air when he talked, as if drawing imaginary shapes. He was never garrulous, his words were an extension of his body. In his dressing-room, before or after a performance, he'd always seem tired. His cheeks were sunken as if he were starving. I don't know whether he drove. I think not. I can't imagine him behind a steering wheel.

Let's examine a typical beginning to one of his plays. The stage is empty; the table has been laid for the family meal; everyone's out. Enter Eduardo holding a bottle wrapped in paper. He'd been out on an important mission – at least that's what we think, judging from the solemnity of his gestures. He unwraps the paper and reveals a bottle partly filled with red wine. He then picks up a carafe two-thirds full of water from the table. He delicately fills the carafe to the top with wine. The carafe now looks full of rosé. Satisfied, Eduardo scrunches up the wrapping-paper and throws it in the bin. He takes the empty bottle and puts it on a shelf. He sits down happily and waits for his guests.

Eduardo's pauses are often long and dense with meaning. The audience waits, impatient, and Eduardo continues, immobile and silent.

Sometimes, the words resemble objects: Eduardo plays with them like a juggler. It's as if we were watching acrobatics, verbal sleights of hand. At other times, the tone of a phrase can be more significant than the meaning of the words it contains.

Charlie Chaplin enters as a zealous waiter, pushing a trolley laden with dishes under a silver cover. He bows rapidly, takes off the cover and the cat, who's been hiding in the warmth underneath, jumps out.

And so I've engineered an amicable encounter between these two giants.

Both have great cities behind them, London, Naples. Both are tireless imitators of human misery, a misery without nationality and without date.

It is, of course, dangerous to compare Eduardo, whose work was based on language, with Chaplin, who staged stories without words, whose sole means of communication was mime and images. And yet the stories Eduardo's words evoke and the silent force of Chaplin's images do have something in common. Both men present human feelings, human misery, with irony but without pity; both are observant, incisive. The audience is transported effortlessly from laughter to emotion.

The characters are believable and true, although built around clichés: authority in the form of priests, night-watchmen, and cops; the petits bourgeois as lawyers, civil servants, and commissionaires; women as wives, adulteresses, dancers. In front of this army of figurines appears the protagonist (played by the author) who invariably depicts an unforgettable character. He is accompanied by a woman or a child, never another male character.

Thanks to the omnipresent irony, realism and surrealism, truth and imagination intertwine effortlessly and in all simplicity.

Eduardo progressed from the most rigorous realism of *Filumena* (a comedy where the female character is of equal if not superior stature to the male) to the fantastic abstraction of *Questi fantasmi*, where his interlocutor is a character we never see or hear, but to whom Eduardo explains with minute precision how coffee is made in Naples.

It makes me think of the finale of *Monsieur Verdoux* when, without batting an eyelid, the protagonist takes part in his own arrest. The character watching the actor, the actor watching the character; it's a double-act typical of Eduardo's theatre and Chaplin's films. In *The Pilgrim*, Chaplin plays an escaped convict who disguises himself as a priest, and performs the most extraordinary games where the two roles, convict and priest, continually keep an eye on each other.

Eduardo's sets are absolutely conventional. Naples reigns on stage in all its reality. But the city disappears once the actors arrive on stage. The set is subservient to the gestures of the actors and their words. The set has no life of its own. It helps to situate the action and give it an atmosphere in the most rapid, direct way possible.

Chaplin was so faithful to his origins that the backgrounds to his Hollywood films always look like the London of his childhood. They look so clichéd. But, precisely because they are a cliché, they refer us to the roots of his comedy – just like the sets of Eduardo's plays.

In his last years, Eduardo recorded all his comedies. He fixed for ever these pictures and sounds which, in other times, would have survived only in the memory of those who had seen them on stage. We can go on studying his work, gleaning ideas, suggestions.

Eduardo was a unique cultural phenomenon, especially in Italian theatre. Like Molière, who also performed his own work and was master of all that surrounded him, Eduardo rose above the Neapolitan tradition and broke the isolation.

Several years after *Tutti a casa*, I worked with him again on an episode of *Cuore*, a long television film. It was another short but important role: an old, retired schoolmaster. With his spindly appearance, his somewhat conventional gestures, his pale face framed by furrowed cheeks – the marks of fatigue and a dignified impecuniousness – Eduardo was the only actor capable of playing this rhetorical, blandly pathetic character who represented an unbearable bourgeois morality. A real 'character'. I think he had fond memories of *Tutti a casa*. When I went to see him, he agreed to play the part without pay. The scene took two days to shoot. He told me not to put aside, out of deference for him, my prerogative as director; I should tell him what to do clearly and with authority. 'You be the director. I'll be the actor.'

It was autumn 1983. He died the following spring.

Roger Corman

Vincent Price as I remember

Vincent Price was a well-educated, highly-cultured man. I cast him in our first film together, *The Fall of the House of Usher*, because the character of Roderick Usher was very close to his own persona: handsome, educated, cultured, and sensitive. In the Edgar Allan Poe story, Roderick Usher is a gentle, aristocratic man who progressively descends into madness. My feeling was that the audience should be frightened of this character, but not in conscious reaction to his sinister features or brute strength. Instead, I envisioned a refined, attractive man whose intelligent but tormented mind operates in realms far beyond the minds of others, and who therefore inspires a deeper fear. In Vincent I found exactly the man I was looking for.

Vincent and I got along so well on that shoot that I ended up using him in seven more films, among them *The Pit and the Pendulum*, *The Haunted Palace*, and *The Masque of the Red Death*. In every case, he was a valued contributor to the creative process.

Only once do I remember Vincent being puzzled by my film-making requirements. In *The Fall of the House of Usher*, he was asked to speak the line, 'The house lives. The house breathes.' He came to me and asked in great bewilderment, 'What does that mean?' 'It means,' I replied, 'that we're able to make this picture.' It seemed that the good folks at American International Pictures, the company providing our financing, were worried that this was a horror film without a monster. To win them over, I had promised that the house itself would be our monster. Now I had to make good that promise. Once this was explained to him, Vincent said, 'I understand totally.' He went on to deliver the line with a subtle intensity that became for me one of the high points of the entire film.

Vincent had been classically trained as an actor in England, but also knew something of the Stanislavsky Method, as expounded by the Actors Studio. I myself had studied the Method, and our approaches to acting meshed extremely well. In the roles he played for me, I admired how Vincent was able to blend his classical training, his Method experience, and elements of his own character to create indelible film portraits.

Aside from his powers as a dramatic actor, Vincent was surprisingly adept at humour. His abilities along these lines were put to the test in *The Raven*, a film intended to combine horror with comedy. Vincent's contribution of jokes and comic bits to the shooting script added greatly to the picture's overall humorous

Vincent Price in *The Raven*.

effect. On the set of *The Raven*, Vincent had to adjust to the presence of two veteran co-stars, Peter Lorre and Boris Karloff, as well as a new young actor, Jack Nicholson. He showed extraordinary flexibility in working harmoniously with Jack (trained in the Method), Boris (schooled in the English classical style), and Peter, who did anything that came into his mind at any given moment.

Peter Lorre's great talent was for improvising, which he did with great wit and panache. This on-the-set spontaneity did not sit well with Boris Karloff who, nearing the end of a long and distinguished career, expected to do his scenes exactly as written. Inevitably, there was some friction between these two strong personalities. Fortunately for me, Vincent was able to strike a balance in his own acting style, adapting to Peter's looseness, but also playing scenes with Boris that were models of the classical approach. His personal graciousness in bending to the demands of two conflicting egos was a great help to me in what could have been difficult circumstances.

Vincent had a well-deserved reputation as a host and a gourmet chef. I was privileged to attend several parties at his home. The food, the wine, the décor: everything was planned in the most exquisite detail. And he had the gift of eliciting sparkling conversation from his guests, so that it was a joy to sit at his table. I suspect that by inviting me to dine, Vincent was trying to improve my eating habits, which tended toward the Spartan back then. In fact, in our filmmaking days he used to joke about sending me CARE packages to keep me from starvation.

In addition to his other achievements, Vincent was also a great collector of art. He gave me invaluable advice when I decided to start my own collection.

There is no question that Vincent Price was a remarkable actor, and a remarkable man. His friendship enriched my life, and for that I will always be grateful.

Alain Corneau

Fritz Lang

Glen Ford in *The Big Heat.*

The name which springs to mind this December 1993 is Fritz Lang. So why Fritz Lang?

Because, many years later, the mystery remains unsolved.

Because it's the question of identity, central to all his films, which determines the smallest nuances in the *mise-en-scène*; and it is this question – both hidden and revealed by cinema's usual stock in trade, the impression of reality – that is the central preoccupation of cinema.

Because Fritz Lang had several contradictory lives and careers; because he made true genre films and, in making those films, stayed true to himself.

Because, although it doesn't speak of cinema directly, *Mabuse*, his last German film, is perhaps the most vertiginous film ever made about cinema.

Because *Moonfleet* was for many of my generation the most 'beautiful' film in the world, although Lang himself didn't seem to like it much ...

Because *The Big Heat* proves once and for all to what extent European and American cinema (amongst others!) need each other and are complementary.

Because the 'secret' will always stay 'behind the door', because for Lang, to whom psychological analysis was anathema, destiny was the only object of the spectacle.

Lastly, because Doctor Mabuse is the most revealing character of the twentieth century, a century which, brandishing the Rights of Man, seems to have been the most bloodthirsty and cataclysmic in history.

In all his films, one feels Lang stepped close to the abyss and gazed in.

Michel Deville

The film of my life

I've made four films with Michel Piccoli. He never turns me down. All the great French film actors have turned me down at least once. But not Michel Piccoli. Not once. I don't think he's turned anyone down. Often, he accepts a part before reading the script. And you have to insist that he reads it. So he does. Not to reassure himself, but you.

Michel Piccoli is the actor one speaks with least before the making of a film. A few words, more or less whispered, a smile – or a burst of laughter – and then, on the first day of shooting, you realize he's the one who's best understood the film, the character, all the things that can only be written into a script below the surface.

There's a modesty and a daring in Michel Piccoli. An emotion and a reserve. An extreme self-control, an infallible measuredness, but at the same time, the most enormous exuberance, the most admirable extravagance. Each moment brings something unexpected, a surprise, an invention, but never does it jar with the text or anything else.

There's also the greatest wisdom and the greatest craziness. He can change from the most miserable, pathetic character to the most grandiose and haughty; from the tenderest humility to the most scathing authority. He can be the funniest, the most farcical, but also the most moving and tragic.

He is priceless. He will make a film for nothing, just for the pleasure or the glory of it or, more often, to help an impecunious beginner.

He is, of course, the greatest, but he's always managed to keep it quiet. No doubt because he doesn't think so. Or because he doesn't think in those terms. Therefore, he is truly the greatest.

What's more, he's always on time and always knows his lines.

Carlos Diegues

Deus e o Diablo na Terra do Sol (White Devil, Black God)

Exactly thirty years ago, I took part in the Cannes Festival where two Brazilian films, Glauber Rocha's *Deus e o Diablo na Terra do Sol* and Nelson Pereira dos Santos's *Vidas Secas*, were presented in the official competition. These films, along with *Os Fuzis*, also represented Brazil at the Berlin Festival of the same year and, thanks mainly to the support of French critics, brought Brazilian cinema to world attention.

I remember the first press screening of *Deus e o Diablo na Terra do Sol* at the old palace on the Croisette. As its strange images and barbaric sounds filled the cinema, the audience looked at each other, in turn amazed, confused, shocked and delighted by the absurd human geography, the savage dramaturgy, by characters and situations never before seen in cinema. About half the audience left before the end. The other half gave the film a standing ovation. But I'm sure most of them didn't really know what they were applauding.

But what is certain is that both those who walked out and those who had stayed had witnessed something new, original and unique, something never seen before.

In my mind, this certainty was fed by a very pleasant sensation: the conviction that it was worth making films in Brazil – films like these, without the commercial constraints and the cultural references that make us the slaves of what's gone before. We were convinced that not only were we inventing a cinema for our country, but also that we were doing it in a way never before employed elsewhere in the world.

Time has passed. The military coup of the same year, 1964, and the ensuing military dictatorship saw the end of our dreams and proved that reality wasn't waiting for them to be realized. History developed in a totally different and, for us, surprising way.

Brazilian cinema, from *Deus e o Diablo* to the films we make today, has yielded some interesting results. Some films have been true successes, by no means all of them have been worthy of praise, and none have been able to reproduce the same international impact Cinema Novo had in the sixties. But Brazilian cinema is not dead and will never die. It is like a weed, a pest, which when least expected springs up in some far-flung corner of the country.

Our principal achievement during these years has been to produce a cinema (not just films) which always corresponds to the reality of the country, which transforms this reality and the crises we have experienced into gestures and language. In a modest way, we have been great when we've managed to do this. That is why these last years have been the hardest test of the collective conviction I first felt during that screening of *Deus e o Diablo na Terra do Sol*.

Brazil, victim of the incompetence of the élite, of corruption and pessimism, of an extraordinary crisis in confidence, and most of all of increasing poverty and social violence, seemed to us more than ever to reflect the view expressed by Lévi-Strauss when he taught at the University of São Paulo: 'Brazil is a country which seems to have passed from barbarism to decadence without having known civilization.'

Deus e o Diablo na Terra do Sol.

It's a phrase I think about, that I repeat to myself obsessively like a refrain, like a teacher trying to prevent his pupils from making avoidable mistakes. We are always on the brink of disaster, as if to be so were inevitable – as if, for us, the eternal 'country of the future', the future itself, were already in the past.

At the end of the eighties, Brazilian cinema was seduced by the foreign pessimism that always follows our crises of megalomania. A new generation, sophisticated, dreaming of an idealized Western world, decreed that our culture is unviable and pushed us towards a melancholic and sometimes cynical cinema, which, as it happens, met with very little success either in Brazil or abroad.

Today, on the eve of a general election, a new law favouring audio-visual production has been brought in, and the cultural climate has been shaken up by a realization of what is happening. I have the feeling that intentions have changed.

In the mid-century, Cinema Novo, and Glauber Rocha in particular, prevented Latin-American cinema from becoming a mediocre reprise of European neo-realism, of a standardized neo-realism full of good intentions.

Nowadays, any new films must examine us with the same urgency and anxiety, with the same feverish desire to know the world that surrounds us. They must conjure up images and sounds which are unique, as ours once were. This will happen soon, I promise you. You can believe it.

Clint Eastwood

Directed by ...

You want me to talk about the directors I've worked with? Let's start with those I didn't get the chance to be directed by. Howard Hawks, for example, the first director I ever met! It was a brief meeting. I was helping him round up his horses when I was about sixteen, seventeen. John Ford? I never met him but, sure, he's one of the ones I'd like to have worked with. I saw a lot of his movies when I was young.

I saw all the big hits like everybody else: *Grapes of Wrath, Gone with the Wind*, etc. I also saw comedies like *Sitting Pretty* and westerns like *Winchester 73*. Very few foreign films were imported in those days, but I do remember seeing an Australian movie, *Forty Thousand Horsemen*. There was a lot of action. It was also the first movie where I heard actors use bad language. They'd say 'Damn!' or 'Hell!' That wasn't allowed here. The Hays Office saw to that. I can't remember who the director was.[1] At the time, I didn't care who directed what.

Going back further, I remember Preston Sturges's comedies. I liked *Sullivan's Travels*, Joel McCrea especially. Maybe he didn't have the stature of Gary Cooper, but he always gave the impression that more was going on inside him than he was revealing. There were also fantastic character actors in Sturges, Capra and Hawks movies. They all had interesting faces. It's very comforting for a director to know he can rely on the same actors movie after movie. I tried to do the same in *Every Which Way ...* and *Bronco Billy* by getting together people like Geoffrey Lewis, Bill McKinney and so on. Someone like Ford liked the same faces around him. When you're an admiral, you play the part. You don't ask any questions. Ford wasn't the kind of director to analyse what he was doing with his actors. He knew their capabilities and what they could bring him. Could I have joined his gang? I don't think so. I'm not the gang type.

I met Capra when I was making *High Plains Drifter* in Mono Lake, North California. I was staying in Silver Lake, four houses down from Capra, and I got the chance to talk to him. Afterwards, every time I came by, I paid him a visit. He was always pleased to see me, but I never worked with him. Did Capra ever see *Bronco Billy*? I don't know. When I read the script, I thought 'Capra could have made this'.

1 Charles Chauvel (1940).

Sullivan's Travels: Preston Sturges's stock company of character actors.

Capra's movies have an underlying energy which, although it's difficult to define, he alone possesses. Anyone can shoot a scene, but like all the greats, Capra added something which was neither written nor visualized, but which permeates all his work. All the greats had this gift to some extent or other. It depended on the material, their enthusiasm, the problems they had to solve.

Hitchcock? He was with another studio when I was under contract at Universal. Years later, I met him once, shortly before he died. I got a call from his office: 'Mr Hitchcock would like to see you. His health isn't good, he may not make the movie, but he'd like to talk to you about the lead part.' We had lunch at the Universal commissary. It took us ten minutes to walk from the door to the table. He walked very slowly and carefully. He ordered his usual lunch: steak and tomatoes. He was still in full possession of his mental powers. He talked brilliantly and I fell under his spell. The movie was set in Finland or Norway, on a train. He'd seen a few of my movies, notably *Misty*. We had a good time. But how could I have been his man? I was a generation too young!

The same goes for Ford and Capra, who were retiring when I was starting out. Anthony Mann? Yes, I'd like to have worked with him at his peak. I liked his movies a lot, especially the westerns with Jimmy Stewart. Nick Ray also did some good things but I never met him. Same with Sam Fuller. He was preparing a film at RKO, *The Run of the Arrow*, and I tried unsuccessfully to get a meeting. I only met him much later, in France.

At the time, Mann, Ray and Fuller were looking for new sources of inspiration and went to make movies in Europe. The top man was Elia Kazan. Ever since *On the Waterfront*, he was the director everyone wanted to work with. The trouble was he did his casting in New York and other places. I never managed to make a movie with him. The same applied to Stanley Kubrick. I saw *The Killing* when it came out. I would have liked to have worked with him, but the opportunity never came up.

On the other hand, I did get to meet Billy Wilder when he was casting *The Spirit of St Louis*. As often happens in Hollywood, the press was full of stories about him looking for an unknown to play Lindbergh. All the young guys, especially the gangly ones, were chasing the part. I met him once ... just for a handshake, not even an audition. His films had marked my youth: *Double Indemnity, Sunset Boulevard,* and so many others. I don't understand why he stopped working so soon. I don't know the circumstances, but I find it amazing that a man of his talent hasn't been more productive in the last twenty years.

I desperately wanted to be in Raoul Walsh's *The Naked and the Dead*. My agent couldn't get me an audition so I didn't get to meet him. Small agencies had no power. Walsh was a fantastic character. And he'd been an actor as well. It's always good to work with directors who've been actors. They're much more receptive. When I gave Don Siegel a part in my first film, *Misty*, I told him that way he'd learn to be more tolerant towards his actors while I'd learn what it's like to be a director. Often an actor only worries about his performance and his character. He doesn't realize a director can only spend 5 per cent of his energy on him, the other 95 per cent being devoted to the crew, the other actors and all the rest.

In my time, Universal mainly made B movies. They had a stable of actors under contract: Rock Hudson, Tony Curtis, Jeff Chandler, Rory Calhoun ... But they couldn't afford stars like Cooper or Gable. I played a small part in *Away all Boats*, and Gable was offered the lead. I was in the studio commissary when he came in. It caused a sensation. No one at Universal had seen such a great star. But, in the end, the part was played by one of the house actors, Jeff Chandler I think.

It was a good period, but Douglas Sirk was the only important director. Universal gave him all their prestige movies, big melodramas like *Magnificent Obsession* and *Written on the Wind*. I tried to get a meeting but failed. When you were under contract, you thought you could get meetings anywhere, at least with the house directors. You even thought you had the edge over actors from outside, but that wasn't the case at all. Sometimes directors were suspicious precisely because you were under contract. Familiarity breeds contempt.

They could see you any time, but actors from outside had the advantage of novelty.

In those circumstances, it wasn't easy to get work with the greats. But I did work with William Wellman at the end of his career, on *Lafayette Escadrille*. It wasn't a great movie, the script wasn't up to scratch, but it was a period when Wellman, the eternal rebel, was trying something new. Perhaps he wanted to do something he hadn't been allowed to do before. I remember we had a conversation on the set of *The Ox-Bow Incident*. It was one of my favourite films. He was surprised by my opinion, because it was a financial disaster. He said it was Mrs Zanuck's fault. Everyone at the studio was very proud of the movie, but when Darryl screened it at home, his wife said, 'But this is terrible! How can you let them lynch Dana Andrews and Anthony Quinn?' The rumour spread that the movie was jinxed. So it only got a limited release. It was only when the movie was praised by the French critics that Fox tried to run it again in New York. But that didn't work either. The movie had been shot fast, in less than thirty days, like a commando raid. That's how Wellman worked best. To save time on *Lafayette Escadrille*, he used two cameras to cover the same scene, something he'd never done before. His idea was that there'd be no continuity problems. He was right, but I think it meant making too many compromises with angles and lighting. I've used two cameras very rarely, usually only for

Wellman's *The Ox-Bow Incident.*

with angles and lighting. I've used two cameras very rarely, usually only for action scenes. I prefer using several lenses rather than several cameras. Wellman retired after *Lafayette Escadrille*, but I carried on seeing him and his family. He gave me a lot of encouragement during *Breezy*. He liked the film a lot, and wrote me some very nice letters. I think that because he was married to a woman much younger than himself, he identified with the William Holden character. He had a big influence in encouraging me to become a director.

I couldn't work with the greats every day. Which is why I worked with unknowns or semi-unknowns, such as Sergio Leone, who only had a couple of toga movies under his belt. *Fistful of Dollars* was his first big break. *The Colossus of Rhodes*, I admit, didn't make much of an impression, but people said he had a great sense of humour. I'd already realized this reading the script. I told myself I should maybe try something new and, if it didn't work out, I could always say I'd had a good vacation in Spain.

Sergio cast me after seeing an episode of *Rawhide*. Anyway, he didn't have much choice: the film was being made on a shoestring. An American representing the producer even asked me whether I could bring my own costume. I was amazed, but I went off and bought some clothes in a shop on Santa Monica Boulevard. I bought a pair of trousers and washed them over and over again to age them, and grabbed the boots and gunbelts I used on *Rawhide*. I put them all in a rucksack and headed off to Europe! And I finally met Sergio. He was a character. I didn't speak Italian and he didn't speak English. Our interpreter was a Polish lady, Elena Dressler, who spoke six or seven languages. She'd been in a German concentration camp and was liberated by the Americans. One of the assistants spoke English and would give me all the necessary instructions. After a while, Sergio and I got to understand each other quite well. The only time we really used the interpreter was when I wanted to cut dialogue I believed irrelevant. We talked a lot, discussed what we were doing, and ended up coming to an agreement. I was playing the character as I saw him, very controlled, with the minimum of gestures. The opposite of playing to the gallery! I showed no emotion whatsoever. If I'd tried to be as baroque as the others, it would have been ridiculous. Sergio understood what I was doing, but when the producers saw the rushes, they thought I was doing nothing, that it was a disaster. When the film was cut together, they changed their minds.

It was fun working with Sergio after *Rawhide*, where the stories were so conventional. I remember that Lee Van Cleef thought Sergio was completely crazy when we started making *For a Few Dollars More*. Maybe Sergio's methods and ideas weren't very orthodox, but they helped me discover another point of view. He was a great admirer of the masters of the western, Hawks and Ford. But he had his own vision of what a western should be, and some of his ideas were truly crazy. Sometimes I'd have to intervene to keep the ship on course. But we made a good team. We were on the same wavelength. Sergio liked to say there were fights on the set; but that wasn't true in this case. Later he got a little jealous because I was more prolific than he was. It was neither his fault nor mine. After the première of *Bird* at Cannes, I went to see him in

Eastwood with Siegel on the set of *The Beguiled.*

Italy and we spent a great day together. I think he held it against me for having turned down Charles Bronson's part in *Once Upon a Time in the West*, then the part of an Irish gangster in *Once Upon a Time in America*. I would have liked doing *Once Upon a Time in the West* if I hadn't done the three westerns before. It was time for me to move on and try something new.

When *Coogan's Bluff* came up, Don Siegel heard I'd asked to see some of his movies. The only one I vaguely knew was *Invasion of the Body Snatchers*. They screened for me his two previous movies for Universal, *Madigan* and *Stranger on the Run*. When he found out about this, Don asked to see the films I'd made with Sergio. He liked them, and that's how our association started.[1]

We only had one argument, right at the beginning. Don always insisted on writing the story where it was set. If the story was set in New York, then he'd go and live there. I'm the opposite. I prefer concentrating on the story and making the necessary adjustments afterwards. He liked going to the locations and planning everything around them. This is what happened on *Coogan's Bluff*. The problem was, Don got so involved in the geography that he completely forgot about the story. When he came back, the script had to be rewritten, which is what we did together.[2]

Don always needed an opponent, either the studio or a producer. This went back to his fights with Jack Warner, and usually the enemy was the producer. When we were getting ready to shoot *Dirty Harry*, I said to him, 'Now you're your own producer, you won't be able to find any scapegoats.' He laughed, but ended up blaming the production manager! Don never liked production people. He must have known them when they'd been assistants or secretaries, and he treated them like they still were.

Don hated the old studio system. And I showed him how to escape it. I'd come up the ladder while the new system came into being. My power wasn't linked to any particular studio. This was the age of Frank Wells and John Calley. They didn't tell you how to do your job; they just let you get on with it. But Don was used to endless interference from studio executives. When I was at Universal, I used to slip into the back of the screening rooms where executives were watching rushes and listen to what they said. There'd be at least twenty of them and right in the middle, forced to listen to their idiocies, would be the poor director. We had a bit of that on *Coogan's Bluff*, but managed to get away from it afterwards. At Warner's it was completely different. When I got Don to come over for *Dirty Harry*, all they said was 'Now it's up to you.' All of a sudden, Don had more time than he'd ever had before in his life. Seven or eight weeks seemed to him an eternity. Don could be anything but extravagant. He

1 Eastwood dedicated *Unforgiven* to 'Sergio and Don'.

2 See Siegel's account of the same episode in his autobiography *A Siegel Film* (Faber and Faber).

was always grumbling but, my, he was efficient! He knew what he wanted and he knew how to take decisions. He kept to his budget and to his schedule. His frugality rubbed off on me, I'm sure. On *Escape from Alcatraz*, I persuaded him to shoot in the air-shafts where the escape happened. Why spend a hundred thousand dollars building a set?

Don knew exactly which shots to shoot. But he wasn't rigid. He could add or change a shot at the last moment. I've worked with directors who are completely pole-axed if you suggest a change in a scene. I bumped my head while we were shooting *In the Line of Fire*. To hide the bruise, I asked Wolfgang Petersen whether I could enter a shot from the right rather than the left. Wolfgang had a lot of trouble reorganizing the scene, because he'd imagined it all from the one angle. A detail had changed and it threw him off balance. This was never the case with Don. Sergio would have taken time to think and then probably have said OK, but Don wouldn't have blinked an eyelid. He believed that there were no rules, or if there were rules, they were made to be broken.

Atom Egoyan

Pasolini's *Teorema*

Teorema: Stamp's gaze.

Terence Stamp glides through the shattered family of Pasolini's *Teorema* with an emotional texture and resonance that has left a deep impression on me.

I am most moved in cinema by those moments that somehow escape a rational explanation, yet are made with a deep sense of conviction. These moments provide a transcendence, since they require the viewer to suspend his belief in the literal reality of a film and look for meaning on other levels.

Teorema has many such moments. What I remember most are the moments of seduction, the expressions of the members of the family as they gaze at Terence Stamp, the bashful admiration of the son, the frightened incomprehension of the daughter, the unbridled lust of the mother, the trusting acknowledgement of the father, and most of all, the spiritual fervour of the maid.

Each of these gazes is locked into my subconscious in an iconographic way. Every relationship in the film assumes a heightened reality which transports the drama from the banal rituals of a bourgeois family to the levels of Greek myth.

The film is shot with a plaintive simplicity and spontaneity which I find very moving. As the Terence Stamp character places the father's legs on his shoulder in an attempt to comfort him, as the maid tearfully lifts her skirt for the strange intruder's pleasure, as the son urinates on his empty canvas ... so many moments of this film are overwhelmingly powerful for me.

Pasolini is one of the few directors who have communicated the true nature of transcendent experience on film. As in his brilliant depiction of Christ, *The Gospel According to Saint Matthew*, he is able to convey the emotionality of belief by the sheer directness of his vision.

His cinema is passionate in its conviction, pure in its form, and profound in its vision.

Stephen Frears

Alexander MacKendrick

Alexander MacKendrick with Alec Guiness on the set of *The Man in the White Suit.*

Because of my character, I have always been interested in the *engineering* of direction. I loved hearing how Mark Sandrich would draw charts of Fred Astaire's musicals to work out where to put the dance numbers. What do you want the audience to understand? How do you make things clear? How do you structure sequences within a film? Afterwards – what have you got away with?

Right now, I'm very interested in story-boards. I've read a lot about Hitchcock. When directors use story-boards, do they stick to them? Or do they make the shots up as they go along? How do you pre-plan and yet stay sponta-neous, letting the life flow from the characters? Other people may know the answers to these questions – but of course, I never got to see other directors working. I'm always jealous of the other people on the set for this reason. Alexander MacKendrick (the great director who died in 1993) began work at Ealing studios as a story-board artist.

I saw Sandy MacKendrick's Ealing comedies at a very impressionable age, between ten and fourteen, when I was first sent to preparatory school. *The Ladykillers* I can remember seeing at a first-run cinema; *The Maggie* at a seaside town with my parents; and *Whisky Galore* and *The Man in the White Suit* at school within a couple of years of their release. *Mandy* I refused to go and see. How could a film about a little girl called Mandy be interesting? How could a film about a deaf child be interesting?

Later, by which time I'd seen *Mandy* – in which a deaf girl learns to speak – I realized his great talent lay in not separating comedy from drama. He had a Scottish friend who had apparently said to him when Sandy showed him the script of *The Man in the White Suit*: 'Oh, this is very good. This isn't funny.'

Anyway, I grew up with his comedies as a part of my life, and I think they were clear and piercing in a way that other Ealing comedies – *Passport to Pimlico, The Titfield Thunderbolt* – were not. Clear as the West Coast of Scotland is clear. Or else they were complex and mucky like *The Man in the White Suit* or *The Ladykillers*, never doing what was expected, never showing you comfortable certainties, although they were enormously popular and had an unusual familiarity, full of actors the audience loved and characters they recognized. I can remember a pianist at a concert at school playing the Boccherini quartet immediately recognizable from *The Ladykillers*. I can still hum the theme from *The Maggie*.

By the time I went to university, *The Sweet Smell of Success* had already entered a young man's mythology as if it had been made by Dizzy Gillespie or Thelonius Monk. You couldn't get hipper than that. I've no idea how old I was when I realized that the man who'd filmed Tony Curtis was the man who'd filmed Katie Johnson and Alec Guinness.

I got to know Sandy in the last few years of his life. Colin Young, who had worked at MGM in the Story Department around the time of *Sweet Smell of Success,* must have formed some Scottish mafia with him, and when Colin came to run the National Film School in England, he eventually persuaded Sandy to teach there for, I think, only one term.

I started coming across students who would go on and on about this course that Sandy had taught, and eventually I got my hands on some notes that Sandy had prepared. I think there was a lot of stuff about Aristotle's *Poetics* which I have yet to understand. Diagrams – one from *On the Waterfront* showing Lee J. Cobb's relationships to everybody else and how that had affected the staging. There was also an exercise. A girl had to get a man who is in bed in a hotel room to a station where a train is leaving in twenty minutes. How do you show the man getting up, getting dressed, getting to the station, given that you don't want just to cut directly, that you want to give some weight to those twenty minutes, maybe to build up tension, for example? This exercise has always reminded me of me – it seems a perfect distillation of Film Direction. How do you solve this dramatic problem? How do you keep the audience interested while a man is getting dressed? How do you speed up time? How do you cross space? How do you stay as graceful and witty and expressive as you want to? What begins as an artistic question is eventually reduced to a series of practical matters. What do you want to show the audience? Where do you put the camera? What do the actors do and say? George Devine used to say at the Royal Court: 'All problems are technical.' It has taken me all my life to see the truth of this.

MacKendrick is the ideal man to study if you are interested in these kinds of problem. In the opening minutes of *Whisky Galore* there is a joke that palpably doesn't work. The commentary refers to the islanders' traditional pastimes over a shot of nine children leaving a cottage. By the time he made *The Ladykillers,* his grasp on the material had become consummate. Look at the introduction of Guinness outside the window beyond Katie Johnson, in silhouette against the evening sky. As Guinness walks right to left, the camera tracks right and pans left, leaving Guinness's silhouette now against the buildings of King's Cross but outlined by the smoke from a train in the railway cutting, whilst a haunting train whistle underlines his arrival in the film. This must all have been planned. The camera which photographed the background plate deliberately pans from evening sky to lit smoke. Guinness's movements in the studio are timed to the back projection. The whistle might have been added later.

There are tapes I have heard of Sandy teaching at the National Film School. Like the Zapruder film, they take your breath away by their immediacy. This was what it was like at that moment for those students sitting in a shabby room talking with this man who had made these fine films. So-and-so was sitting there. So-and-so had a bad cold that day. So-and-so was late that day. And Sandy talks about his films, about other people's films, about the students' films.

MacKendrick was spectacularly both an intellectual and a draughtsman; he tried to extract lessons about why certain films, or maybe certain sequences within films, worked – worked in the sense of gripping and interesting audiences. And this had taken him back to the most fundamental drama, back to the Greeks, back to Aristotle. You can hear him sitting at an editing machine with his students, watching these wonderful films he had made thirty years before, saying, 'Oh, I should have shown Alec Guinness earlier, I should have delayed his entrance, I should have photographed him from over here, I tried to do this, I tried to do that'; self-critical, still analysing how he could have made *The Man in the White Suit* better, given the audience still more pleasure.

(Perhaps it was this perfectionism which made him uncomfortable with Hollywood, and vice versa.)

I think what must have happened is that when he retired as a film director in the mid-sixties, he must have been very startled to find himself no longer making films, although he had in his head all this experience and knowledge about how you could construct a credible film, how you could tell stories, how you could prepare audiences to believe the unbelievable. So it was our good fortune that he became a teacher – and, very slowly, through individuals tapping on pipes, the lessons that he taught are being spread.

'Still,' I said to the student who had had the grace to take a tape recorder to class and turn the bloody thing on, 'this is all retrospective. He can't have thought like that at the time. It must have been instinctive. No matter how clever and analytical you are, there's a point when you simply have to invent what the characters are going to look like, what they're going to do and say, etc, etc.'

Everyone knows how films had changed by the mid-sixties, how the world's cinema had opened up, how the changes in equipment had caused different films to be made, how films had been revitalized by the young people who now made them. Sandy, who seemed younger than anyone else, had been brought up on German silent films; he had filled his films with himself, his intelligence, his humour, his quirkiness, his morality; but he was trained in a more classical school, to put everything at the service of the film and the audience. What he learned, what he practised, and what he taught is everything I believe in. Of course, there are also things you can't learn, that you get from God. He had plenty of those.

Samuel Fuller

How John Ford and Max Steiner made my favorite movie

John Ford popped up during the shooting of *Shock Corridor*. Ignoring the chair I shoved behind him, he chewed on the corner of his handkerchief and watched mental hospital inmates pushing their asses across the floor, rowing boats with invisible oars down an invisible river. Catatonics silently frozen to the wall in the long corridor. Then a young black inmate stood on a bench, pulled a white pillow-case over his face, and believing he was the founder of the KKK, he spoke to the inmates: 'We must keep our white race clean.' He told them 'to get rid of all the niggers', commanded them to 'pile every pic-caninny into boats and drown the goddamn nigger babies and children!' He spotted a black inmate ... The Negro KKK leader shouted: 'There's one of them niggers! Let's kill him before he marries my daughter!' The riot takes place as inmates chase the terrified black down the corridor.

Shot finished. I walked with Ford down the deserted corridor.

'Why are you shooting in this two-bit rented stage?'

'The majors turned down my story.'

'Why?'

'It's a mirror of a sick America in the sixties.'

'Rougher on Uncle Sam than *Steel Helmet*?'

'No war this time, but a helluva lot rougher.'

'Those words he spoke through the pillow are damn familiar, Sammy.'

'Words spoken by Southern senators and congressmen, John.'

'Going to be controversial as hell.'

'I *have* to make this story.'

He grunted. We walked in a silence that he broke.

'This corridor was my street in *The Informer*.'

I was stunned.

He pointed. 'The church was there. The set of the informer with the whore was here on the other side of this corridor. Over there the IRA grilled the informer.'

I was still stunned. To me it made no sense. He glanced at my face and read it.

'RKO,' he said, 'was queasy about a movie about the Irish Republican Army still fighting English rule. They wouldn't greenlight me shooting at the studio. They gave me a bread-and-butter budget. I had to make it cheaply in this rented stage of an independent studio, which only rented stages and made no movies.'

To me, it was an outrage – and it was the first dark side of a director's fairy-tale – especially to a director of Ford's stature and to a movie based on Liam O'Flaherty's great proletarian novel of 1925. What a goddamn insult to Ford and O'Flaherty!

Again Ford glanced at my face, and again he read it and said, 'I *had* to make this story.'

We kept silent, but to me the corridor was slowly changing into a fog-filled street with pubs, church, alleys, and the 'Black and Tan' English cops looking for the IRA fugitive for murder.

I found myself in that fog, which was unlike any I've seen in movies because the story Ford shot was in an emotional fog: the IRA operated in a fog, the informer moved through the fog.

I was suddenly back with him in the street, and found myself humming a few notes of *The Informer* score.

'What made you pick Max Steiner?' I said.

'Heart.'

Of course! I remembered the time Victor Young died before he finished the score of one of my movies. The cream of the crop offered to finish the score because they loved Victor Young. I chose Max Steiner. The credit card in that movie read: 'Music by Victor Young, extended by his old friend Max Steiner.'

Ford wanted no canned music for *The Informer*.

Knowing exactly what Ford wanted, Max ran the movie many times all alone in the projection room. He told me he cried every time he ran it. And he ran it until he was completely immersed in the IRA, and in the characters on the screen, and in Ford's arrow-straight emotion always in flight.

And never did Max's music swerve from that flight.

All his notes sought to define a character and contributed a precisely-charged emotional colour to the overall spectrum desired by the director.

RKO released the picture, gave it little publicity and lukewarm distribution. It was shot in twenty-odd days.

Victor MacLaglen won the Oscar as the informer. The picture became a box-office smash. It remains today one of the greatest classics in motion pictures.

All this was the result of a controversial low-budget film.

Every time I see *Gone With The Wind*, Max's music for it remains unforgettable. Every time I see *The Informer*, Max's music makes me cry, simultaneously with Ford's direction of a superb cast.

István Gaál

Henri 'of the Cinémathèque'

The first print of my film *Sodrásban (Current)* has just been made, and I'm just putting the finishing touches to the editing of short films by Sándor Sára and Zoltán Huszárik, when I get a call from the Film-Makers' Association telling me that Langlois is in Budapest. He's seen my film and wants to meet me.

I have never yet had the chance to meet the great guardian of our cinematic kingdom. I introduce myself. Henri looks at me. One rarely encounters such a gaze. His eyes radiate a comforting warmth and ease. One feels safe with him.

I understand him, thanks to my sketchy knowledge of French, but in order to hear the good news twice, I let the interpreter speak for him as well: the Cinémathèque will be screening films made by the Béla Balázs Studios, my film *Sodrásban* included, since I am the first member of the Studio to have had the opportunity to make a feature. Not bad. A world première screening in Paris ...

Paris. The Royal-Monceau Hotel, rue de Courcelles. The smell of fresh ink on the posters, dear Mary Meerson like a character from Chagall, Lotte H. Eisner, a life-size Marie Epstein smiling warmly, and further away, photographs of Clark Gable and Gloria Swanson. The smell of film stock – a bewitching perfume – and of film cans, conjuring up a metallic taste in one's mouth, fills the rooms.

The screening. The Palais de Chaillot and the rue d'Ulm. In the evening, I stand up in front of the audience and say a few words in my appalling French. Then I hand over to the film-maker next to me. Langlois has invited members of the *Nouvelle Vague* to introduce the works of colleagues from a faraway country: Agnès Varda, Eric Rohmer, Claude Chabrol, Jacques Rivette. *Sodrásban* is presented to the public on 5 February 1964. From time to time, Henri appears, organizing, making phone-calls, talking. Mary takes me to a wonderful little shop where the owner, who has a long beard, serves us himself. Occasionally, he slips a few Russian words into his French.

The day for saying farewell arrives too quickly.

Four years later, also in February, I hear that there is a move to relieve Henri of his duties. I don't know the circumstances, but my reaction is unambiguous. I immediately send him a telegram saying simply, 'I'm with you.'

A year later, something extraordinary happens to me. A wing of the Palais de Chaillot, smelling of glue and mortar: Henri, with the air of a man possessed, is showing me round the empty rooms. We walk past half-built walls as he explains to me which periods of world cinema will be represented where. Sometimes he runs into one corner of a room or another, strikes a pose with an agility belying his enormous bulk, and talks.

The next time we meet it's in a different palace. And here he is genuinely in his element. I couldn't say how many films are being shown in how many rooms at the same time. Those who enter are all celebrating cinema. Henri rushes back and forth, his long hair flowing behind him, his face radiant. He delights in the event, in its success. He is happy.

He puts his arm across my shoulder and we walk along. 'We must honour you, my dear István. A retrospective.'

It happened in 1978. Organised by my dear friends Mary, Lotte, Jean-Michel Arnold, Claudine Arnold and Annick Demeule, and introduced by Jean Rouche. But no Henri.

A year earlier, at the end of January 1977, we had planned to go to Tours. We would both have been members of the Jury.

But Henri had other things to do ... [1]

Nowadays, when cinema is on the defensive, or is about to lose itself through being captured by associated arts, it is a real pleasure to talk about the role of the *Cinémathèque Française* to the young people who are bold enough to choose this profession! It was a wonderful, permanent refuge where one could arrive with a film under one's arm and always find someone to whom one could show it, with whom one could discuss it. And if this person wasn't a film-maker, he might be one of the passing students who always watched films with pleasure because they truly loved cinema ... It may be that some of these students are now generals in the armies sent to our rescue. By various stratagems they sometimes succeed in making the projection machine work, so that scratched and stained images can still follow one another on the screen, and a sign can pierce the darkness; the individual sign of each one of us, like a fingerprint, like the impression of our faces and our thoughts.

[1] Henri Langlois died on 13 January 1977.

Peter Greenaway

Just place, preferably architectural place

Fellini's *Roma.*

Place in preference to people. I know my enthusiasms to be stronger for a sense of place than for a sense of people. Yet I like crowds. Perhaps that is not so contradictory. Sufficient numbers of people on a flat and empty plane make a place, a *genius loci* with its own shape. And smell. And temperature. And when the crowd disperses, you are left with a pregnant void that's tangible enough.

At the moment, there is a pregnant void at the back of the Wallace Collection in Manchester Square that is causing me some tangible anxiety.

74

Some disquiet. Disquiet is concomitant with a *genius loci*. It's a large and empty well or basement open to the air. There is no way down into it except from above, over the spear-headed railings, and I doubt whether the sun ever reaches the paving-stones at the bottom. More than once, freakishly, I've seen the shadow of an aircraft flick up the brick façade. The space is about six metres by seven and of triangular shape. It's kept clean and swept. Who sweeps it? The Wallace Collection is full of swords. I have some notion that this basement should be coloured brown and black, and heaped high with swords, and the window should be criss-crossed neatly with strips of sticky brown paper to prevent shattering by bomb-blast. I'm sure that there will have to be a film to justify the place.

This disquiet is not an infrequent occurrence. The island of Sark does it for me, and the house in Robbe-Grillet's *Jealousy*, and Tigerlily's pagoda in *Rupert Bear*, and the bridge of San Luis Rey, and Birnam Wood, and e.e. cummings's *Enormous Room*, the stairway in Kitaj's *Smyrna Greek*, and the open, unprotected country roads of *Uccellacci e uccellini*. Is the *genius* of the *loci* reconvertible? Consider working the situation backwards, and attempt to re-create a real location solely on the information given by a book. Or a painting. Or indeed a film. Very rapidly, that real landscape would be full of voids and blanks and grossly ill-fitting, disquieting details. Long practice has accustomed us to this misalignment of real space. Cinema audiences have well learnt to hide their anxieties and conspire in the great 'location-deception'.

Really to impress itself on the imagination, the place undoubtedly has to have been fashioned by humans. At the very least, it has to have been touched – even if briefly – by human hand. And then it preferably has to be 'untouched', released again a little from human grasp. This applies to the country landscape as well as to the city. Little in England has not been fashioned by human touch; there is little in England of what you could call wilderness. And a very long and extended and continuous human presence in a landscape is going to excite particularly. There aren't too many serious films about continually-used landscape, about excavations, about serious archaeology, about a serious 'love of ruins'. Indiana Jones is no serious archaeologist.

If the delight in place is strong, if you can drive a car or catch a plane or take a boat to visit it, it is just as strong, if not stronger, if the place is physically unreachable. If it exists solely in words. In a painting. In a film. This way you can add your own disquiet. Are you going to find an audience who want to watch a film solely about place? There aren't going to be any people in this hypothetical film – no actors, no extras, no crowds – but just the marks they have made, preferably the marks they made a long time ago. Maybe there could be just a few Chirico shadows on a wall in the middle distance. But the film would be full of quotations, like those impressive eighteenth-century *capriccios* which, avoiding the inconvenience of the unobtainable vantage-point and the uncooperative weather, could put your favourite building in a location of your choosing, could mix up chronologies and styles, could build a Utopian city of immaculate perspectives like della Francesca's Ideal Town. Make your ideal city. Put St Paul's on the Grand Canal and Cologne Cathedral in the Black Forest. You could go better, like Hadrian collecting all the great buildings of his empire and putting them together in his garden. More humbly, like Ellis at Portmeirion – though an Italian campanile in North Wales is problematical. Piranesi must be the most pre-eminent exponent, though Desiderio is more mysterious and Boullée more monumental. Delightfully, you can always pre-fabricate the same architectural deceptions in cinema, in a studio, with an armoury of devices – glass-painting, multiple light-sources, blue-screen back-grounds, *trompe l'oeil* artifices. Architecture built solely for the camera. At noon you can make dawn, and after lunch you can make midnight, with a moon that can be manipulated to shine right into the peristyle and separate out seven separate shadows from seven different pillars.

In this hypothetical *genius loci* film, I would quote the Italian suburbs in *La Strada* – town-edges smelling of burning rubbish and noisy with the echo of sentimental trombones bouncing off bleak tower-blocks. And the long autumn perspective of the cemetery at the end of *The Third Man*. The tree grove in Giovanni Bellini's *Death of St Peter Martyr* – though we would have to clean up the bloodstains. The isolated barns in the background of innumerable Stubbs paintings – new brick, new tiles, the smell of horse urine and the sound of skylarks. The damp ditch in Hunt's *Hireling Shepherd*, a patch of reed and dragonflies in C. S. Lewis's *Out of the Silent Planet*. All wet places are good – as long as there's no fear of drowning. I remember a Po-valley rice drama with Sophia Loren or Gina Lollobrigida – or was it Anna Magnani? I cannot see the actress's face or her bare legs, but I remember the low horizons and the pud-dled rice. I can hear mosquitoes.

Space with architecture. Is there much true interest in the cinema in archi-tectural space for its own sake? Happily, I would say there is – often. Tisse photographing tenements for Eisenstein's *Strike*, Muller photographing New Orleans for Jarmusch's *Down By Law*, Coutard looking at Godard's Paris, especially (and unexpectedly) the tourist monuments, Fellini looking at Rome. With Fellini at the top of the list, there should certainly be two great directors of place – Resnais and Antonioni, with Vierny and Venanzo as cameramen.

I can think of Bogarde in Resnais' *Providence* taking a drive along a street of bourgeois buildings and middle-class palaces, accompanied by the most proud and celebratory music. Narratively slight, unaccountably disturbing. I have rarely looked at comparable buildings without experiencing an exciting disquiet. I remember the English equivalent all too well; every day I walked past similar ivy-covered domestic mausoleums on my way to school – each of their driveways was like a dual-carriageway main road. Resnais is an

excellent placer of architecture. The black-and-white streets of collabora-
tionist Nevers, the sunset casinos in *Muriel*, and the slumbering architectural
nightmare-dreams of *Marienbad*. Post-*Marienbad*, I have now seen Atget's
Versailles and St. Cloud in still, photographic black-and-white. And they
link me to Kurosawa's mists and fogs. How can you have a *genius loci* with
dense mist and fog? Kurosawa's mists and fogs come with charging cavalrymen enveloped inside them like architectural details to help you find the
scale.

To see how best to scale and pitch people, not against fog but against solid,
shiny walls and dead brick and melancholic, end-of-the-day street-corners,
look at any Antonioni black-and-white movie. Superb, atmospheric architectural montages. Even in Antonioni's London, which I am supposed to know –
in *Blow-Up* – why didn't I see the quiet, urban parks in the wind, looking as
dangerous as those Magritte houses at lamp-lighting time, and those isolated
Carel Willink houses, northern Europe's answer to Hopper? I remember the
fuss over the mushroom water-towers in Antonioni's *The Eclipse* – harbingers
of the atomic cloud. I like water-towers. And I like beach-houses. In northern
Europe, they are both touched and then untouched places, without being
archaeology. They are abandoned, not-abandoned places. You never see a
water-tower and a person together. And nobody – in England – ever lives in a
beach-house. Except us. As children. As a family. My father liked the smell of
creosote and methylated spirits – the first to keep out the water and the second
to boil it with. For tea. My father liked the damp, and he was a keen apprecia-
tor of the *genius loci*.

Hilla and Bernd Becher are for taking pictures of water-towers as
Meyerowitz is for taking pictures of beach-houses. I had photographed water-
towers along the River Humber in Yorkshire, perverting their purposes, imagining they had been converted into echoic film-vaults, having in their blunt cir-
cularity much sympathetic resemblance to a stack of empty film-cans that
clanged when kicked. Meyerowitz's white-frame, damp-floored beach-houses,
variously photographed in conditions of thunderstorm or bright noon light,
inspired a canvas-sailed, pavilioned beach-house from the art department of
Drowning by Numbers. That beach-house pleased and entertained so much
that prints from the film-frame were demanded by German and American
viewers, thinking perhaps that they too could build themselves such a country
cabin or seaside gazebo. One gentleman from Maine sent us a cheque for five
thousand dollars for the plans. But our building was pasteboard to the winds
of the North Sea, and it blew right away in October 1987, on the night of the
one and only English hurricane of the twentieth century.

The strongest remembrances of a sense of place I have as a child were of
beaches – any beaches – the unfamiliar places of summer vacations. If possible, I was the last to leave the shore, shut the beach-house door, close the

curtains, pull down the blinds, never certain I would see the world outside again just as I left it.

I was hesitant about travel because of the unlikelihood of being able to repeat my coveted experience of place. As a child, I especially disliked travelling fast in case I failed to understand the connections between places. I slept on trains to avoid consequent misalignment, and I was happy that there were superstitions enough to legitimize my fear of not seeing a place again. I threw coins in every fountain. I begged the use of a cheap camera, but twenty-four black-and-white snaps of the sea and sand in poor focus were not good enough. I still felt uncomfortable in an unknown city until Sacha Vierny encouraged me to carry a compass. He always carries one – it's about the size of a squashed pea. He uses it to be certain from which direction the sun's going to attack him and thwart his control. With a compass at least you can know where north is. A map usually fixes the discomfort. At least a map will offer a spurious sense of capture, and will situate the details and continuity of a place even if you cannot experience every single street. I need to see the back of buildings. Perhaps that's the interest of the basement at the back of the Wallace Collection in London W1.

I am certain now that those early anxieties were not irrelevant to the question of light, because night so often annihilated the problem. I well knew the possibility of change in a location was less likely after dark. Perhaps it is an English preoccupation, since the light changes quickly in England and cannot be relied upon to be repeated. Constable knew this. So did Turner. Constable faced it out and stayed. Turner became exasperated and went to Italy. The value of my anxiety has changed; it has now become professional not personal. I suspect one of the unadvertised reasons for the claustrophobic studio shoots of my past three feature films has to do with anxiety about volatile light-changes outside the film-maker's control.

No architectural excitement of place can be separated from the excitements of light. In *A Zed and Two Noughts*, much of the background architecture was the Hollywood-Dutch Art Deco of van Ravenstyn. At night, through the camera, the architecture seemed to be newly minted. Lion and tiger prowled with beautiful incongruity among the softly-moulded edges. In daylight, all the camera persisted in seeing was the decay of rusting bars and stucco falling off the rococo concrete. Architecture of space after dark is almost a genre in itself, with a particular and curious rule that, for once, the camera can sometimes see what the human eye cannot – unless, that is, the director uses the light of a wartime explosion or the flare of a firework display. The celebrated train-spotter, O. Winston Link, setting out to trap fast-moving locomotives in the blink of a startled eye, also incidentally trapped small-town railway architecture, throwing the brightest of lights uniquely into front porches and dead-of-night sitting-rooms. Bergman's moonlit forests in *The Seventh Seal* should be reprised in this hypothetical film of place, and it is unsettling and comforting at the same time to know that these are not rolling broadleaf oak forests that stretched from Sweden to the Urals in thirteenth-century Europe, but were a thicket of softwoods on the set backlot in the 1950s. You can cheat the *genius loci*.

Architectural space on film is stubborn. To film architecture is to become aware of multiple curiosities of vision and downright retinal deceptions.

On the film *Belly of an Architect* Sacha Vierny and I paced and re-paced selected buildings in Rome to find the exact required emphasis of man and building. We never found it with the impossibly-sited Augusteum, which refused to permit its totality to be seen in any conceivable wide-shot, but maybe the Pantheon and the Victor Emmanuel building were more lenient. If your favoured architectural setting is classical, then you have to fight the frustrating immutability of verticals that persist in pretending not to be diagonals – not every film can shoot its architectural verticals on the angle like Reed's *The Third Man*. You have to accept the disappointment of the refusal of carefully stage-managed entasis to work for the camera lens. All the important horizontals sag in wide-shot. A painter can cheat. Canaletto painting Venice. Saenredam painting Amsterdam churches. Piranesi drawing Rome. Even Sickert painting Camden Town. The painter easily invents multiple vanishing-points. He is cavalier with scale. He keeps an arbitrary palette. His ubiquitous vision is enviable. He can see – with apparent conviction – both sides of the same wall at once. However, if a painter cheats within his very agreeable licences, it is not to say that the architect has not cheated before him. I have come to believe that, in terms of classical perfection, the architect, or perhaps it is his builder, has taken just as many liberties, for the camera – which of course never lies – refuses to agree that the spot chosen by the architect as the centre of all things really is the centre of all things: it's five metres to the right, up a bit, and facing south-south-west – not west at all.

I have, on more than one occasion, been accused of wasting actors in the interests of praising architecture: 'Why employ such talent if all you want is an architectural mannikin, a scale figure for a façade, a body to measure off a curving space?' However, I am pleased to know now three actors, self-consciousness permitting, who are happy to sit in front of a fine piece of architecture and clap it if it pleases them, like the architectural enthusiasts applauding the Roman Pantheon in *The Belly of an Architect*. The architecture in these three cases was first, not surprisingly, the Taj Mahal, then more surprisingly the Wrexham gasometer, and then, most disturbingly, anything by Quinlan Terry – you may create the habit, but there is no telling the result.

Why can't we simply applaud the excitements, the drama and the changing light of a sense of place? One day, I'm going to do it. No actors. No dialogue. No plot. No narrative. No extras. No crowds. It was said of the Great Mosque at Córdoba – a place that is truly architecturally astonishing – that 'there is nothing crueller in life than to be blind in Córdoba'. Now that would be some epitaph for a film.

The Belly of an Architect: applauding architecture.

James B. Harris

Woody Allen – check him out

This is great! I get to shoot my mouth off and say what I want about whomever I want and nobody's around to correct me, argue with me, or just plain tell me to shut up. Now I know what it's like to be a critic.

OK, here we go. I'm going to say right here and now that, all things considered, Woody Allen has to be one of the five best American film-makers active today. *You* can name the other four (may I strongly suggest you include Kubrick and Scorsese?) – I'll stick with Woody.

Not that I feel obliged to defend my opinion, but you may some day be lucky enough to be asked to write about film directors, as I have, and you'd be doing your readers, as well as yourself, a huge disservice if you didn't carefully consider Woody's accomplishments. So for your sake, and the sake of your readers, I'll waive my right of no obligation to defend, and pass along some food for thought. I'd suggest an open mind for better digestion.

Here's a joke: When they make *Schindler's List* 2, they're going to use as the main musical theme 'Send in the Kleins'. End of joke. Do I hear silence?

In order to appreciate this joke, one must be knowledgeable about its three elements: (1) *Schindler's List* deals with the extermination of the Jews in a Nazi concentration camp; (2) Klein is a Jewish family name; (3) There exists a popular song from the musical play *A Little Night Music* entitled 'Send in the Clowns'. Even with this knowledge, one might not respond to this joke if sensitive to anything connected with the Holocaust.

Woody, to a great extent, faces the same problems inherent in that joke when his films play before world-wide audiences. There are prerequisites of knowledge the viewer must bring with him in order fully to enjoy the experience, otherwise it's doubtful he'll ever get below the surface, thus finding Woody's films to be nothing more than amusing.

The same requirement applies, although to a lesser extent, when evaluating Woody as a film director. Without having directed yourself (therefore not being able to bring with you the knowledge acquired by doing so), you can only make surface judgements.

A director's first responsibility when making a film is to begin with a flawless script. Most directors fail to do this. They either don't have the ability to recognize the flaws, or they are of a mind that gives top priority to cinematic techniques and visual effects. This mind-set is getting more and more popular these days – simply because young people with underdeveloped minds (having been weaned on television) are in some cases making these kinds of film, but in most cases strongly supporting them at the box-office.

Unlike most film-makers, Woody begins his directing in the writing stage. He's one of the few directors originating the basic material (story, concept, situations, etc) from which he either writes or co-writes the screenplay. Check out how many directors are capable of doing this. And while you're at it, check out their body of work and see if it compares with the dozens of quality films Woody has made. Take a tip from Woody – the play is definitely the thing.

Casting is another thing that's definite. Just look at Woody's impeccable selection of actors to portray his characters. A mistake at this early stage of a project is almost as fatal as flaws in the script. But scripts and casting are both Woody's strong points. It seems as if he always eliminates the problems these can cause before a single frame of film has run through the camera.

The formula is simple, and it works out every time: 'The better the script and the cast, the lesser the difficulty in directing the film.' Maybe it's an over-simplification, but I've always found that, after those two elements have been dealt with, directing the film was for the most part a question of taste – the ability to discern and select what plays, where it plays, how it plays, and in what order it plays (editing the film). Woody is master of all this. Maybe it's because he's an actor also. But, on the other hand, think how difficult it is to direct the other actors while acting in the film as well. It's amazing how, in spite of this, all the performances in his films are outstanding.

Don't think I'm unaware of negative reactions to Woody's work, especially here in Hollywood. But that's to be expected. When Lenny Bruce was alive and performing as a stand-up comic, he was referred to as 'too hip for the room'.

That's the case with Woody today. His films are too hip for the general public. It's like playing jazz for an audience that gets off on country-and-western music.

If we can make that analogy, we can understand some of the limitations Woody's films have for mainstream audiences.

As you know, jazz deals mostly with improvisations and variations on themes. You might say the same for Woody's approach to film-making. It's a fact that, whether it be film or music, the general public wants to hear the melody (that is, the film's narrative) played loud and clear at all times. When the variations and improvisations take over, audiences get lost and usually become confused, if not hostile. They are unable to follow due to their inability to retain the original melody in their minds and match it with what's being played at the time. Needless to say, they have no way of appreciating the expertise or creativity of the artist.

If there is some validity to the jazz-film analogy, it's just possible we can make the jazz connection with Woody.

Let's start with the fact that Woody *is* a jazz musician. His instrument is the clarinet. He's been playing publicly for years at Michael's Pub in New York City. It really doesn't matter how well he plays – I imagine he's no threat to other jazz clarinet players such as Eddie Daniels, Tony Scott, or Buddy de Franco. But the mere fact that he plays is more than enough for me. It might just account for his impeccable sense of timing, both as a director and comedy actor. Woody's use of variations on a theme (*Bullets Over Broadway* was originally a sketch by television comic Sid Caesar) and the improvisations apparent in many of his films, could also support the possibility of a jazz connection.

At any rate, whether it's jazz or just the hipness in his soul, Woody has given us an incredible body of work, for which I'm most thankful.

Incidentally, 'hip'[1] is defined in Webster's Dictionary as 'characterized by a keen, informed awareness of, or interest in, the newest developments.' I take 'newest developments' to mean what's happening, what's going on. And believe me, Woody knows what's going on.

There's a lot more to be said on Woody's behalf – but I'm going to let *you* say it. I'm sure you will, once you check him out.

1 Some say 'hep' – but it's unhip to say 'hep'.

Monte Hellman

Victor Erice's *Spirit of the Beehive*

'A work of art should also be "an object difficult to pick up". It must protect itself from vulgar pawing, which tarnishes and disfigures it. It should be made of such a shape that people don't know which way to hold it, which embarrasses and irritates critics, incites them to be rude, but keeps it fresh. The less it's understood, the slower it opens its petals, the later it will fade.'

Jean Cocteau

Nestor Almendros told me to look at Victor Erice's *Spirit of the Beehive* because he knew I needed a Spanish director of photography, and thought Luis Cuadrado's work was the best he had ever seen. He knew Cuadrado had lit the film when he was nearly blind, by having his assistant describe the sets to him, and telling him where to put the lights. He didn't know that Cuadrado had since died of a brain tumour.

I have now seen the film more than a dozen times – more than any other of my favourite films. I never tire of it; in fact, I am more enriched by each successive viewing. It reveals its secrets slowly.

It is a secret and mysterious work, concerned with the biggest mysteries of all: creation and death. It is also concerned with family relationships – husband and wife, father and daughters, sister and sister – and with each character's attempts to communicate, as well as with their ultimate isolation and loneliness. Finally, it is about cinema itself, and the power of cinema to invade our dreams and awaken our knowledge and fears.

There are no accidental images nor extraneous scenes. The opening shot of the father, his face distorted by the screen of the beekeeper's hood, foreshadows the scene near the end where he becomes the Frankenstein monster in his daughter's fantasy. In other scenes, the children watch Dr Frankenstein, on screen, create his monster from parts of bodies; then later they create their own monster in the classroom by adding arms and legs to a chart of the human body. Even the image of the hexagonal cells of the honeycombs is repeated in the small hexagonal window-panes and the hexagonal screening of the apiary.

The film opens with the arrival of a travelling projectionist at a small town in Spain during the early forties – his film is the original *Frankenstein*, starring Boris Karloff. The central character in our film is a five-year-old girl, Ana,

Spirit of the Beehive.

who along with her slightly older sister Isabel, attends the screening. Ana is disturbed by the killing of the little girl in the film, and doesn't understand why the monster is also killed. Isabel pretends to have the answers to Ana's questions, but when pressed, can say only that they're not really dead. It's a movie and nothing real. Besides, she's seen the monster. He's a spirit, and she can make him appear whenever she calls him.

In subsequent scenes, the children play with and at death. Isabel experimentally attempts to strangle her cat, stopping when the cat scratches her. She applies the blood on her finger to her lips, as if it were lipstick. Later, she pretends to be dead to frighten Ana. Finally, Ana experiences the death of a real person, an escaped prisoner whom she befriended. We feel Ana's crisis as our own, for we have all passed from innocence to knowledge of mortality at some time in our own childhood.

The adults remain more enigmatic. The wife writes letters to a young man in the army in France, perhaps a former lover. The husband works late into the night at his desk, eventually falling asleep in his chair. The wife goes to the train station to mail a letter to her soldier, and sees another soldier sitting in the train as it slowly pulls away. They are separated by the glass window of the compartment as they watch each other, each in their own sound-proof universe, isolated.

The most difficult thing to portray in cinema is privacy. The very process of making films is public, with so many people looking on. Actors have been trained to communicate with the audience, so they too are uncomfortable just being. Many directors try to achieve this level of reality by using non-actors, but rarely successfully. Erice succeeds extraordinarily well, using professional actors. His greatest achievement is with the children, where there is a fine line between amateur and professional.

Victor Erice has only made a new film every ten years. I'm sure part of the reason for this is economic; his film *El Sur*, shown at the 1983 Cannes Film Festival, was really only the first half of a two-part work, the second half of which was never made. But part of the reason may also be his meticulous striving for perfection. His last film, about a painter trying to paint a quince tree over the period of a year, and finally giving up because he cannot capture the motion, I feel may be as much autobiographical as biographical. I regret there aren't more films from this brilliant artist, but if there were only *Spirit of the Beehive*, he would still be a master.

Otar Iosseliani

About Boris Barnet

In order to choose a film-maker whom I respect and to whom I owe my joy and love of film-making, I have to observe certain criteria. He could be cultured, but that's not essential. He could be honest; it's necessary, but not sufficient. I prefer to apply Cauchy's criterion for mathematical analysis which holds that a subject must be both necessary and sufficient. So the film-maker must be humane, good, serious, and not a cheat; he must know what he is talking about, how to communicate his message, and why he is doing so. He must also be, throughout his whole life, the sole owner of his thoughts and the work he has accomplished. In no way can he follow ready-made clichés or waste his energies using methods invented by others. Above all, he must show imagination and a sense of fantasy by refusing, for example, to adapt famous literary works or film the biographies of famous people. That is also a moral position. Faced with a great text, one knows that the author has expressed himself fully. There is no need to translate it into a another, more primitive language than his own.

So for all these reasons, I'd like to talk about Boris Barnet. He was a large man, physically at ease and determinedly generous. Since God had endowed him with enormous gifts, he could be neither mean nor stingy, nor the thief of other people's ideas.

More importantly, he lived in the Soviet Union and behaved as if the state didn't exist, except as a paradox. *Okraina*, for example, dealt with the relationship between a Russian woman and a German, both of whom had lived through the First World War. It was also a film about dressmakers and shoemakers, artisans who, by the very fact of having to work together, cannot be enemies. This was a point of view directly opposed to that of the Communists, who held that only the proletariat, who made nothing, could unite and build a socialist paradise on earth. As a poet, Mayakovsky, also a great talent and a generous man, fell into the trap of believing this Communist dream due to his lack of education. Where Barnet would project himself into the past and knew that all on this earth was vanity and that everything ended badly, Mayakovsky believed that the socialist revolution would be a decisive turning-point. And on that unfortunately mistaken belief, he built his poetic achievement. Barnet did not make such an error. Dovzhenko did because he was a peasant, revelling in having learnt to read and write. He had been accepted into a circle of great men who impressed him deeply: Pudovkin, fellow-believers like

Mayakovsky, and the arrogant, cynical and cold Eisenstein, who tossed off paradoxes left and right, manipulated words and images, but who was ideologically empty, believing that art existed merely as form.

When Barnet realized it was no longer possible for him to follow the only profession he knew, he escaped into genre films – adventure movies, police and spy films. Mikhail Romm – a man who deserves our respect – had made *Boule de Suif*, adapted from Maupassant's story, and then was broken by the system because of his weakness, fear or desire to be obedient. He went on to make films about Lenin, but always dreamed of returning to his first love. Barnet, however, stopped practising his art. He spent his time playing practical jokes. His friend Nikolai Chenguelaya recounts how Romm was shooting *The Thirteen* in the Kara-Koum desert. At the time, Barnet was living with the very beautiful Elena Kouzmina, a famous Soviet actress who was playing in the

Boris Barnet with his actors.

By the Bluest of Seas.

film. A small plane flew over the location, and at the same moment Kouzmina disappeared behind the sand-dunes. A week later, the little plane flew over again, but in the opposite direction. They discovered dozens of empty champagne, vodka and beer bottles behind the dunes. Barnet, who'd been flying the plane, and Kouzmina had spent the entire week drinking and making love in the desert! And the filming could only start again when Barnet flew away! Barnet was a charming, honest man, solid but impecunious. He was much loved by women who were obliged to live with mediocrities who protected them materially, but whom they detested.

He later lived with an editor, thirty years his junior, from the Mosfilm Studios. She told me a great deal about him and said she had never met anyone quite like him.

Why should we follow Barnet's example? Because he did everything himself without adapting anyone else's work. He believed one must never betray oneself, that a film must be clear, precise, articulate and its subject well-fashioned and identifiable. As far as he was concerned, it was impossible not to be faithful to one's own project because it was a 'decree from heaven'. I rediscovered this notion of a 'decree from heaven' through Dovzhenko, who was my professor at VGIK. He told me that every act in one's life must be accomplished as if it were one's last. He'd say that one could be knocked down by a bus in the street and

Okraina.

leave the world having done something badly. One must never believe that one can repair what one has done badly, for death can come at any moment.

I particularly like Barnet's *By the Bluest of Seas*. It's a marvel, full of an admiration for life, for love, desire, and fidelity. All with a *kolkhoz* for a setting! But Barnet places this *kolkhoz* on an island and cuts it off from the rest of the world. In fact, it's a fishing community linked to a beautiful, powerful, glittering sea, ploughed by sailing boats and overlooked by clouds. Two men fall in love with the same woman, only to discover she's waiting for a man who is far away. Anything is possible at any moment of this film. One moment, you think she is falling for one of the men, then the next moment the other. In the end, it's neither. The pain which arises out of unrequited love is transformed into beauty. There is the scene where the two men, unhappy with their lot, eat a bitter lemon which makes them grimace; or the equally wonderful scene when, during a storm, a wave throws the woman into the hold of the boat where people are sitting.

I knew Barnet a little. We met once or twice over a bottle of vodka. We talked of insignificant things. He showed me how to win at arm-wrestling, told me stories about the time of the tsars. We were drinking and suddenly he said, 'By the way, the pleasure of refusing a gift is a privilege one can get a real kick out of.' And it's noticeable that he never had the kind of charm which predisposed the Bolsheviks either to kill him or to be taken in by him. For example, Bulgakov, another giant of the period, provoked the authorities to such an extent they killed him. As for Barnet, he was absent from the social stage. He didn't want a flat, or an Order of Lenin, or favours, or any of the things that pushed some Russians to compromise themselves and betray others. Mikhail Romm, who was the only film-maker to confess publicly, as an example to others, the errors he had committed, received a state *dacha* as thanks for the films he made about Lenin. He once asked the forester why the elms had been chopped down around the house, and the forester answered, 'Because they were beautiful'. Romm would go on to say that Barnet was not the kind of tree one could cut down. Barnet was a phenomenon apart, because he asked for nothing.

Nothing Barnet made later can erase the memory of *By the Bluest of Seas, Okraina* or *The Girl With the Hatbox*. There are film-makers who are thinkers, but too much thought can deprive a director of the lightness which is vital to his art. One can detect the metaphysical dimension in Barnet's work, but thought never dominates. His art is nonchalant and superficial, like life. At no stage do serious ideas stultify his work, as they sometimes do in Thomas Mann or Tolstoy. Oddly enough, Barnet's method reminds me of Anatole France's, as exemplified by *The Opinions of Monsieur Jérôme Coignard*. That is why, out of all the directors who've influenced me – Clair, Vigo, Tati – I chose to speak about Barnet, less well-known than they but nonetheless belonging to the same family.

Okraina.

Elia Kazan

The Hyphenated Americans

Question: Why have I disappeared from the film world? Years ago, when I decided to turn to the novel, I was propelled by an unfulfilled wish to make films for my heart rather than for Twentieth Century Fox. I began to ask myself questions that were so simple they are childish. I remember the morning I asked the face in the small, circular mirror I use when I'm preparing to shave, the most childish of all questions: 'Who the hell do you think you are?'

I discovered that I'd never answered that. I was not as I wished to be, truly an American, rather than someone who had slipped into this country long ago holding his father's hand. It took me years before I answered my question in the small, round mirror. I then accepted the basic fact that I was an American dash Anatolian – or Anatolian dash American. Which do you prefer?

I discovered I was not alone. Now we have, in plain view, African-Americans, Italian-Americans and, before them, Irish-Americans, and so on, all people separated from their own traditions and character and mysteries. When I thought about it, it seemed to me that most of these *hyphenates* became truly American (which is what I wanted) when they most became separate, special and apart, and that this was the worth of the country – much more than other things.

I thought about this problem when I had trouble attracting funds for the films I wanted to make about hyphenated Americans. I concluded I would always have this trouble, which was about the time I disappeared from the world of film-making and took to the novel.

To tell the rest of the truth, the moving-over was not easy. But there I was, I made the choice. And there was one result I was proud of: the autobiography I called *A Life*. But it was a difficult choice to make. I went ahead with it and am now writing another novel, which is not a novel so much as an extension of *A Life*.

I wish all this had not happened as it did, but there are advantages and gains. I don't have to beg and scrounge and bend away from how I truly see things. A novel is a clean thing, it's all mine and I can say in this way that I am satisfied.

But the truth is that this is not what I wished for. What I wanted was to make a film with my son Chris. It was to be called *Beyond the Aegean*. I spent four bitter years trying to raise the money for this film. Now I have written a novel with the same title and it will be published in New York by Knopf this spring.

Am I satisfied with this? Of course I am. And of course I am not. Probably I wasn't a good enough screenplay writer. I can accept that. So, OK.

But the regret and the considerable pain are still there. I failed myself and I failed my son Chris, that's for sure. And that is not forgotten.

Zsolt Kézdi-Kovács

The Round-Up

It is said that, at the end of the 1966 Cannes Festival, the jury of venerable sages – Achard, Genevoix, Giono, Pagnol, Salacrou, Maurois – were so tired that they slept during the entire screening of the last film to be shown in competition. Thus *The Round-Up*, perhaps the best Hungarian film of the sixties, failed to win a prize. The value of Jancsó's film is hard to underestimate; from the political, ideological and artistic points of view, it is the most important of his works.

The political aspect

We must not forget that the film was made only nine years after the repression that followed the 1956 revolution. The last political prisoners had just been released, and people still remembered those who had been executed. The dictatorship had softened, there was no longer any open repression, but the state, present in all aspects of day-to-day life, still held society in its grip. The state wanted to make itself acceptable internationally. One could not speak openly about what had happened under Stalinism; nevertheless, one had to find a way of expressing what one had lived through, if not openly then at least through symbols and parables. The film is set in 1860, eleven years after the great revolution of 1848-49: political prisoners are being released and the Habsburgs are attempting to rein back the repression. The audience of 1965 immediately understood the historical parallel. But, beyond this, Jancsó touched on the basic mechanisms of modern dictatorships. Pure violence (prison, handcuffs, chains, whips, death) are only one aspect of the relationship linking the oppressor (dressed in black) and the oppressed (the 'enchained'). The manipulation of the oppressed, the fate of prisoners – made to turn on each other, blackmailed into betraying or killing their fellows, renouncing consciously or unconsciously their principles, their humanity even – is what really holds the audience's interest. The brigand denouncing his companion in exchange for freedom, the imprisoned policeman, or the images of hopeless escapes over the endless plains are not events from a previous century, but the stories of prisoners of war and internees in gulags and concentration camps (both Jancsó and Hernadi, his writer, had been imprisoned in the Soviet Union).

The revolution had failed, the state still pulls all the strings, traitors are amongst us, one cannot escape this world: this is the message of the film. And the audience was grateful to hear it, because it meant that others knew this too, and therefore all was not yet lost.

A million people went to see the film in Hungary.

The cinematic aspect

Formal innovations had already appeared in some of Jancsó's previous work, for example *Cantata* and *My Way Home*. Scenes filmed in one shot are more and more common, and the camera follows the characters like a detached observer. Jancsó consciously uses lessons drawn from Antonioni (a rigorous use of tracking-shots, the dissolution of filmic time and space will only come later in the seventies). The dialogue is increasingly 'dry' (the keyword for Jancsó during this period was precisely that – 'dry'). The music is functional; it never underlines emotion.

The characters have a particular movement, a kind of dance. They do not look each other in the eye and rarely stop – as if they were avoiding each other.

The space is vast and the distance incalculable. One cannot see an end to it: does it exist? All this communicates a sense of insecurity to the audience: the world is not present, it is beyond our comprehension, impossible to know. But we remain the subjects of a power which is always visible.

The work

Jancsó began his career making documentaries. After a brief expressionist period, he made realist fictions. By the end of the sixties, abstraction, the imaginary became dominant. It's above all a story of film first abandoning reality – as in *Winter Sirocco* – then space and finally, with *The Heart of the Tyrant* at the beginning of the eighties, time itself.

But in *The Round-Up* there is a rare balance between the real and the imaginary. The film is almost entirely shot in real locations. The fortress with its white walls shaped like cubes, the black clothes of the interrogators, the incessant noise of the wind anticipate the abstract sounds and images of the later films. Jancsó's characteristic style is present here in all its rough freshness. And that is precisely why the film is so perfect and unique. His desire to use single-shot scenes systematically to show large movements and characters is not yet evident. Even though the film is not totally polished, its story, characters and style were already perfectly conceived at the writing stage. I had just returned from Paris in September 1964 when I, who was about to become Jancsó's first assistant on the film, took part in a read-through of a first draft of the script in his tiny apartment. At that moment, those of us who were sitting around the yellow stove in the apartment realized that a masterpiece was being born.

The Round-Up.

Abbas Kiarostami

From Sophia Loren to *La Dolce Vita*

To avoid all misunderstandings, I should confess at once that I haven't been particularly struck by either a director or a film. My films are much more influenced by events which occur in daily life, and which, without realizing it, I store in my memory well before they make their appearance in a new film. I haven't seen a film for ages. I don't know why, I've simply lost the habit of going. Recently, I attempted a reconciliation with cinema, but I was disappointed.

It was no longer the cinema I had given up several years previously. It was a cinema that was hollow, violent and, more often than not, devoid of identity. But I did see some good films on video. Unfortunately, the tapes were of such poor quality I found them difficult to watch.

I only know the contemporary directors by name. If asked whether I'd actually seen the films of Kieślowski or Angelopoulos, I'd have to say no. But they do interest me. I'd also like to see the work of the Portuguese director Botelho and the Spaniard Almodóvar, but I haven't had the chance. I doubt these artists would wish me to see their films on poor-quality video cassettes.

So I have to admit that I rarely go to the cinema, and that this isn't solely due to the poor quality of the screening. I can't even bear seeing my own films, either on tape or in the cinema, with the exception of course of *Close-Up*. In general, I walk out half-way through a film because I can't stay any longer. This may have nothing to do with the film.

Therefore, if I must talk about the influence, if any, cinema has had on me, I should mention the films I saw thirty years ago, in my youth.

First I'll talk about when I was very young. Before knowing cinema, I encountered film itself. At the time, schoolboys like me would collect little bits of film and stick them into albums like stamps. I'd sometimes have images of men and women and not even know which actors or actresses they were. For example, I knew Tarzan, but I only discovered many years later he was Johnny Weissmuller. I also had a picture of man with neatly-combed hair, a moustache and a splendid smile. I later found out he was Clark Gable. I identified Susan Hayward in the same way after seeing her films.

We swapped these pictures – mostly close-ups of actresses – amongst ourselves before sticking them in our albums. The only difference between them and a stamp collection was that, in order to see them, one had to hold them up to the light.

Amongst the actresses there was one who was unique, Sophia Loren, and it was she more than anyone else who attracted me to cinema. I went only to see her. The rest of the film didn't matter. Her splendour put everything else in the shade. She filled the universe of my adolescence. She resembled no one: she was both wife and mother.

At the suggestion of a friend, my elder sister took me to the cinema for the first time when I was eleven. The first image I saw was the MGM lion. He roared and I was terrified. I groped in the dark for my sister's hand to hold. I remember a man in the film with a big nose who played the piano. I found out who he was later – Danny Kaye – but I don't remember the name of the film. I also don't remember why I fell asleep before the end.

When I was sixteen or seventeen I started to go to the cinema more seriously. Darkened auditoriums, Italian films, young girls, Vespas, long, narrow alleys, frivolities and American tourists were all mixed in with the exhilaration of youth. Or there'd be other, heroic films, full of emotion, like those with Ulysses or Maciste ...

I only went to the cinema for entertainment. I can't remember having seen during this period one single intelligent or exceptional film, except of course for the one that made an immediate impression. An impression that was both different and profound. The film is not perhaps one of the director's best. I know it doesn't appear amongst the ten best films ever made. But it deeply influenced me. For the first time, I became interested in the director of a film and understood what role he played in the making of it. For the first time, the impact of the performers, such as Mastroianni – the 'Marcello' of those days – and the beautiful Anita Ekberg, was eclipsed by the brilliance of the work. The film belonged to the director. While we watched, my girl-friend grumbled constantly, saying she wanted to leave. She complained that the story made no sense. Perhaps she thought that the attention I was giving the film meant I was losing interest in her. This kind of reaction was perhaps due to our youth: going to the cinema together had a particular significance at that age. We left the cinema and for hours I walked the streets alone.

That's become a habit. Every time I see a beautiful film, I walk for hours afterwards, getting lost. But, thirty years later, I'd like to know what I was thinking that particular day, what I discovered on my walk.

Why was this film so different? What distinguished it from all the others? Unfortunately, I can't recall. I simply remember a few ambiguous images. I saw *La Dolce Vita* when I was twenty-one. At the time, making films hadn't even occurred to me, but I do remember thinking a great deal about Fellini, the film's director. I would have liked to have met him, to have known how a film-maker could transform such a seemingly incoherent story into such an overwhelming film, a film which would stay etched for ever in the spectator's mind.

La Dolce Vita.

In my opinion, *La Dolce Vita* is the very image of moral and social degeneration. People who have taken part in their own self-destruction observe their decadence in a state of complete passivity. *La Dolce Vita* is a spectacle of futility, powerlessness. Men hopelessly chase will-o'-the-wisps, and Fellini – like

Dante before him – sees, through the poetic incoherence, a destiny that is both obscure and uncertain. Thirty years later, we feel this destiny approaching. Fellini announced the decadence of contemporary civilization and the decay of morality in the bourgeois, intellectual world. This is my present interpretation of the film. But I'd be curious to know what it was when I was young. Of course, at the time I wasn't capable of analysing any film, but I'd like to know what part that film played in the evolution of the young man I once was, who looked for emotion and imagination in those darkened theatres.

In *La Dolce Vita*, Fellini feels responsible for the life of that man. His film is the autobiography of an artist who can continue to live because he has found a motive for existence. The final scene is the response of a director who is trying to find a way to breathe and to live. And it's the only scene I can remember. On that sad, damp morning, on the edge of the sea, a fresh, intelligent young girl stands her ground against the actors, the intellectuals of the film: that is the only hope the director offers us. This ideal, unreal hope is my ideal universe, not just as a director, but as a man. I believe we men don't have the right to live in such a lugubrious manner or to take such a pessimistic view of the world. I think I read somewhere – perhaps they were Fellini's words – that the film was a 'tender incident'. And I believe it. Must one possess some kind of power to analyse a work? Or is it enough to have feelings, experiences similar to its maker, apart from what one may have in common ethically, religiously, linguistically and geographically? Feelings and experiences which link the present to both the past and the future, and unite different peoples.

In *La Strada*, which is my favourite film, Fellini is God. The film was more powerful than a work of neo-realism. With *La Strada*, Fellini composed a lyric poem, the great epic of man's pain and joy.

La Strada: Masina with trumpet.

Krzysztof Kieślowski

The Sunday Musicians

In the name of the friendship I feel for you and *Positif*, I am answering your three questions. In all sincerity, though, I don't believe this type of enquiry can help us to grasp either the state of cinema or the state of mind of us film-makers. With the approaching centenary of cinema, many newspaper and television journalists have tried to make lists of the directors, actors or films which are the favourites of other directors, other actors or the public. This can often lead to amusing results. I was recently asked by the editors of *Sight & Sound* to make a list of the ten films which have most affected me. Here is my list – although the order is by no means significant (film number one could be number ten and vice versa):

La Strada by Fellini; *Kes* by Ken Loach; *Un Condamné à Mort s'est Echappé* by Robert Bresson; *The Pram* by Widerberg; *Intimate Lighting* by Ivan Passer; *The Sunday Musicians* by Karabasz; *Ivan's Childhood* by Tarkovsky; *Les Quatre Cents Coups* by Truffaut; *Citizen Kane* by Orson Welles; *The Kid* by Chaplin.

Nine of these films you know. So I shall speak about the one you don't know, which for me is as important as all the others.

The Sunday Musicians[1]

Twenty, perhaps thirty, men enter a small and dimly-lit hall. We recognize it to be in one of those places, so redolent of the period, that were called a 'medium-sized industrial unit'. The sort of place where all the chairs are broken, the tables are scratched, the walls are peeling, and the floor hasn't been cleaned for ages. Night has fallen. The men have the faces of workmen, their thick hands and fingers indelibly stained by labour. The director doesn't attempt to place them socially, but as we see them in close-up for ten minutes, we guess them to be men involved in hard physical labour.

Most of them are already in their forties or fifties.

They take musical instruments out of battered old cases. Horns, trumpets, trombones, mandolins, guitars, accordions. If I remember rightly, there are no violinists or pianists; all the instruments are rather crude. The conductor is

1 *The Sunday Musicians (Muzykanci)*, Polish documentary by Kazimierz Karabasz (1958; 10 minutes)

even older: over sixty, with grey hair and moustache. They put their music on rickety stands. The only thing which evokes the grander world of the concert hall or opera house is the conductor's baton. It's a baton of good quality. It stands out. The men sit down.

Almost all of them solemnly put their spectacles on. The conductor too. Unlike the baton, the spectacles belong to their world – almost all are held together across the bridge of the nose or at the hinges by Elastoplast. Sellotape didn't yet exist, so people used Elastoplast bought in chemists. You can see this very well on the screen. A few of the spectacles, the conductor's for example, have cracked lenses.

Karabasz's *The Sunday Musicians* won the Grand Prix at the Oberhausen Short Film Festival in the late fifties. At the time, this was the most important documentary festival in the world. The film was then shown in several countries. A Dutch spectacle-maker saw it in Holland. He wrote to Karabasz, who then asked the heroes of his film what their sight defects were. A few months later, they all received brand-new spectacles from Holland. In those days, in Poland, such a gift had great value.

The men start playing. They play clumsily and, even though the music is as simple as their instruments, it's rather difficult to make out a melody. The conductor quickly interrupts them by tapping the table with his baton. It isn't the first time they've rehearsed the piece, and he's annoyed that the musicians seem to have forgotten everything they learnt at earlier rehearsals. He loses his temper and even starts shouting. But he comes from Vilnius (the city was part of Eastern Poland before the war) and his accent, so soft and pleasing to the Polish ear, gives even his most terrible outbursts a soft, lilting quality. They rehearse again and again. Gradually, and after many interruptions – during which the conductor takes various musicians to task and, humming, shows them how and when to play – the melody starts to appear. By the sixth or seventh minute the music becomes recognizable.

For a couple of minutes we watch the men: we see their hands, their faces, we follow their fluid, uninterrupted playing. Then the camera leaves this dark place. A wide shot reveals a tram depot at dawn. We see men in overalls covered in grease-stains. They have hammers of various sizes, pincers, anvils. Sparks fly from soldering machines. The first trams leave the depot. In the maintenance pits, the men work on the trams that won't be running in town that day. During this little scene, the sound of the music mixes with the sounds of the depot. Final credits.

I know that Karabasz spent several months with his musicians and that he was with them during rehearsals. It's rare for a short film to express so much, in such a beautiful and simple manner, about the fundamental human need to create.

Because, apart from satisfying our elementary needs – survival, breakfast, lunch, supper, sleep – we all aspire to something more, something that can give a meaning to life and elevate it. The more difficult this is to achieve, the greater the joy when one succeeds. For two minutes of *The Sunday Musicians*, this is the joy one reads on the faces of a few dozen middle-aged men with broken spectacles who together play a simple melody in a 'medium-sized industrial unit'.

Since I need a few more lines to fill the required three pages, I'll answer your other questions. Amongst directors, Ingmar Bergman affected me the most. I consider Giulietta Masina in *La Strada* to be the greatest actress, and Charlie Chaplin, up to and including *The Great Dictator*, to be the greatest actor.

Matjaz Klopcic

Vertigo

To choose a film that has particularly struck me and to describe its merits, as I've been asked to do by *Positif*, seems to me a difficult, thankless, and even pretentious task. Apart from the great achievements of world cinema (*2001: A Space Odyssey, La Règle du Jeu, Hiroshima mon amour, La Dolce Vita*), the first great shock I experienced was Alfred Hitchcock's *Vertigo* (1959). It's quite possible this film was decisive in making me choose cinema as the art of the century. In it, I saw the realization of my dreams; from the moment I saw the film, cinema obsessed me as the craft of the chosen. I saw *Vertigo* in Ljubljana, a small town in Slovenia, which seems to me, even now, hardly the place in which to judge the achievements of world cinema. Since then, alas, I've never felt the extraordinary sensation that overwhelmed me when I first saw *Vertigo*.

Amongst all its themes, one struck me particularly: the influence of the dead, the influence of dreams on the life of men. *Vertigo* transports us into the world of dreams. One could say this, with varying degrees of conviction, about all its themes. This constant tendency in the film corresponds to the kind of imagination that produced the literary motifs of the beginning of this century. The significance of these motifs did not lie in sentimental confessions or descriptions of a supposedly scientific or realist nature, but in dreams, myths and symbols. What is a dream? 'A dress woven by fairies' as Nerval described it? Is it an escape, the opposite of action, as is commonly thought? A denial of reality? An insufficiency of existence or a supplement to it? A reflection of desires we know to be mortal? Dreams are perhaps all of these things, but when they are as lucidly delineated as they are in Hitchcock, they become both a refusal to adapt to life and, most of all, a desire to adapt life to oneself. The dream – *Vertigo* shows this – can very well be defined as a privileged moment, a celebration of the spirit ...

In this search for an identity that Hitchcock's heroes never cease to pursue – often with a woman by their side – the slow work of time also makes an appearance. A man does not destroy himself *in abstracto*, but in time. We also see that, from the sequence under the sequoias onwards, time itself makes its own notable appearance in the film – all great film-makers have either praised or deplored this moment. The escape from time, the linear escape which drags everything with it, especially happiness ...

'There is nothing more terrible in history than the fall of empires,' said

Nerval, 'They signify the death of religions; the fate of a unique, subtle love, impossible to hold on to!'

The great achievement of the film lies in its promise of time regained, a time, however, which is more promise than actuality. The realities of disappearance and dissolution impose themselves just as much on things as on people. The great sadness which permeates the film is the discovery that everything is mortal ...

Another great film, *Barry Lyndon*, expresses the same idea. William Faulkner put it very well when he wrote: 'A man struggles many years against misfortune, hoping that this misfortune will tire with time, and time will then become full of promise. In this way, it is the work of time that becomes the source of our misfortune.' In these sentences I see the true and cruel fact that frames an utterly brilliant thriller!

Robert Kramer

In and around Godard's *Hélas pour Moi*

When what's left is all gathered together afterwards, when what's left is the radiation of what was, an *after-image*, the order and chaos of *Hélas pour Moi* is 'how we're living these days.' Or rather, 'what we're living with.' Or even, 'what we made of what we were given.' This was there anyway as the movie went by on the screen: the rhythm and density, the odd, uncomfortable content of our days. As if you said to yourself, 'How can I bring the pieces together? And above all, how this breathless, golden light fits with the night. Or how my insistent foolishness brushes up against a whisper (only a whisper!) of meaning. Or if "meaning" itself is much too rigid and pumped-up, then a whisper that is only a different awareness, only a suspicion of another way. And that it has come to that! *Hélas pour moi.*'

'All fixed and fast-frozen relationships, with their train of venerable ideas and opinions, are swept away, all new-formed ones become obsolete before they can ossify. All that is solid melts into the air … .' That's *The Communist Manifesto*, but it could be *Alice in Wonderland*, or Jacques Tati on one of his missions – especially Tati. Especially in relation to *Hélas pour Moi*. It is not certain what happened. Or when it happened. There was a sense of order and everyone knew their place. Then the order is gone. Or perhaps there never was an order. Or perhaps it is always happening, over and over, the little order that was there melts, and little humans … But then, there are always a lot of confusions and mind-games about the 'golden age', about the past.

Of course, just now we are surely floating without a place or a prayer, and we do not even know what part of the forest to go to to find help. '*Hélas pour moi!*' It is difficult to say these words. It is difficult to gather up the courage necessary even to play with self-pity. Especially in front of the absolute satisfaction of this light (and the ability to 'capture it' so well!), of this golden Swiss light, of this ultimate lake, of this golden hair. In fact, there is even a breath of indecency. That comes from wealth. From what money can buy. Money that buys time, stillness, health, peace. Money that buys actors with very smooth skin and fields that are still plentiful, graceful, ancient trees whose outstanding attribute is that they survive, and 35 mm film stock, film and the rest. Our collective wealth in the West relative to the rest. And then Switzerland as this caricature of all that! And then our '*métier* of cinema' which is like a further caricature of all that, and where God the director can always lift young skirts to admire the perfect asses with just the right white panty. That's how it is. I'm not pointing fingers, or, if I am, it's in the mirror or at all of us. This whole story is about a certain 'us' and 'how we live'.

And still (and this is a main point and why it is all so great), and still a whisper is there! The sense of a sense. That although this sound makes much fury and often signifies only itself, still there is the *intimation*, the *insinuation* of something miraculous. Miraculous in the sense that it belongs to our capacity to choose how we live in this world.

But really all this myth, Greek and Christian, is part of the same sound and fury. Is (for me at any rate) at about the same level of volume as the TGV ripping apart the air, or the endless repetition of *'Monsieur! Madame!'* like an instinctive and pathetic prayer, a reminder of a community/society/tissue-of-relationships that has long ceased being the tissues of a living body (again Tati, again!). But what foolishness! Of course it is living ... in its own way. There are sexes and social classes. There is a garage, a café by the lake, there are students who are convinced they need to know something, and there are teachers who have answers, there are ideas floating around, and there are as many stories (as usual) as you have patience for.

Myself, I can't really listen attentively to the Judaeo-Christian thing any more, and even to the Greeks. Although in the case of the Greeks I sense a vitality, but I've lost the living feel. I say, 'I should go back and reread the Greeks.' But saying this is already a warning sign. So all this aspect of the movie is lost on me. You could ask, 'Do we have the time or patience for this?' The answer is, it's worth dealing with one's inheritance. Maybe it will turn out to be something different from what we thought. At any rate, the inheritance is history-in-us, and above all a crucial sign (if signs are lacking) of what a culture is, and how limiting; of how education works to channel and shape; and, in the context of this movie, it is a way of saying (since it is best never to forget) who we are. This is what background noise is, or 'room tone'. The particular roar of each city, the continual shake and rattle in our imperfect heads, or the reverberation of the Big Bang that has never stopped echoing through the universe. Room tone is there, it's what's happening on the shooting stage when nothing's happening. I take this golden age and Greek culture and Christian gods a little like that. And that is where I am stuck. Those are my liberties or my limitations, or probably both. *'Le passé n'est jamais mort – il n'est même pas passé.'*

Indeed. In that space between what is no more and what still is. I am thinking of the ritual, whose place/fire/prayer, and even whose spirit, we have forgotten. So it is put forward in the beginning of the movie. And yet it is precisely this ritual (of longing and need and assistance) that is reconstructed in the movie itself. Or rather in those spaces (those luminous gaps that pierce the leaves, those still moments like the swollen belly lit by a shower of sparks). We leap into those spaces, having abandoned all intention of going somewhere specific, having given up all hope of story or meaning. In those spaces, those moments, which are also the absence of all the noise around them, the movie offers itself up. The movie, like these moments, is indifferent and vulnerable. And the fact that this ritual is enacted here, in this tiny part of the forest, in a Switzerland of such power and privilege and exceptionalism that it staggers the imagination to contemplate – the fact that it happens here, and that it may be possible in part because of this great, golden calm of security, only contributes to the strange bewilderment that it could work at all. That the movie could be something other than game/exercise/excuse, and that adding it up, and not just living with it, but letting it live with me, it leaves such a strong after-image of our life in the forest.

Alberto Lattuada

One film, one director, two actresses

Amongst the films that have made an impression on me, Fritz Lang's *M* is undoubtedly the most important. It was one of the films that the nascent Italian Cinémathèque (then known as the Ferrari Cinémathèque), of which I was a member, screened semi-clandestinely during the reign of the Fascists, at the end of the thirties. The director of the French Cinémathèque, Henri Langlois, sent it from Paris in a diplomatic bag. A copy was hidden in the Vaprio d'Adda warehouse, along with other objectionable films such as *La Grande Illusion, The Blue Angel, Foolish Wives, The Kid, A nous la liberté*.

The narrative is based on a wonderful idea: the criminal underworld joins in the hunt for the maniac terrorizing Düsseldorf. The police have turned the town upside down in their search for the monster, to such an extent that the gangsters' businesses have been disrupted. So the gangsters decide to join in the hunt for him. At this point, the story has a brilliant moment: the maniac is recognized by a blind man who hears him whistle a tune from *Peer Gynt*. When he is near the killer, the blind man draws in chalk the letter M (for *Mörder*, killer) on his back. The maniac is captured and taken to a basement. There follows a brutal, violent trial. He defends himself, saying he's sick. The trial is one of the most interesting scenes in the film: the gangsters play all the roles of a traditional court – judge, prosecutor, defence lawyer. When the police arrive they all put their hands up. And the film ends with an image of justice enforced by the law, with the three mothers of the victims weeping in black.

M is a thriller with a perfect mechanism. I'd describe it as a 'mechanical masterpiece'. I remember its visual originality, details such as the maniac's twitching as he peels an orange with his knife. The film is recognizably the work of Thea von Arbou, a great screenwriter, who stayed in Germany when Lang decided to go to the States. My films, at least in the beginning, were profoundly influenced by Lang. The hold-up scene in *Il bandito*, when the women give up their jewels to the rhythm of a drum beaten by one of the gangsters, is very Lang. Lang's characters were the inspiration for the hero of *L'imprevisto*: his neurotic cough, the speech about money delivered to a new-born baby, some of his monstrous traits, the dehumanization of the character.

But there's another German too, a contemporary of mine, Edgar Reitz; a German who's gone beyond the experience of Wenders, Fassbinder, Herzog, Kluge, of those film-makers figuring in the renaissance of German cinema at the beginning of the seventies. Seeing *Heimat*, I was struck by the sense of organization which, though seeming haphazard, in fact linked one part of the narrative to the other, one situation to another, one character to another, while retaining an extraordinary freedom of conception.

Certainly, Reitz's way of making films is very different from mine. But I find it highly attractive, especially his way of 'losing' characters only to 'find' them again later in another place. Such freedom of construction is hard to find in traditional cinema. It's a freedom far removed from the temporal progressions of film narrative, therefore better adapted to television. And the decisive, courageous support given to Reitz by German television is another surprising aspect of the project. Altogether, *Heimat* was an agreeable discovery, especially the philosophical or didactic appendices at the end of some episodes; at such moments, the image becomes less important than the written message, which is a kind of lesson.

As far as actresses are concerned, two names spring to mind: Francesca Neri and Chiara Caselli. Neri has great qualities of interiority. In *Le Età di Lulu*, an orgasm was for the first time represented on screen in an exemplary fashion from the point of view of the actress's performance.

She's been less well-used in other films. Troisi keeps her too much in the shade in *Pensavo fosse amore invece era un calesse*. What attracts me in Caselli is her look of surprise when faced with life, the continually interrogative expression in her eyes.

Both actresses show that they possess a great interior dimension, a portmanteau of experience that manifests itself in the intensity of their gazes. Behind their eyes, we can see knowledge, curiosity, a questioning, a desire to discover, to know.

Neri and Caselli embody perfectly the problem of their generation: not being able to understand what is happening. Their questioning sometimes seems a sign of limited intelligence, or the impossibility of understanding the world. Their gaze is a merciless denunciation of the almost total absence of instruments through which to understand this world. For example, I can't imagine what they read. This may explain their freedom from taboo and prejudice, their belief that the world can be understood simply through itself – through sexual experience, for example – and that that suffices.

Their gaze shows that they are alone before the world. But, I repeat, this is the tragedy of their generation. Family roots, political and ideological certainties no longer exist. Think of the difference between them and the young postwar generation, in neo-realist films, or those I showed in *Dolci inganni* and *Guendalina*, on the brink of love and sexual experience. In their characters, Neri and Caselli reflect the present confusion of values.

PS. In any case, the greatest *auteur*, the greatest actor of all time, is Buster Keaton.

Patrice Leconte

If there were only one ...

I've always been interested in everything. With the enthusiasm of an incorrigible eclectic. Which I have totally come to terms with. Hence my embarrassment – a weak word, I'll admit.

Because the least thing I could do would be to pay homage to Jean Gabin. But then that leaves out Groucho Marx.

Or I could speak of Miou-Miou, the actress who has never failed to touch and move me. But at the cost of Michelle Pfeiffer, Judith Godrèche, Katherine Hepburn, Sandrine Bonnaire, Julia Roberts, Fanny Ardant ...

The simplest thing would be to mention *Les Disparus de Saint-Agil*. But at the cost of *Close Encounters of the Third Kind*, *Pépé le Moko*, and *Trop Belle pour Toi*.

It's no easier as far as directors are concerned. Can you like at the same time Duvivier and Luc Besson, Coppola and Bertrand Blier, Eric Rohmer and the Coen Brothers? Yes, you can. Of course you can. It's even a pleasure to be able to do so, because you will never be bored with such disparate loves, loves which I couldn't care less whether they're coherent or not. So?

So, all things being equal, if I were to say to myself that there was only one to keep, only one to isolate, protect and love, only one I could take to that desert island – which, thank heavens, one never goes to – I'd take him, that extraordinary, talented New York Jew in whose company I always feel happy. Who else would be capable of offering, with such pleasing regularity, a new film, a film which never seems less important than the next one? Who else amuses himself, tries, searches, questions, doubts, changes, advances? Who else can imagine these masterpieces of which one can also say that, after all, they're only movies? And finally, who else can give me the courage and the energy to carry on writing stories, inventing images, and getting back on my feet when I've fallen flat on my face?

Not a day goes by when I don't think of Woody Allen. And I thank him for being there.

Mike Leigh

L'Albero degli Zoccoli

A priest instructs an illiterate peasant to send his son to school. The boy walks
12 km every day, until his clog breaks. His father cuts down a tree to make a
new clog, but the tree belongs to the landowner. So does their home, and the
whole family is evicted.

The landowner is plump and lazy. He is more interested in opera than in his
estate. As he dozes off in his study one morning, the peasants outside stand
silently, listening to the gramophone playing by his side.

A young peasant couple court. On their wedding day they travel by boat to
the big city, arriving during a political riot. They spend their nuptial night in a
convent, where the girl's aunt is the Mother Superior. In the morning, she
offers them a one-year-old foundling boy. They do not refuse him.

A poor widow takes in laundry. Her cow falls sick. She ignores the vet's
advice to slaughter it, preferring to go to church and pray for it. She gives it
'sanctified' water from the stream by the church. The cow lives. Her adoles-
cent son gets a job in a flour-mill. The priest wants to put her youngest daughters in the care of nuns, but the boy asserts his manhood and refuses to let
them go.

A dishonest peasant fights with his sons, puts stones in his bags of maize to
make up the weight, and finds a gold coin on the ground whilst listening to a
socialist address a crowd in the town. He hides it in his horse's hoof, and when
the horse reacts violently because he beats it for losing the coin, the man has a
fit and takes to his bed. They have to send for the local wise woman, who
cures him with an obscure, mystical remedy.

An old man creeps out at the dead of a winter night to spread chicken-dung
on his tomato patch. A secret formula. He shares it with his granddaughter,
and in the spring, when they both take their new tomatoes to town, the little
girl smiles as the townsfolk wonder at such early produce.

A pig is slaughtered in the pouring rain. Its terrified shrieks pierce the landscape. Men, women and children wait, watch and scurry about with buckets
of steaming water, umbrellas, bowls of precious blood, wheelbarrows of
offal. As the carcass is hacked in two, the priest arrives and cracks some
jokes.

The passing of a year. The four seasons. Fresh, bright, clear days. Cold, dark
nights. Rain. Snow. Early-morning mists. A baby is born. Workers sing.
Children laugh at a simpleton. A girl steals logs from a neighbour. A fat youth

wets his bed. The harvest. The fair. Bread. Soup. Polenta. Wine. Prayers. And all the while, the church bells toll, never far away.

All this, and much more, fills the brief three hours of Ermanno Olmi's greatest work, *L'Albero degli Zoccoli* (The Tree of the Wooden Clogs).

This remarkable and wonderful film, which I love deeply, is one of the few true epics. For although it offers neither great romance, nor lengthy voyages, nor wars, nor even death (except for the poor pig, and a goose), this masterpiece succeeds effortlessly and with monumental simplicity in getting to the essence of the human experience.

Directly, objectively, yet compassionately, it puts on the screen the great, hard, real adventure of living and surviving from day to day, and from year to year, the experience of ordinary people everywhere.

And it does so in a way that has no equal in the cinema. Flaherty, for all his integrity, managed somehow to romanticize his subject matter. Kaneto Shindo's *The Island*, although it captured the pain of toil, was ultimately emotionally limited. And even Satyajit Ray's beautiful *Pather Panchali* (or indeed the whole *Apu Trilogy*), which I also love, does not quite achieve the breadth of Olmi's canvas, nor the sense of the total reality of these people's lives. Few films are as successful as this in making you feel you were actually there when it all happened.

L'Albero degli Zoccoli: the eviction.

L'Albero degli Zoccoli: arrival in the city.

As a film-maker with pretensions to making films about real life, I am often asked whether I have used actors or 'real' people. My answer is of course always appropriately shocked and outraged: how could I possibly achieve this reality with people 'off the street'? Only highly sophisticated, professional actors could possibly achieve such performances, never amateurs!

Yet there is Olmi, returning to his native Lombardy, assembling a fairly large cast of ordinary working folk from the district around Bergamo, and achieving a set of the most solid performances, not least from the children.

How does he do it? These people cannot merely be acting out their own lives, as the film is set eighty years before it was made. Nor are they supplying the flat, unemotional, humourless 'non-acting' of Bresson's films, insular and schematic by comparison.

Instead, they inhabit their characters fully and, whilst never withholding a grain of emotion, they also never succumb to histrionics or theatricality.

Why is this? Perhaps for two main reasons. Firstly, because this is a film about living on the land and surviving in all weathers. And the players have the land and all weathers to work with. This is the ultimate location film, and that elusive condition to which some of us aspire, which is to create a world that the audience believes existed before the film ever began and will go on existing long afterwards, is here fulfilled fully.

Here the actors have no problem of motivation or background research: they live and breathe the characters and their world because they are in that environment.

Secondly, and following on from this, Olmi has created a working atmosphere in which his actors achieve great ensemble playing. Whilst this applies in the more intimate moments, like the beautifully subtle relationship of the newly-weds, or the scene where the central character, Batisti, baths his son, it is most remarkable in the bigger communal scenes.

For this is also a film about community, concerning several tenant families living side by side on a farmstead at the end of the nineteenth century.

They harvest the maize together; they pray together; they gather together in the evenings to sing songs and to tell stories; the men work together and fight; the women deliver each other's babies. And the children play together in the yard.

And this natural ensemble makes for strong, clear, truthful acting. Not that the quality of the performances is restricted to the characters in these communal situations. The local priest, the uninterested landowner and his trusty, beady-eyed bailiff, the Mother Superior, and any number of minor characters are equally well-realized.

An actor's director, certainly. But this consummate *auteur* here directs his own script, perfect in its construction, its economy and in the simplicity of the story-telling.

And as if that weren't enough, the maestro is also his own cinematographer and editor!

Now you might reasonably expect that the style of a film about basic peasant life, shot on location in all weathers on 16 mm with a bunch of amateur actors by a director/cameraman might well be in the erratic, *cinéma vérité*, newsreel, semi-documentary, grab-what-you-can, improvised mode.

But this is not so. *L'Albero degli Zoccoli* is a visual feast. Every shot is masterly in its control and its precision.

From close domestic interiors to the empty landscape and streets, from the busy harvesting and the Spring Fair to the tranquil river journey to Milan, even to the slaughter of that legendary pig (did he get it right first time, or did they have to go again with a second pig?), the camera is always in exactly the right place, unobtrusively, unpretentiously, clear and pure.

Much of the film is set in the farmstead, a two-storey construction around a courtyard in the middle of a field, and it is a measure of Olmi's endless visual resourcefulness that we never see the same shot twice. He re-investigates the location again and again, always motivated afresh by the specific needs of the scene.

I do not share Ermanno Olmi's religious views, although I empathize with his spirituality; and, in some ways, I am not entirely sure that I don't see the behaviour of the Church in this film as somewhat coercive and paternalistic.

However, as a political film *L'Albero* resonates with me completely. For the politics are clear, but always implicit. They are never discussed, but they are always there.

The film is about the iniquity of the landowner's cynical control over his tenants' lives, but although there are glimpses of a political world beyond the immediate lives of the characters, they always seem unaware of these forces.

Thus the important thing that happens to Finard when he is listening to the socialist orator is not that he is instantly politicized (he isn't!), but that he spots the gold coin on the ground.

And when the newly-weds get to Milan, they gaze innocently at the chain-gang of political prisoners being led past them, and wait patiently in a doorway as the insurgence erupts around them.

But at the centre of the film is the future twentieth-century educated citizen, the small boy Minek, for whose daily trudge to receive his education his father is forced to cut down the tree, the act which causes the family's disastrous eviction.

And here it is impossible to divorce Olmi's politics from his religion, for surely this tree, the tree of the film's title, is somehow the Tree of Knowledge in the Garden of Eden?

There is indeed a holiness about the film, but not a piousness. Olmi allows his characters their state of grace, which is beautifully underpinned by his occasional use of J.S. Bach.

Behind the wholesome simplicity of the characters' lives is their faith, and for all one's own late-century urban atheist scepticism, one cannot but be moved by the total harmony of their lives; of their inevitable relationship with the land and the elements.

And it is this very harmony that motivates Olmi himself, making him so uniquely capable of telling his story in such a real, unsentimental way, and with such warmth, humour and clarity.

Interestingly, although there are central characters and conflicts, Olmi never ultimately allows us to become too involved with any of them in too intimate, detailed or idiosyncratic a way.

For all his compassion and humanity, he always manages to maintain a distance from his subject: no one story is given greater importance than any other.

In this way, he succeeds in painting this wonderful, broad canvas, his extraordinary vision.

But for me, the big question remains: how does he really do it?

Ken Loach

Death of a Nation

The film that is most in my thoughts as I write is a documentary by John Pilger and David Munro called *Death of a Nation*. It tells the story of the brutal occupation of East Timor by its neighbour Indonesia. Some of the filming was done in secret, without the approval or knowledge of the Indonesian authorities. Journalists are not welcome. Two Australian television teams were murdered in 1975 by the Indonesian Army for trying to break the wall of silence that the Jakarta regime and its Western allies have built around East Timor.

The silence was to hide the fact that 200,000 people, a third of the population, have died in this invasion. This has happened with the complicity of Western governments, despite Indonesia's defiance of many UN resolutions calling on it to withdraw from East Timor. A British ambassador is quoted: 'We should let matters take their course.'

The military coup that established Suharto's power in Indonesia met with the approval of the US. The American Ambassador says, 'Washington is sympathetic with and admiring of what the army is doing.' This is juxtaposed in the film with pictures of Indonesians uncovering a mass grave of the victims of that same army's brutality.

The story of the destruction of East Timor's emerging democracy is heartbreaking, particularly as Western intelligence knew in advance every move the Indonesians were making. The archives show appeals by the Timorese leaders to 'stop the Indonesian isolation of our territory'. They got no response.

The film shows why in a telling exchange between John Pilger and Alan Clark, the British Minister of Defence. Britain sold arms to Indonesia during its attack on the Timorese people.

PILGER: Did it ever bother you personally that this British equipment was causing such mayhem and human suffering?
CLARK: No, not in the slightest, never entered my head.
PILGER: The fact that we supply highly effective equipment to a regime like that then is not a consideration as far as you're concerned?
CLARK: Not at all.
PILGER: It is not a personal consideration?
CLARK: No, not at all.
PILGER: I ask the question because I read you are a vegetarian and you are quite seriously concerned about the way animals are killed.

CLARK: Yes.

PILGER: Doesn't that concern extend to the way humans, albeit foreigners, are killed?

CLARK: Curiously not, no.

Film-makers with access to mass communications have a responsibility to expose the lies and hypocrisy of politicians and the interests they represent. This film is more valuable to us than a hundred self-absorbed movies, however prettily shot.

Dusan Makavejev

Life as a remake of movies

During my first extended visit to America, we were somewhere in the country-side, passing by beautiful detached houses in green spaces, with nicely-cut grass, no fences between the neighbours, bushes here and there, and patches of well-groomed flowers. A strange and pleasant (but slightly uneasy) feeling began to overwhelm me. I felt enveloped by unreality. The landscape I was observing with enjoyment was as painfully clear as a hyper-realist painting, but it was as if I were seeing double. I was experiencing a psychological phe-nomenon that I realized I knew about from my school-days. It was called *déja vu*. I was recognizing places where I had never been!

Then the appearance of someone with a lawn mower triggered my memory. I had only seen this kind of machine in Walt Disney comics. Mickey!

Later on, in California, in glorious houses with interiors 'like a movie set' and picture windows unifying interiors and exteriors, again there was that same sweet, itching *déja vu* feeling, like when you are falling in love. Sweet haze: where am I?

Most of America's interiors (and exteriors) were built after similar ones – or even the same ones – had first appeared on film. American landscapes look as glorious as their pictures in *National Geographic*; they often seem as if they are 3-D projections from some Kodak photo on slide.

Is it partly because Americans document themselves so thoroughly, have so much of their daily lives captured on film, tapes, slide or photograph? In many ways, because Americans are so much freer, as well as having a much larger margin of tolerance for deviant behaviour, you sometimes simply cannot say who copies whom: Silver Screen copies life, or vice versa?

I have a similar real/unreal feeling these days as I watch the ex-Yugoslavia/Bosnia war, which in so many ways is more horrible than any oth-er war because there is no foreign army or invader here; it's all 'our guys'. This time, the *déja vu* comes from horror and sci-fi B-movies: *The Island of Doctor Moreau* and similar monstrous inventions, such as *The Night of the Living Dead* etc. The banality of evil.

Boys in paramilitary units dress and behave as if they were acting in a remake of *The Deer Hunter* or *Platoon*, with Sly Stallone's bandanna from *Rambo*. And they *do* remake these films in their own and other people's lives.

Before Disney went into feature production, he did a lot of stories for daily newspapers and syndication.

In these stories, Mickey and his entourage tracked down secret treasure, published a newspaper, started a detective agency, served in the Foreign Legion. Lots of fantastic moments from Spielberg's movies or *Romancing the Stone* seem to me as if I have already seen them in comics with good old Mickey Mouse, hero of my childhood. Stories with social content, about fighting gangsters, about fighting corruption in local politics etc, remind me as well of Frank Capra films.

Trying to decide who did it first will not work with American culture. From the famous radio programmes of the forties to the movies and now to television, and of course all the time through an extraordinary and powerful tradition of photography, it is actually life, and the precise registering of it, that makes this country, the USA, so unique: a constant, dream-like flow from images to life and back into image ...

Louis Malle

Libera Me

I first saw *Libera Me* at its only showing at the Cannes Film Festival. The film quite literally struck me, as if in the darkness of the theatre I'd been hit by something hard. It made me think of a sculpture by Anthony Caro, opaque and formidable. And as the film went on, I felt the shock of the familiar several times, in several shots.

Six months later I saw the film again in a movie theatre and this time, from its very first images onwards, it spoke to me directly: this is my own memory, fixed in time and place, the collective memory of my generation, of those who were children during the Second World War. The faces, the gestures, the clothes, the silences, the light of *Libera Me* belong to that age of. shadows, power-cuts, curfews, Radio London hardly audible, rumours of arrests, escapes, underground networks. Many people hide, or disappear. Words are dangerous; one doesn't mention names. Children try to guess their destiny in the eyes of adults, who dare not raise their voices to pronounce on either the present or the future. I hadn't seen the faces of Cavalier's film for fifty years, yet I recognized them at once. They are lit by a dim lamp, dressed in heavy materials – the heaviness of that epoch. They carry with them their anxieties, their anticipation of the nights in 1943 or 1944 when, instead of fairy-tales, reality fed our nocturnal terrors.

For me, *Libera Me* is a succession of signs, such as the close-up of the fingers deformed by chilblains. Of course, there are other keys to the film, other readings. But from time to time a film speaks to you personally, like the messages from Radio London. It struck me in the face and short-circuited my entire adult life, which is of little importance by comparison with my childhood.

Chris Marker

A free replay (notes on *Vertigo*)

'Power and freedom'. Coupled together, these two words are repeated three times in *Vertigo*. First, at the twelfth minute by Gavin Elster ('freedom' underlined by a move to close-up) who, looking at a picture of Old San Francisco, expresses his nostalgia to Scottie ('San Francisco has changed. The things that spelled San Francisco to me are disappearing fast'), a nostalgia for a time when men – some men at least – had 'power and freedom'. Second, at the thirty-fifth minute, in the bookstore, where 'Pop' Liebel explains how Carlotta Valdes's rich lover threw her out yet kept her child: 'Men could do that in those days. They had the power and the freedom ... ' And finally at the hundred and twenty-fifth minute – and fifty-first second to be precise – but in reverse order (which is logical, given we are now in the second part, on the other side of the mirror) by Scottie himself when, realizing the workings of the trap laid by the now free and powerful Elster, he says, a few seconds before Judy's fall – which, for him, will be Madeleine's second death – 'with all his wife's money and all that freedom and power ... '. Just try telling me these are coincidences.

Such precise signs must have a meaning. Could it be psychological, an explanation of the criminal's motives? If so, the effort seems a little wasted on what is, after all, a secondary character. This strategic triad gave me the first inkling of a possible reading of *Vertigo*. The vertigo the film deals with isn't to do with space and falling; it is a clear, understandable and spectacular metaphor for yet another kind of vertigo, much more difficult to represent – the vertigo of time. Elster's 'perfect' crime almost achieves the impossible: reinventing a time when men and women and San Francisco were different to what they are now. And its perfection, as with all perfection in Hitchcock, exists in duality. Scottie will absorb the folly of time with which Elster infuses him through Madeleine/Judy. But where Elster reduces the fantasy to mediocre manifestations (wealth, power, etc), Scottie transmutes it into its most utopian form: he overcomes the most irreparable damage caused by time and resurrects a love that is dead. The entire second part of the film, on the other side of the mirror, is nothing but a mad, maniacal attempt to deny time, to recreate through trivial yet necessary signs (like the signs of a liturgy: clothes, make-up, hair) the woman whose loss he has never been able to accept. His own feelings of responsibility and guilt for this loss are mere Christian Band-Aids dressing a metaphysical wound of much greater depth. Were one to quote the Scriptures, Corinthians I (an epistle one of Bergman's

123

characters uses to define love) would apply: 'Death, where is your victory?'

So Elster infuses Scottie with the madness of time. It's interesting to see how this is done. As ever with Alfred, stratagems merely serve to hold up a mirror (and there are many mirrors in this story) to the hero and bring out his repressed desires. In *Strangers on a Train*, Bruno offers Guy the crime he doesn't dare desire. In *Vertigo*, Scottie, although overtly reluctant, is always willing, always the one taking the first step. Once in Gavin's office and again in front of his own house (the morning after the fake drowning), the manipulators pretend to give up: Gavin sits down and apologizes for having asked the impossible; Madeleine gets back in the car and gets ready to leave. Everything could stop there. But, on both occasions, Scottie takes the initiative and restarts the machine. Gavin hardly has to persuade Scottie to undertake his search: he simply suggests that he see Madeleine, knowing full well that a glimpse of her will be enough to set the supreme manipulator, Destiny, in motion. After a shot of Madeleine, glimpsed at Ernie's, there follows a shot of Scottie beginning his stake-out of the Elster house. Acceptance (bewitchment) needs no scene of its own; it is contained in the fade to black between the two scenes. This is the first of three ellipses of essential moments, all avoided, which another director would have felt obliged to show. The second ellipse is in the first scene of physical love between Judy and Scottie, which clearly takes place in the hotel room after the last transformation (the hair-do corrected in the bathroom). How is it possible, after such a fabulous, hallucinatory moment, to sustain such intensity?

In this case, the censorship of the time saved Hitchcock from a doubly impossible situation. Such a scene can only exist in the imagination (or in life). But when a film has referred to fantasy only in the highly-coded context of dreams and two lovers embrace in the realist set of the hotel room; when one of them, Scottie, thanks to the most magical camera movement in the history of cinema, discovers another set around him, that of the stable at the Dolores Mission where he last kissed a wife whose double he has now created; isn't *that* scene the metaphor for the love scene Hitchcock cannot show? And if love is truly the only victor over time, isn't this scene per se *the* love scene? The third ellipse, which has long been the joy of connoisseurs, I'll mention for the sheer pleasure of it. It occurs much earlier, in the first part. We have just seen Scottie pull Madeleine unconscious out of San Francisco bay (at Fort Point). Fade to black. Scottie is at home, lighting a log fire. As he goes to sit down – the camera follows – he looks straight ahead. The camera follows his look and ends on Madeleine, seen through the open bedroom door, asleep in bed with a sheet up to her neck. But as the camera travels towards her, it also registers her clothes and underclothes hanging on a drier in the kitchen. The telephone rings and wakes her up. Scottie, who's come into the room, leaves, shutting the door. Madeleine reappears dressed in the red dressing-gown he happened to have draped across the bed. Neither of them alludes to the intervening period, apart from the *double entendre* in Scottie's line the next day: 'I enjoyed, er ... talking to you ... ' Three scenes, therefore, where imagination wins over representation; three moments, three keys which become locks, but which no present-day director would think of leaving out. On the contrary, he'd make them heavily explicit and, of course, banal. As a result of saying it can show anything, cinema has abandoned its power over the imagination. And, like cinema, this century is perhaps starting to pay a high price for this betrayal of the imagination – or, more precisely, those who still have an imagination, albeit a poor one, are being made to pay that price.

Double entendre? All the gestures, looks, phrases in *Vertigo* have a double meaning. Everybody knows that it is probably the only film where a 'double' vision is not only advisable but indispensable for rereading the first part of the film in the light of the second. Cabrera Infante called it 'the first great surrealist film', and if there is a theme present in the surrealist imagination (and for that matter, in the literary one), then surely it is that of the Double, the *Doppelgänger* (who from Doctor Jekyll to *Kagemusha*, from the *Prisoner of Zenda* to *Persona*, has trod a royal path through the history of the medium). In *Vertigo*, the theme is even reflected in the doubling-up of details: Madeleine's look towards the tower (the first scene of San Juan Bautista, looking right, while Scottie kisses her) and the line 'Too late' which accompanies it have a precise meaning for the naïve spectator, unaware of the stratagem, but another meaning, just as precise, for a watchful spectator seeing it a second time. The look and the line are repeated at the very end, in a shot exactly symmetrical with the first, by Scottie, looking left, 'Too late', just before Judy falls. For as there is an Other of the Other, there is also a Double of the Double. The right profile of the first revelation, when Madeleine momentarily stands still behind Scottie at Ernie's, the moment which decides everything, is repeated at the beginning of the second part, so precisely that it's Scottie who, the second time, is 'in front' of Judy. Thus begins a play of mirrors which can only end in their destruction. We, the audience, discover the stratagem via the letter Judy doesn't send. Scottie discovers it at the end via the necklace. (Note that this moment also has its double: Scottie has just seen the necklace head-on and hasn't reacted. He only reacts when he sees it in the mirror.) In between, Scottie's attraction for Judy, who at first was merely a fourth case of mistaken identity (the constant of a love touched by death; see Proust) Scottie encountered in his search through the places of their past, this attraction has crystallized with her profile in front of the window ('Do I remind you of her?') in that green neon light, for which Hitchcock, it seems, specially chose the Empire Hotel: her left profile. This is the moment when Scottie crosses to the other side of the mirror and his folly is born ...

... If one believes, that is, the apparent intentions of the authors (authors in the plural because the writer, Samuel Taylor, was largely Alfred's accomplice). The ingenious stratagem, the way of making us understand we've been hood-winked, the stroke of genius of revealing the truth to us well before the hero, the whole thing bathed in the light of an *amour fou*, 'fixed' by what Cabrera (who should know) called the 'decadent *habañeras*' of Bernard Herrman – all that isn't bad. But what if *they* were lying to us as well? Resnais liked to say that nothing forces us to believe the heroine of *Hiroshima*. She could be mak-ing up everything she says. The flashbacks aren't the affirmations of the writer, but stories told by a character. All we know about Scottie at the beginning of the second part is that he is in a state of total catatonia, that he is 'somewhere else', that it 'could last a long time' (according to the doctor), that he loved a dead woman 'and still does' (according to Midge). Is it too absurd to imagine that this agonizing, though reasonable, and obstinate soul ('hard-hitting' says Gavin), imagined this totally extravagant scenario, full of unbelievable coinci-dences and entanglements, yet logical enough to drive one to the one salvatory conclusion: this woman is not dead, I can find her again?

There are many arguments in favour of a dream reading of the second part of *Vertigo*. The disappearance of Barbara Bel Geddes (Midge, his friend and confidante, secretly in love with him) is one of them. I know very well that she married a rich Texan oilman in the meantime, and is preparing a dreadful reappearance as a widow in the Ewing clan; but still, her disappearance from *Vertigo* is probably unparalleled in the serial economy of Hollywood scripts. A character important for half the film disappears without trace – there isn't even an allusion to her in the subsequent dialogue – until the end of the second part. In the dream reading of the film, this absence would only be explained by her last line to Scottie in the hospital: 'You don't even know I'm here ... '

In this case, the entire second part would be nothing but a fantasy, revealing at last the double of the double. We were tricked into believing that the first part was the truth, then told it was a lie born of a perverse mind, that the sec-ond part contained the truth. But what if the first part really were the truth and the second the product of a sick mind? In that case, what one may find overcharged and outrageously expressionistic in the nightmare images preced-ing the hospital room would be nothing but a trick, yet another red herring, camouflaging the fantasy that will occupy us for another hour in order to lead us even further away from the appearance of realism. The only exception to this is the moment I've already mentioned, the change of set during the kiss. In this light, the scene acquires a new meaning: it's a fleeting confession, a reveal-ing detail, the blink of a madman's eyelids as his eyes glaze over, the kind of gaze which sometimes gives a madman away.

There used to be a special effect in old movies where a character would detach himself from his sleeping or dead body, and his transparent form would float up to the sky or into the land of dreams. In the mirror play of *Vertigo*

Vertigo: the spiral of Madeleine's hair.

there is a similar moment, if in a more subtle form: in the clothes store when Judy, realizing that Scottie is transforming her piece by piece into Madeleine (in other words, into the reality he isn't deemed to know, making her repeat what she did for Elster), makes to go, and bumps into a *mirror*. Scottie joins her in front of the mirror and, while he's dictating to an amazed shop assistant the details of one of Madeleine's dresses, a fabulous shot shows us 'all four of them' together: him and his double, her and her double. At that moment, Scottie has truly escaped from his hospital chair: there are two Scotties as well as two Judys. We can therefore add schizophrenia to the illnesses whose symptoms others have already judiciously identified in Scottie's behaviour. Personally, though, I'd leave out necrophilia, so often mentioned, which seems to me more indicative of a critic's neurosis than the character's: Scottie continues to love a truly living Madeleine. In his madness, he looks for proof in her life.

It's all very well reasoning like this, but one must also return to the appearance of the facts, obstinate as they are. There is a crushing argument in favour of a phantasmagoric reading of the second part. When, after the transformation and the hallucination, Madeleine/Judy, with the blitheness of a satisfied body, gets ready for dinner and Scottie asks her what restaurant she'd like to go to, she immediately suggests Ernie's. It's the place where they first met (but Scottie isn't meant to know this yet – Judy's careless 'It's our place' is the first

Vertigo: the Golden Gate Bridge.

give-away before the necklace). So they go there *without making a reservation*. Just try doing this in San Francisco and you'll understand we're in a dream.

As Gavin says, San Francisco has changed. During a screening at Berkeley in the early eighties, when everyone had forgotten the movie (the old fox had kept the rights in order to sell them at a premium to TV, hence the cuts for commercials and the changed ending) and the word was that it was just another minor thriller, I remember the audience gasping with amazement on seeing the panoramic view of the city which opens the second part. It's another city, without skyscrapers (apart from Coppola's Sentinel Building), a picture as dated as the engraving Scottie looks at when Elster first pronounces those two fateful words. And it was only twenty years ago ... San Francisco, of course, is nothing but another character in the film. Samuel Taylor wrote to me agreeing that Hitchcock liked the town but only knew 'what he saw from hotels or restaurants or out of the limo window'. He was 'what you might call a sedentary person'. But he still decided to use the Dolores Mission and, strangely, to make the house on Lombard Street Scottie's home 'because of the red door'. Taylor was in love with his city (Alex Coppel, the first writer, was 'a transplanted Englishman') and put all his love into the script; and perhaps even more than that, if I am to believe a rather cryptic phrase at the end of his letter: 'I rewrote the script at the same time that I explored San Francisco and recaptured my past ... ' Words which could apply as much to the characters as to the author, and which afford us another interpretation, like an added flat to a key, of the direction given by Elster to Scottie at the start of the film, when he's describing Madeleine's wanderings; the pillars Scottie gazes at for so long on the other side of Lloyd Lake – the *Portals of the Past*. This personal note would explain many things: the *amour fou*, the dream signs, all the things that make *Vertigo* a film which is both typically and untypically Hitchcockian in relation to the rest of his work, the work of a perfect cynic. Cynical to the point of adding for television – an anxiously moral medium, as we all know – a new ending to the film: Scottie reunited with Midge and the radio reporting Elster's arrest. Crime doesn't pay.

Ten years later, time has continued to work its effect. What used to mean San Francisco for me is disappearing fast. The spiral of time, like Saul Bass's spiral in the credit sequence, the spiral of Madeleine's hair and Carlotta's in the portrait, cannot stop swallowing up the present and enlarging the contours of the past. The Empire Hotel has become the York and lost its green neon lights; the McKittrick Hotel, the Victorian house where Madeleine disappears like a ghost (another inexplicable detail if we ignore the dream-reading: what of the hotel's mysterious janitress? 'A paid accomplice' was Hitchcock's reply to Truffaut. Come on, Alfred!) has been replaced by a school built of concrete. But Ernie's restaurant is still there, as is Podestà Baldocchi's flower-shop with its tiled mosaics where one proudly remembers Kim Novak choosing a bouquet. The cross-section of sequoia is still at the entrance to Muir Woods, on the other side of the bay. The Botanical Gardens were less fortunate: they are now parked underground. (*Vertigo* could almost be shot in the same locations, unlike its remake in Paris.) The Veterans' Museum is still there, as is the cemetery at the Dolores Mission and San Juan Bautista, south of another mission, where Hitchcock added (by an optical effect) a high tower, the real one being so low you'd hardly sprain an ankle falling off it, complete with stable, carriages and stuffed horse used in the film just as they are in life. And of course, there's Fort Point, under the Golden Gate Bridge, which he wanted to cover with birds at the end of *The Birds*. The *Vertigo* tour is now obligatory for lovers of San Francisco. Even the Pope, pretending otherwise, visited two locations: the Golden Gate Bridge and (under the pretext of kissing an AIDS patient) the Dolores Mission. Whether one accepts the dream reading or not, the power of this once-ignored film has become a commonplace, proving that the idea of resurrecting a lost love can touch any human heart, whatever he or she may say. 'You're my second chance!' cries Scottie as he drags Judy up the stairs of the tower. No one now wants to interpret these words in their superficial sense, meaning his vertigo has been conquered. It's about reliving a moment lost in the past, about bringing it back to life only to lose it again. One does not resurrect the dead, one doesn't look back at Eurydice. Scottie experiences the greatest joy a man can imagine, a second life, in exchange for the greatest tragedy, a second death. What do video games, which tell us more about our unconscious than the works of Lacan, offer us? Neither money nor glory, but a new game. The possibility of playing again. 'A second chance.' A free replay. And another thing: Madeleine tells Scottie she managed to find her way back to the house 'by spotting the Coit Tower' – the tower which dominates the surrounding hills and whose name makes visiting French tourists laugh.[1] 'Well, it's the first time I ever had to thank the Coit Tower,' says Scottie, the blasé San Franciscan. Madeleine would never find her way back today. The bushes have grown on Lombard Street, hiding all landmarks. The house itself, number 900, has changed. The new owners have got rid of (or the old owner kept) the cast-iron balcony with its Chinese inscription 'Twin Happiness'. The door is still red, but now blessed with a notice which, in its way, is a tribute to Alfred: 'Warning: Crime Watch'. And, from the steps where Kim Novak and James Stewart are first reunited, no one can see any more the tower 'in the shape of a fire-hose', offered as a posthumous gift to the San Francisco Fire Brigade by a millionairess called Lilli *Hitchcock* Coit …

Obviously, this text is addressed to those who know *Vertigo* by heart. But do those who don't deserve anything at all?

---

1 Coit means 'coitus' in French.

Gianfranco Mingozzi

Two images

My meeting with Leonardo Sciascia occurred during an episode which, through its dramatic conflicts, marked my entire experience as a film-maker and is (or so it seems to me) emblematic of the struggles and difficulties encountered by anyone who wishes to make films reflecting the society we live in.

In 1963 the making of my first film, La violenza, a feature-length documentary about Sicily seen through the eyes of the sociologist-poet Danilo Dolci, was mysteriously suspended. Its financier, Dino De Laurentiis, who was producing the film through Baltes Film, one of his companies, had suddenly halted the shoot without giving a reason. The truth was that he was trying to find money amongst Catholic organizations for his huge project The Bible, and therefore didn't want to be involved in a work of denunciation. The material we had already shot for La violenza dealt with highly controversial matters such as the Mafia (it was the first documentary to be made specifically about this subject), illiteracy, misery – all the tragic problems Sicilians face.

Along with some friends – particularly Cesare Zavattini, who had had the idea for the film – we tried to finish the second half on our own. But joining together the two halves was made impossible by the fact that the first half, Dino De Laurentiis's, had in the meantime been caught up in the bankruptcy of Baltes Film. After two fruitless years spent trying to find Italian or foreign buyers, I decided to finish the material we owned by turning it into a medium-length film no longer reflecting Dolci's point of view, but showing my personal, visual meditation on Sicily and its dramas. However, I still needed a genuinely Sicilian voice to furnish an authoritative complement to my images. I thought of Sciascia, who by then had already published, amongst other books, The Day of the Owl. Not knowing him, I wrote him a letter explaining my predicament. Though I was hopeful, the speed of his reply astonished me: he suggested a meeting in Rome at ten o'clock on 6 June 1965.

The Hotel Mediterraneo, built in the thirties and renovated in the fifties, was (and still is) one of those big, anonymous hotels near the Termini station. In this rather lugubrious setting of square columns, windows looking out on to traffic-choked streets, functional and uncomfortable furniture, I was to meet Sciascia. I knew him only from the photographs on the back covers of his books – serious, official, sombre images – and I was sure I'd recognize him at once; I trusted my own ability to recognize faces, a skill acquired through long

131

years as an assistant looking at actors. The hotel lobby was deserted, or so it seemed. I asked the receptionist whether Sciascia had arrived; in reply, he pointed him out to me. I then saw the writer, backlit by the sun pouring in through the window, sitting in the corner of a sofa and almost disappearing into the cushions. Was it my director's imagination, this professional conditioning which insists on applying a character, a profession, to each physique, to each facial feature? But I do think they were genuine: the penetrating, inquisitorial eyes, the thin lips of a determined thinker, the stocky body of a fighter, the voice, somewhat hesitant yet so sure of the ideas it was expressing. He welcomed me cordially enough, but my initial embarrassment and timidity were not dispelled immediately. It was only after an hour's conversation that I began to relax, and more importantly, that my ideas began to coincide with his desire to participate, to contribute his experiences to the knowledge I wanted to set forth about Sicily and its problems.

He sent me his text a few days later. It was so dense, compact and full of tension, that I guessed he had written it in one sitting, inspired by the images I had screened for him that day. I believe his beautiful commentary was decisive in *Con il cuore fermo, Sicilia* winning the Golden Lion for Documentaries at the 1965 Venice Festival. I'd like to quote, for example, his lucid definition of the Mafia: 'Mafia. Under this name are united, albeit mistakenly, two types of violence: the first, the violence of personal interests, secretly allied for mutual and illicit financial benefit, imposing a discipline which is both inviolable within its organization and respected outside it; the second, a violence born of pride, a tribal law designed to safeguard property, honour, possessions, and women. There is no doubt that both forms of violence have their roots in the same feeling, in the same conception of the world. It is a despairing, pessimistic concept – the kind that a people who for centuries have been frustrated and molested, whose property and dignity have both been violated, may well possess – a people who have known not the virtues, but the vices of their oppressors!'

For twenty years after 1965, I never had another opportunity to meet Sciascia. My work developed along other lines: my fictional films were a kind of indirect autobiography, and my documentaries dealt with other problems, either anthropological or linked to my experience in films.

But Sicily – even though I had never really abandoned it during the intervening years – returned with a vengeance in 1987. The footage of *La violenza* that had been blocked by the bankruptcy of Baltes Film, and which I had bought back from the receivers in the seventies, had caught the attention of public television. RAI 3 was interested in a project I had written with my habitual collaborator Lucia Drudi Domby called *La terra dell'uomo*. I had proposed a comparison between the Sicily of the sixties – to be shown in black and white – and the Sicily (alas, still bloodstained) of the eighties. I shot this documentary, comprising three one-hour episodes, in 1987. I immediately got in touch with Sciascia, not for a commentary, but in order to talk to him about the Sicily of those years. But the writer was ill and couldn't grant me an interview. It was only at the end of the year, in a Palermo covered in Christmas decorations, that I managed to film this vital sequence.

Although he arrived at our location, the villa of La Favorita, leaning on a stick and accompanied by two young people whose job was to escort him and, I imagine, to help him, Sciascia didn't seem ill. The gaze hadn't changed, those sharp and penetrating eyes, and the voice, which I remembered being a little weak and hesitant, trembled no longer.

I planned to sit him in front of a television set and show him a video of our old documentary, but he said he'd prefer not to see it, that he didn't want to be influenced by what he had written so long ago. He asked me to show him only the final sequence, where the camera follows, without commentary, some innocently happy children playing in Cortile Cascino, a miserable district of Palermo – a sequence which had particularly impressed him ...

So I started the interview and his image immediately filled the screen and completed my film, even though a technical hitch meant I had to continue the interview without pictures. But I had enough: the light that, through his words, illuminated the drama of Sicily was, as ever, clear, lucid and dispassionate; enriched and shaped after so many years by humanity, rage, and pity for his 'land of man'.

Mario Monicelli

Mamoulian, Langdon, Rossellini

At the beginning of the thirties I was a very young man living in Milan when, mad about cinema like my friends Lattuada, Freda, Mondadori and Ponti, I went into a suburban movie theatre where they were showing Mamoulian's *City Streets*, a film I wanted to see again. It was the first American gangster movie: with its pacy rhythm, tight action, tough characters and hard lighting, it had the essentials of a psychology, a style that would later become associated with Warner Bros.

Harry Langdon in *Long Pants*.

Mamoulian represented a change from the sentimental, sugary romances and the fairy-tale adventure stories, typified by Robin Hood and Douglas Fairbanks, which had until then dominated the screen.

At the time, second or third-run cinemas – the kind of cinema I could afford to go to – often showed two films for the price of one, usually a comedy and a drama.

This is how, without meaning to and not even knowing he existed, I saw Harry Langdon in *Long Pants*. I can't remember the Italian title, but I do remember being overwhelmed by the emotional and psychological depth of a film which, though billed as a comedy and supposedly aimed at titillating the most superficial sensations of the audience, in reality awakened the most profound feelings. By its use of irony and the grotesque, both pushed to the edge of farce, the film touched the deepest and most varied emotions. And it did this with the minutest changes of tone, without ever beating a big drum, as so often happens in serious drama.

This seemed all the more surprising given the fact that both the films I saw dealt with the same subjects: the brutality and cruelty of relationships within the big cities, the absence of pity and the characters' indifference to feelings.

I've only seen the film once since then. I think it was directed by Frank Capra. I'd like to find it again, and to see Langdon, an actor who had bad luck, take his place alongside Chaplin, Keaton and Lloyd – perhaps with a touch of his own caustic irony, devoid of the sentimentality found elsewhere, especially in Chaplin.

Many years later, I experienced the same psychological and aesthetic shock on seeing Rossellini's *Francesco, giullare di Dio* (*The Flowers of Saint Francis*). The tenderness, spontaneity and joy of the little monks were filtered through a thin veil of irony, an irony which impregnated not only the characters but also the places, the light, the seemingly arbitrary gestures, the tone and the camera movements, and gave the impression that nothing had been 'directed' but instead joyously 'stolen'.

Here again, the director's sense of comedy, his ability to bring out the most intimate movements of the soul, endowed his work with the same spontaneity, the same ecstatic joy one finds in *The Song of Songs*, where everything is so simple as to seem obvious.

This admirable film was the fruit of irony. All subsequent lives of St Francis, whether by directors of stage or screen, lack this essential filter and offer nothing but whining, lachrymose, tedious monks. O what a comic vision of the world, so terrible and merciless and yet so true!

Leopardi wrote in the eighteenth of his *Pensieri*: 'Great amongst men and formidable in its power is laughter. Against laughter, no one can feel that his conscience is entirely protected. The man who has the courage to laugh is master of the world, much like the man who is ready to die.'

Marcel Ophuls

The last of the Good Guys

Max Ophuls hated auditioning actors. He found such public declarations of the power of megalomaniac directors over the life, the professional destiny, and the bank balance of actors not only vulgar but also embarrassing and largely pointless for both parties concerned. Even those classic Broadway scenes where the Great Ziegfeld or some other cigar-chewer, often played by Ned Sparks, sits slumped in the stalls watching the girls parading for Busby Berkeley's next show discomfited him and he'd suddenly start shifting uncomfortably in his seat. He found such scenes disagreeable, even crypto-fascist: they gave the public a totally false impression of a profession he pursued with such energy and grace, an impression that was at the same time sordid, lazy and megalomaniac; in short, they were the fantasy ... *of a producer*. How then would he have reacted to the more recent fashion amongst the new 'masters of the screen' of 'auditioning' technicians and other potential collaborators? What miserable festivals of humiliation, set in gloomy, sordid production offices or in plush apartments in fashionable areas, have we here? Damn it!

(My wife, to whom I'm reading this before supper, cruelly reminds me that twenty years ago, when I was in London preparing *The Memory of Justice*, I also 'summoned' two potential cameramen in turn to the bar of the Westbury Hotel. The first one was utterly charming; he must have been at least ten years younger than me, with long, curly hair. The second, older and greyer, politely apologized that he could only stay ten minutes because he'd promised his kids he'd take them kite-flying on Hampstead Heath; at the very place where, during the Franco-Prussian war, the elderly Karl Marx, ferociously beating out the tempo with his cane, once sang Prussian patriotic songs accompanied by his goose-stepping brood. And so I decided on the spot to work with this devoted family man on a film about the Nuremberg trials! Don't ask me why! As it happened, by the time we next worked together, Mike had left his wife and children and gone off with an American girl.

The other day, in Sarajevo, my cameraman and friend Pierre Boffety told me how another great friend of mine, Claude Lanzmann, had recently summoned him to his house and interviewed him for more than three hours about his 'concept of his profession', only to call him the next day and say, 'I've been thinking. If you get on with Marcel, you can't possibly get on with me.')[1]

[1] How can I resist criticizing Claude Lanzmann's article about *Schindler's List* in *Le Monde*? It's a film I feel no compulsion to see, but the stills and extracts I've seen on television seem to suggest a

136

But to return to my father. I remember the morning when, during the preparation of one of his last films, he was shaving in the bathroom at Chevreuse and cursing all those responsible for having saddled him with a 'bloody audition'. The audition was to take place on the Champs-Elysées at midday, either at the Hakim brothers or at Deutschmeister's. Finally I said to him, 'But if you hate auditioning actors so much, why do you still agree to do it?' His answer was immediate and cutting: 'To eliminate in one go all the ones who say "Monsieur, I shall play a character for you".' He thought for a moment, and then added quietly, 'Anyway, who knows? We might find a young Jimmy Stewart!'

True, it's difficult to imagine this greying man of almost fifty – who returned to Hollywood after the war, during which he had been a highly-decorated general in the reserves, and revealed that he was still capable of playing for Capra, in a touching, amusing and superbly credible way, a young student from the Midwest who can't dance with a girl without falling into the swimming pool – saying to a studio head in that nasal, eternally youthful voice: 'Sir, I shall play a character for you.' [1]

Nowadays this magisterial artist, the magnificent star of so many great films, has become the last survivor of a generation of actors who for many of us symbolized what the USA, the great power of this sordid and tragic century, had to offer in terms of the representation of noble, beautiful ideas and feelings: generosity, fair play, a sense of justice and humanity. Cary Grant, his greatest rival, more handsome than he was and certainly smarter – the man who stole an entire scene from him in *The Philadelphia Story* with one movement of his head – died a long time ago. Gary Cooper, the most handsome and seductive of them all, but a much less credible Capraesque hero in *Deeds* than Jimmy was in *Washington*, died even longer ago. John Wayne, the quiet man who denounced Communists but zealously protected horses from the creative fury of certain violent but mediocre directors of westerns, has been felled by

brilliantly talented and intelligent work. I'm a fervent admirer of *Shoah*, but this mean-spirited, élitist, impoverished Left-Bank attitude which forever bans the Holocaust from fictional cinema seems to me suspect, tinged with literary provincialism. I'd like to telephone L at once to tell him this: 'It's obvious you know nothing about cinema. You start by saying that you admire Spielberg's other films, then go on to explain why you find this one bad, when everything indicates that it isn't.' In the end, we get the intellectuals that chance sends our way. Once, when I explained that one of the differences between *Shoah* and *Hôtel Terminus* was the difference between the teachings of Sartre and those of Capra-Lubitsch, I meant it as a joke for the use of press agents. I now realize that it is a fundamental difference, totally serious and nothing to be ashamed of.

1 According to Max Ophuls, the worst thing a director can do to an actor is to tell him he's 'doing too much'. According to him, human beings aren't dishes to be seasoned with a little salt and pepper. 'Anyway,' he'd say, 'there is nothing in this profession more dangerous than the bourgeois sense of decorum (*der bürgerlicher Sinn für Mass und Ordnung*).' For him the greatest quality an actor could possss was surprise (*die Überraschung*), the inventiveness which can create the kind of suspense where one never stops asking: 'What's he going to do or say next?'

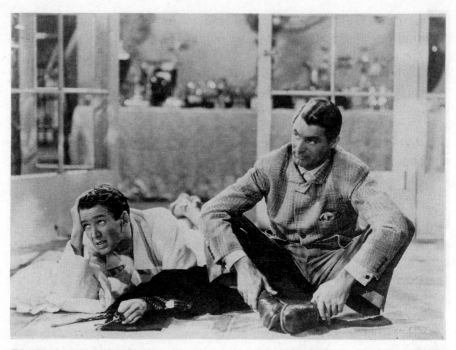

The Philadelphia Story: Stewart with his rival Cary Grant.

cancer. And Stewart's great friend, the marvellous Henry Fonda, after having been led astray by Sergio Leone and arguing on camera with his rebellious daughter, has left us too. Yes, James Stewart is truly the last of the great WASP gentlemen, of the Dead White European Males so derided by the ignoble practitioners of political correctness,[1] the last of the Good Guys of our childhood and adolescence. For the fortieth birthday of my favourite cinema magazine, I – who am condemned to the slavery of documentaries, the cinema of 'truth' (*sic*) without actors (like a meal without wine and sunshine), a cinema where no one is meant to *act*, where authenticity (*sic* again) precludes one from playing with life – suddenly feel a desire to pay homage to this genius of show business, to this inimitable inventor of the lives of others, to this authentic 'creator' (in the best sense of the term), to this model of discretion, modesty, humour and compassion. Long live Mr James Stewart, ladies and gentlemen: the shoe salesman from Matusek's in Budapest, the detective stuck behind his steering wheel in San Francisco, the photographer trapped in his wheel-chair with his leg in plaster, a zoom lens in his hand and a beautiful woman on his arm, the young millionaire sitting on a studio park bench in *You Can't Take It With You* explaining in black and white to his sweetheart Jean Arthur why, 'scientifically speaking', the grass is green, the provincial lawyer who prefers

1 Oh, the terrible backlash against Capra! They can never say enough nasty things about him! Never!

Rear Window: Stewart and the zoom lens.

going fishing to exhibiting Lee Remick's underwear in court in order to defend the arrogant, unsympathetic young lieutenant who is accused of the murder of his wife's rapist.

In cinema, the passing of time sets everything to rights. Who would have thought that Louis Jouvet's asthmatic, deceptively monotonous style would now seem ten times more 'modern' than that of his pre-war partners? Who

A credible Capraesque hero in *Mr Smith Goes to Washington* ...

would have thought that James Cagney, that Irish ham strutting like a cock in the yard, would one day interest us much more than the sober, dignified and O so 'naturalistic' style of Humphrey Bogart ?[1] Who would have predicted that the most discreet actor of his generation, who hardly seemed to change from one film to the other, would now seem to us the most subtle, human, surprising and inventive?

But what a beautiful profession acting is. As Philippe Noiret once said so calmly to Anne Sinclair on *Sept sur Sept*, 'You know, madam, we're the stars, not you.'

Didn't this same wonderful man also say, at the end of a particularly chaotic and sinister evening at the European film awards, presided over by the inevitable Frédéric Mitterrand: 'This was an evening even the Americans couldn't imitate.' Which makes me think of the moments in recent years when,

1 The great German actor Fritz Kortner, reduced to playing more or less Hungarian butlers in Hollywood, once said to us, 'When we go back to Europe after the war, we shouldn't let ourselves be too much influenced by the American school of *Hosentaschenschauspieler*, the actors who play with their hands in their pockets,' and he'd cite Bogart as an example. Long ago, people used to say Bogart's naturalism authenticated any situation, even the most unbelievable stories. Nowadays, isn't it Stewart who has this effect on us?

... and *It's A Wonderful Life.*

during those interminable Oscar ceremonies and Life Achievement Awards – choreographed orgies of self-congratulation in which all the guest appearances and all the witticisms have been thoroughly rehearsed beforehand – Jimmy would appear and everyone would gasp at seeing him so fragile and hesitant. But the second he opened his mouth and spoke in his quavering and deceptively timid voice, one suddenly felt genuine warmth and humour filling that room full of fading and rising stars; and this true 'courtesy of the heart' would once more, and for perhaps the last time, cross the Atlantic towards us.[1]

When I learned that, this time, *Positif* would let us choose a favourite actor

---

[1] My wife, as usual, contradicts what she considers my over-nostalgic memories: 'Remember when we were at Princeton and he didn't want to join the annual graduates' parade because the university let in women and blacks? He said, "They're all a bunch of Commies".' It's true! Life is complicated. It also reminds me of Capra's visit. The students sat in the ceremonial amphitheatre as if in a circus or an anatomy class. Below, the great but diminutive Capra, his nose barely reaching the top of the podium, patiently and amiably answered their questions. Then a polite but scarcely audible student mumbled a question which contained the word 'commercial'. In a flash, Capra lost all his poise. Under his Palm Springs tan he became scarlet with rage, and literally stomped with fury behind the podium: 'Commercial? What do you mean, "commercial"? You blame me for wanting to entertain? That's just stupid. What do you think we're trying to do in this goddamn business apart from surprise and entertain?'

instead of a favourite film or director, I asked my friend Michel Ciment whether I could talk about the 'author's rights' of an actor. I remarked that French law's only loophole in this area was that it took no notice of the major protagonists of a film. They are the ones who should profit from the 'moral rights' rather than the producers. Michel immediately replied: 'And how! And it's all the better because Robert Altman wrote much the same thing!' Brilliant!

Robert Parrish

University of Southern California Film School, Hollywood 1926-50

When I was growing up in Hollywood during the twenties, thirties and forties, there was no Cinémathèque, but there were plenty of films being made, even during the Depression. People all over the world were hungry, but they still needed to be entertained. John Ford, Charlie Chaplin, Lewis Milestone, Ernst Lubitsch, Cecil B. de Mille and other film-makers knew this, and during that period made some of the best films ever made.

I worked as a child actor and as an extra in some of them, such as *City Lights, Wings, Mother Machree, The Informer, King of Kings, etc.* I also worked some nights on the labour gangs at Paramount and FBO (now RKO) studios.

When I graduated from Fairfax High School in 1933, I was seventeen years old. I wanted to be a cameraman, so I signed up for the Southern California School of Cinematography. There was no television then, and only foreigners used the word 'cinema' rather than 'movies'. The class was to be taught in a sub-basement at the university. Fourteen young men and two young girls showed up the first night.

The teacher (professor?) was a gentle, long-since retired cameraman named Lewis D. Phisioc. One of the reasons he got the job was because the university didn't have a 35 mm camera and Lewis D. Phisioc did. He also had a handle to crank it with when he wanted to show us how to expose film.

On the first night, before Professor Phisioc taught us anything, a man who said he was Dean of the USC Drama Department came in, introduced himself, and said that if any of the students were taking the course with a view to getting employment in the Hollywood motion-picture industry, would they please raise their hands.

Sixteen eager hands shot up, and then this Dean said, 'Well, I think it's only fair to tell you that there's practically no chance to break into film-making in Hollywood by taking this course. The industry is overflowing with experienced technicians, the unions won't accept new members, and I regret to say that the university has no influence at the studios.'

The sixteen hands floated down, and most of the sixteen dreams of Hollywood movie glory floated out of the sub-basement window.

The Dean of the Drama Department, anticipating a mass wrist-cutting, then said, 'Don't look so downhearted. Jam Handy in Detroit and other companies that make commercial films throughout America are coming up

143

fast, and what you can learn in Professor Phisioc's class might well train you for work in some other part of the country.'

He walked to the door, then turned to the sixteen young Hollywood residents, smiled, and said, 'Hollywood's not the only place in the world, you know.' He looked over at Professor Phisioc and said cheerily, 'Carry on, Professor.'

As he left the room, both of the girls and seven of the young men followed him out. The rest of us stayed and looked hopefully at Professor Phisioc.

I kept track of the seven young men who stayed in the Professor's class. Eventually, every one of us got good jobs in the Hollywood motion-picture industry: electricians, cameramen, directors, sound men, make-up artists, editors, etc.

I became a film editor, then spent five years as a combat cameraman during the war. When I came home, I became a film director.

May 1954

Twenty years after I left USC, William Wyler, a good friend of mine and one of Hollywood's top directors, called me and said, 'How about lunch? I've just been offered what I think is an honour and I need your advice.'

'Take the honour,' I said.

'Didn't you go to the University of Southern California School of Cinematography?' he said.

'Yes, I did,' I said. 'Are you trying to get in?'

'I'll meet you at Musso Franks at one o'clock.'

We each had a Bloody Mary, and Willy said, 'I've been invited to give the Commencement Address at the USC School of Cinema.'

'Congratulations,' I said.

'What'll I say?' said Willy. 'Those kids are thirty years younger than I am. What are they interested in?'

'You,' I said. 'They're interested in you. They're interested in the movies. You know everything about the movies. Tell 'em what you know. Tell 'em what it's like directing Bette Davis, Humphrey Bogart and Laurence Olivier. Tell 'em what it's like to win Academy Awards. Tell 'em what it's like to argue with Samuel Goldwyn.'

'You think that's all there is to it?'

'No,' I said. 'That's just bullshit to fill in the time.'

'Then what do they really want to know that I can tell them?'

'After the bullshit period, you say, "Any questions?"'

'Any *what*?' Willy said. One of Willy's ears had been blown out in an air raid over Germany during the war. He turned his good ear to me and repeated, 'Any what?'

'Any *questions*,' I said again, louder. 'They'll ask you about the change from silent movies to sound movies and about your experiences in making documentaries in the Air Force, who was the best cameraman you ever worked with, the best cutter, the best producer, the best writer, and anything else they can think of, and finally, one of them will ask you the key question – the real reason why they came to hear you speak.'

Willy sat silent for a moment and then said, 'What's that?'

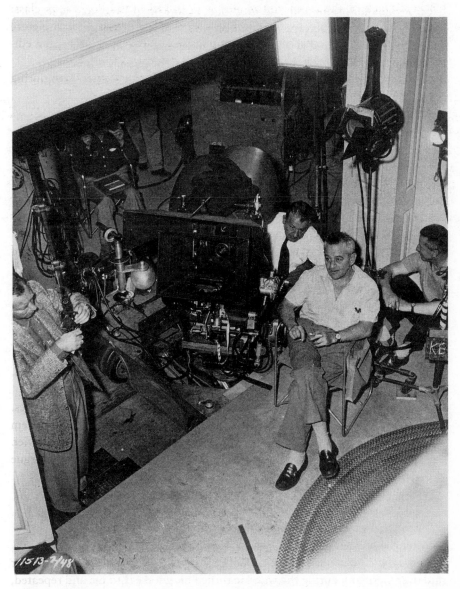

William Wyler on the set of *The Desperate Hours.*

'Someone will eventually ask, "How do you become a film director?"'

Willy sipped his Bloody Mary, smiled and said, 'Will you come to the Commencement Exercises with me?'

'I thought you'd never ask,' I said.

Willy was wonderful. He stood at a microphone in the centre of the stage and performed brilliantly. I sat in the front row. After about thirty minutes, during the question and answer period, a young Burmese student rose in the back of the auditorium and said in a loud, clear, slightly accented voice, 'Mr Wyler, how does one become a film director?'

The audience applauded wildly. Willy looked down at me in the front row and smiled. I smiled back and lowered my eyes. The audience finally stopped applauding, and waited silently and anxiously for the secret words from the great man.

Willy looked up and said, 'I've known many directors in my day, some good, some bad and lots in between, but I don't know of any two who became directors in exactly the same way. Ernst Lubitsch, John Ford, Lewis Milestone, Bill Wellman, Charlie Chaplin, Jean Renoir, Billy Wilder and others are great directors, but I don't think any of them became great directors by following the same rules.'

He paused for a moment to let that truth sink in. Then he said, 'What I can do is to tell you *my* story, how *I* became a director. There may be something along the way that will be helpful to you. I'll start at the beginning and try not to leave anything out.'

Three hundred students sat on the edge of their seats, their ears wide open.

'First,' said Willy, 'be born in Alsace-Lorraine.' Pause. 'Preferably in Mulhouse.' Another pause. 'Have a father who owns a store in Mulhouse and an uncle who is head of a movie studio in Hollywood, California.

'When you get tired of working in your father's store, write to your uncle and ask if you can come work in his movie studio. Your uncle won't answer this letter, so you keep working in your father's store. A year later, if you still want to be a movie director, ask your mother to write to her brother, your uncle, and ask if you can come to Hollywood and work in his studio.

'Your uncle likes his sister, so he answers her letter and sends a steerage-class boat ticket for you to come to New York. He writes that a studio representative will meet you at the dock in New York.

'You pack your skis and your violin and take off for America. A studio representative (Morris) meets you at the boat and puts you on a cheap train to Los Angeles, where another studio representative (this one's name is Jerry) meets you and drives you to your uncle's studio in the San Fernando Valley. He takes you to a one-room bungalow on the studio backlot where you leave your skis, your violin and your suitcase.

'Then he takes you to your uncle's office. Your uncle greets you warmly and asks about your mother and the rest of the family in Mulhouse.

'He then says to Jerry, "Show him round the studio and tonight get him started on the swing gang." You leave your uncle's office, he gives you a five-dollar bill and two one-dollar bills, and says, "Here's your first week's pay in advance. You can have your meals free in the studio commissary until you get a raise, then you start paying like everyone else. It's good to see you, son. Good luck."

'You learn that night that the "swing gang" is the night-shift labour force that strikes the set and cleans up the stages for the next day's shooting. You work at that and other menial jobs for about a year.

'One of your jobs is to sweep up the street in front of the cutting department. As you are doing this one day, you will see a man standing outside, leaning against the building. He'll be the head of the cutting department, and he'll have an unlit cigarette in his mouth. He'll say, "Gotta match?" and you'll say "Yes," because you smoke too.

'He'll light his cigarette and offer you one. You'll light your cigarette and lean against the building with him. After a while, he'll say, "We can't smoke inside the building because we work with nitrate film and it's highly flammable." He thanks you for the match, you thank him for the cigarette, and you go your separate ways.

'The next time you're on a night shift, you sneak into the head cutter's room and set up a "long-distance smoking arrangement" for him.

'You get a piece of copper tubing from the machine shop, put an ivory cigarette-holder at each end of it, and run it from the cutting bench through the window to the outside. You light a cigarette and put it in the cigarette-holder on the outside end of the copper tube. Then you run inside to the head cutter's bench and suck on the cigarette-holder at the other end of the copper tube. The smoke finally comes through. It works. You can now smoke inside the cutting room without blowing up the studio.

'The next day, when the head cutter discovers the set-up, he sends for you and offers you a job as an apprentice in the cutting department. You jump at the chance. You like the work, you learn fast, you keep the copper tube supplied with cigarettes, and you're soon promoted to assistant cutter.

'After a while, you get a chapter of a serial to edit yourself, then a B-feature. You do it so well that they give you a cowboy western to direct, then a feature with real stars, then another, and then you win your first Academy Award, and later you win a few more, and before you know it, you will be invited to address the graduating class at the University of Southern California School of Cinema-Television, and some student will ask you how one becomes a director, and you can tell him how *you* did it.

'Next question?'

Arthur Penn

Actors and directors/directors and actors

(from remarks delivered at the Actors Studio)

Brando, Bancroft, Beatty, Dunaway, Fonda (Henry and Jane), Duvall, Hackman, Hoffman, Newman, Nicholson, Parsons, Redford, Stanley: my career has offered me the privilege of working with some of the finest actors of our time. For many years I have been active at the Actors Studio in New York and have watched and participated in the development of young actors who have now gained great and deserved fame. My working life is inextricably connected with the craft of the Actor. I have learned so much from them. I owe them an inestimable debt.

My career began in 'live' television. The plays we did were by extraordinary writers. It was the time before videotape existed, so we went on the air with direct transmission and 'cut' the camera angles and lenses as we sensed what the actors were doing. Often they reached performance nuances that had only been hinted at in the rehearsals. So we, the directors, controlling the cameras, *identifying with each actor*, searched their changes of emotion and performance. We then manipulated our cameras to catch those exquisite, fleeting moments.

This is how some fine actors approach a play or film: they receive a role to play. I am not talking about the words of the playwright that the actor will eventually speak. The actors are not ready to speak the words because they have not yet found in themselves their identification with the nature of the characters they are going to portray. So they must first begin to 'inhabit' the role. They search out correlative events and emotions *from their own lives* and apply them. Slowly, the role begins to wrap itself round them, and themselves round it.

After analysing their roles in the construction of the play, they, *with the director and playwright*, decide what their character *must achieve* (the objective); and what, in their character's nature (the obstacles), *prevents* them from immediately accomplishing those objectives. The objectives are usually clear. Hamlet: 'I must revenge my father's murder.' The 'obstacles' are not so clear. And they are the most important: because *in the obstacles lies the characterization*. Traits, behaviour, fears, beliefs and doubts: these personality definitions are where the actor finds his character. In the insight that defines the obstacles, the originality of choice, and its fulfilment lies the actor's art. It is in

148

the *tension* between objective and obstacle that true characterization exists.

To put it simply: 'I want this to happen!' (Hamlet wants to revenge his father's murder.) 'But what is it in my nature that *prevents me from accomplishing it immediately?*' That is my character; my 'obstacles' *define* me. In *Hamlet*, Prince Hamlet's *obstacles* give birth to some of the finest poetry in all drama. Soliloquy after soliloquy is devoted to his anguished battle with his

Hamlet: a Freudian obstacle.

149

own nature that prevents him from directly confronting the King, his uncle, as his father's murderer and killing him.

Let's examine some obstacles employed by actors we recognize. Laurence Olivier, for instance, chose a Freudian basis, taken from the writings of Ernest Jones, for his obstacles. Hamlet's strong sexual attraction to his mother, his jealousy that she has moved so swiftly into the marriage-bed with his hated uncle, sends him to near-madness and impotence. He projects on to Ophelia his version of female frailty, female sexual appetite, and drives her mad. He contemplates suicide, but is paralysed because with his own death the opportunity to kill his uncle is lost. These dysfunctional actions and inactions are derived in part from an Oedipal displacement that positions him as his dead father's surrogate: *his mother's lover*. He cannot confront his desire for his mother, and turns it into the strangely dispassionate killing of old Polonius before her.

At the Actors Studio we speculate that if Macbeth played Hamlet, the play would be over in ten minutes. Nothing in Macbeth's nature offers him the obstacles that prevent Hamlet from accomplishing revenge. Macbeth's ambition and reckless love of action would propel him into a swift dispatch of his uncle, bedding Ophelia, a kick in the ass to Polonius, and wrapping his mother in widow's weeds to be worn for the rest of her life. And he would crown himself King! Only after carrying out the 'objective' would he then suffer the nightmares and delusions of the witches' predictions.

Another example: the exquisite moment in *On the Waterfront* when Rod Steiger pulls out a gun and threatens Brando, his brother. Our expectation is that Brando will react with fear or violence or panic. No. Instead, he responds with pain for his brother, who has had to resort to such desperate measures. In that single moment, in Brando's moan, is the epitaph for all the early aspirations and bonding of these two brothers. That is an actor, *in the moment*, inventing one of the rare, ineradicable moments in acting.

Surely the director, Elia Kazan, deserves credit as well, because we know that the atmosphere he creates on the set, the permission he gives the actor to 'follow his impulses, moment to moment', provide encouragement of major importance.

At last we have arrived at the director, and why he is needed by the actor. When an actor is venturing into dangerous emotional territory, it is wise to have someone who will encourage him, dissuade him from one 'choice' and lead him towards another. *Someone to believe the lie*. Someone who is, as we were in live television, 'deeply identified with them'. Someone to trust, because the task of the actor, after all the decisions of rehearsal have been made, is to remain emotionally open *in the moment* as it arrives in each performance. They must summon up their courage to respond in unplanned, idiosyncratic, anarchic ways that violate the conventional and scare us, the audience, into

On the Waterfront: Steiger and Brando.

the belief that this moment is unique. And it must be unique, accidental, dangerous; not a mere copy of the rehearsals, but a leap into space where they have not precisely been before.

Of course, there is interpretative work the director does that does not immediately involve the actor. Before the acting, there is the narrative. The screenwriter, a painfully uncelebrated author in film, has fashioned a film narrative that is a composite of words spoken and images to be constructed. The director has innumerable responsibilities towards the conceptual level of the film. How will the film live, what will its rhythms be? What will it look like? Where in the film can he spare the purely narrative obligations for the improvisatory invention where the craft and art of actor and director join? Which will be the dominant images? Much of that work comes, as with the actors themselves, out of the events and emotions of their own lives that they must search out and apply to those images.

In my work, for example, the family reunion scene in *Bonnie and Clyde* was drawn from my memory of photographs, faded into almost neutral shades of sepia, of my young parents in arrested frivolity at the beach.

Or the end of *Alice's Restaurant,* where the camera dollies back and away from the final image of Alice on the church steps. This was for me the defining image of the film. The camera is pulling away and away, and yet Alice's image

Bonnie and Clyde: the reunion scene.

remains the same size. It refuses to be diminished by passing time. The objective vision of the eye is being contradicted by the 'vision' of the mind. Memory: a photograph of the soul.

Now to return to the collaboration between actor and director, but from a different perspective: improvisation. By improvisation I certainly do *not* mean actors substituting their words for those of the screenwriter. I believe it is an unfortunate turn in film-making that actors' mouthings in front of the camera all too often end up as the 'dialogue' in the film. To call that improvisation, at least as we mean it at the Actors Studio, is to defame an important part of the actor's training. To call it 'dialogue' is obscene.

Improvisation is concerned with matters more personal and unpredictable than simply changing a few spoken words. Improvisation is a way to find personal correlation to the emotions and circumstances in a given scene where the actor has experienced difficulty or lack of inspiration. Here the director becomes a vital part of the process. Improvisations are *structured* for the actor to draw closer and closer to his own experience, however painful that may be.

For the director and actor, it is the way to dislodge themselves from the obvious and facile. Here is where discoveries are made, where original behaviour not specified by the script comes into being. The actor and director collaborate in the discovery of the unexpected, the 'inappropriate', the odd and unpredictable behaviour that we all know resides in us and which can then be carried forward into the performance of the play.

Only now, *after the basic work is completed*, should the actor turn to the words of the play. *Not before*, or the actor's invention will go into 'line readings'. He or she will then be listening from outside their stage life to how they *sound* in the part. At last, the actor joins his or her personal material to the language of the play or film.

An example: Dustin Hoffman in *Little Big Man*, wearing a cavalry uniform but also vestiges of 'Indian war-paint', is apprehended by the cavalry. He is accused of being a 'renegade' and is about to be hanged when General Custer, the murderer of Hoffman's Indian wife and child, intervenes. Hoffman must convince him that he is indeed a cavalryman, and that he was a 'prisoner of the Indians' and tortured mercilessly by them. A difficult task, because Hoffman has been caught as the Indian he has become, and because Custer is quite mad.

Hoffman and I struggled with the scene, trying to find a personal basis for it. We struck upon a Nazi concentration-camp experience, a man trying to deny 'Jewishness' in order to survive long enough to kill his oppressor. He must persuade his Nazi adversary that he too has suffered at the hands of their common enemy, 'the Jews'. It was delicate and extremely painful.

This was meant to be a funny scene in the film, but with the use of such anguished, improvisatory material Hoffman filled with tears and was racked by identification with the Jews who had died in the Nazi madness. In turn, Custer (Richard Mulligan) had to prove to his cavalrymen that he was such an acute reader of human behaviour that he 'believed' the doubled lies, which *proved the truth to him*, and immediately set Hoffman free to become his orderly. Each actor was reaching for an ever-higher intensity in his choice of objective, and was forcing himself through difficult obstacles to achieve them. The scene results in considerable desperate humour – yes, humour – because of the *intensity* of their choices.

What Dustin brought to that encounter were levels of human emotion I had not anticipated when I approached the scene. Until we are on the set and the actors are beginning to inhabit their portrayals, it is easy for the director, because he is so burdened with the logistics of making a film, to have already settled in his mind for an *adequate and familiar* version of the scene ahead. Yet this is the very opportunity for the director *to learn from the actor what the life of the character truly is*. Having two fine actors on fiercely-conflicting lines of action is to witness a great bout.

After all that has been said about film being a director's medium, the truth is that it is not the director but the actor who faces the relentless eye of the camera. Here, the courage of the actor to *be*, to be bold, reckless, unpredictable, is brought to fruition. The director controls excess, and if the actor trusts him, the process is fulfilled. To have an environment, *created by the director*, that releases and liberates the invention of the actor is to avail oneself of the greatest of assets: talented actors who are freed to invent. Actors are not to be feared. But I'm afraid many directors do fear them, and that causes each to deny the other the wonderful opportunity to make magical moments that shed light on the screen or on the stage: the light of true life. And sometimes art.

Nelson Pereira dos Santos

The Grierson comet in Latin America

In 1958 the Uruguayan Cinémathèque invited the master, John Grierson, to Montevideo to chair the first assembly of Latin-American film-makers, including youngsters such as Fernando Birri, Manuel Chambi, Jorge Ruiz, Mario Handler and Patricio Kaulen.

Meetings and debates open to the public – mostly students and film-club members – were preceded by screenings in the presence of the directors of the films. With the exception of my films, *Rio 40 Graus* and *Rio Zona*, these were mainly documentaries.

The film-makers, all taking their first steps in their profession, were nervous of the master's opinions. He had invented documentary films and produced them for years in England. He was also the author of our bible: *Cinema and Reality*.

Imagine our surprise when Grierson, instead of giving lessons in reality, exclaimed with pleasure on seeing Birri's *Tire Die* or Chambi's bland documentaries. Every time he was asked to express his opinion as a 'master', he would decline with a humour that was sharp and curt. As far as he was concerned, the youngsters had found their real master: the reality of their country. It was alive and breathing in all of their films.

Of course, he would comment on the structure of the films, but he never imposed theory on us. He would speak out loudly during screenings whenever clarity fell foul of immaturity or complications of style. Seeing a dissolve, for example, he would shout from the back of the hall, 'Make up your mind!' He was speaking to the screen, not to the director. He spoke to the film.

He liked to talk about his experiences, about his films, about the relationship between politics and cinema. He said of the Brazilian director Alberto Cavalcanti, some of whose documentaries he had produced in England, that he had every quality except that of being political. He couldn't forgive this lacuna in the education of a film-maker.

John Grierson was so fascinated by the Latin America he'd discovered through the films that he decided to extend his journey to Bolivia, Peru and Rio de Janeiro, where he arrived on the same day as the Brazilian national football team, who had just won the World Cup for the first time. He watched the team parade through the city from the balcony of his hotel near the Presidential Palace. This was when I discovered the sentimental side to a man who had, until then, seemed so straightforward, rational and dry. He turned with tears in his eyes to the Brazilians in his room and said, 'God bless you! For your people, footballers are heroes, not soldiers!'

The next day he went to the Maracana stadium and met Manuel Garrincha, one of the greatest Brazilian footballers of all time. I don't know what language they spoke in, but they understood each other perfectly.

Four years later, I met him in a hotel bar during the Leipzig Festival. 'Let's have a drink, Santos!' he said to me, as if we'd never parted.

'How are you, Mr Grierson?'

'I'm not leaving now. I'll wait for the next plane.'

Lucian Pintilie

The meeting

'I left the studio and started to cry – crying for real – my face pressed against the wall.'

Many years ago I was in London. I didn't owe the occasion, alas, to the sublime circumstance of a slender purse, but to the horror of an official visit. No other moment in my life has been marked by such a deep sense of unreality; it was a nightmare lit with fantastic events, such as the (blessedly brief) period I spent being ferried from one banker to another by Rolls-Royce, as if I were a character in some Technicolor Kafka story. The madness reached its height on the day the Archbishop of Canterbury in person granted us the honour of an audience amidst the Gothic ruins of Coventry Cathedral; this was because, by some freak of fate, our group of film-makers had been mistaken for a government delegation whose visit was due the same day.

I shall always cherish a fond memory of the Archbishop of Canterbury who, although an aide had told him, by means of a subtle code, of the vaudevillian error he was about to commit, continued after a moment's hesitation, betrayed by a few blinks, to speak to us as if nothing had gone amiss; visibly, the prelate knew that the spirit of continuity was important even in error.

The rest had the consistency of cardboard – nothing real occurred during the soporific ceremonies we attended – until the morning we were told that, through the channels of friendship or sympathy, much more effective than official channels, the Rumanian delegation had been invited to watch, on a set somewhere near London, the shooting of a prestigious production directed by an old and venerable artist.

Many, many years had passed since this great artist, a prelate too in his way, had practised his religion. We also knew that this great artist never tolerated intruders on his set, which made this honour granted to three strangers seem even more arbitrary.

The next morning we found ourselves at the entrance of an ancient, tumbledown studio which was nevertheless equipped with the latest technology; such is the perversity of the English.

After the normal wait, the great artist quite naturally made his appearance on the set. Actors, technicians – all the participants quite naturally mixed together – greeted him with a quite natural politeness. He replied quite naturally with a joke, or two at the most; and then, just as naturally, everyone set to work.

157

When the venerable artist saw us, the three intruders, his brow darkened as he remembered how, in a moment of weakness, he had agreed to invite us. He looked at us like Monsieur Puntilla must have looked at Matti, his valet, the morning after a binge. Naturally though, he said nothing and continued to work.

At that moment, I selfishly left my colleagues in order to find a more discreet vantage point (so my curiosity should not be too visible). In a way, it was a more illuminating one too: behind him, so that I could watch his profile, his hands (much more interesting seen from behind), the tension of his entire being, and the way he projected this tension on to Marlon Brando's face.

He whispered some instructions into Brando's ear. Brando listened with a quite natural attentiveness. His face expressed nothing but attentiveness – not a molecule of it showed his joy at collaborating with this venerable artist, and the unbelievable luck of meeting him. The artist ended his brief monologue, left Brando and started to make his way towards his chair, behind the lights, in order to give the signal to begin.

Strangely, or so it seemed to me, instead of taking the shortest route to his chair, by walking back a few steps behind the lights, he embarked on a bizarre circular journey that took him outside the ample space occupied by the set.

The trouble was that I happened to be standing at the edge of this circle. The venerable artist approached, and when he was less than a metre away, he suddenly looked up at me with great curiosity.

As I had been watching him with great intensity, meeting his gaze made me feel as if a trap door had suddenly opened at my feet. I fell into the abyss of his eyes and melted – yes, melted – into them. I remember it with a dizzying precision.

It all happened in a flash. He continued his journey and, completing the second half of the circle, took up his position behind the camera.

The others were waiting for the order to turn over when, struck by an idea, he went back to Brando and again whispered some instructions. Perhaps they were a little more precise this time.

After which, instead of returning straight to his place behind the camera, he embarked on the same journey, during which he was bound to encounter my gaze once again. This time, however, like a boxer waiting for an adversary's punches, I had my guard up. I was standing with both feet firmly on the ground, my weight balanced, and leaning a little forward. I waited for him. Arriving in front of me, he looked at me, considered me, and continued on his way.

The others calmly waited for the signal to turn over.

He raised his arm – and then, to the general stupefaction, he changed his mind and again went up to Brando to give him new instructions, many more of them, even more subtle, with a good deal of explanation and gesture. It was becoming a spectacle in itself. And it was only when he re-embarked on his circular journey that I understood that he was 'testing' me, weighing me up, as if he were looking for some confirmation in my face.

The game went on repeating itself, each time increasing in magnitude, but augmented by a vicious, irreversible nuance: the circular journey was now automatic; our exchange of looks, the return to the chair, and the postponement of the command were predictable.

Suddenly, I realized that *this great artist was quite simply nervous*, that what he was looking for in my increasingly naked, infantile face was a reaction to the instructions he was giving Brando; that he was instinctively searching for confirmation of his genius; that at eighty, at the summit of a career one could only contemplate on one's knees, he felt he had to pass an exam in front of me, a humble stranger; that I should confirm his genius as I would the result of a biopsy.

And so I left the studio and started to cry – crying for real – my shoulders shaking, my face pressed against the wall.

The name of the artist whose sublime, angelic pride I've just denounced is Charlie Chaplin.

Roman Polanski

Odd Man Out

The film that probably most influenced my life when I was very young was
Odd Man Out (literally translated in Polish as 'Those not needed can go',
while the French title, literally 'Eight hours' grace', seems to me useless). I saw
it in Cracow when I was sixteen. At the time, I remember, a great many films
were banned to under-eighteens, but I'd always manage to see them because,
as it happened, they always let us in. After the war Western films were very
rare in Poland, and there were always huge queues in front of the cinemas that
showed them. There'd always be a policeman present. That day, there was a
soldier at the entrance who said to me in a half-Russian accent (he must have
served in the Red Army), 'We don't let in kids like you.' I was livid, but I managed to slip in all the same.

It was the expressionist atmosphere of *Odd Man Out* that struck me most.
The film is a little theatrical, in spite of the fact that the credit sequence is composed of aerial shots and that several scenes are shot on location in Belfast
streets. Nevertheless, *Odd Man Out* continues to be something special for me.

About twenty years later, I saw it again in a London repertory cinema and
was terrified I'd be disappointed. But I wasn't in the slightest; the film held up
wonderfully well. Not long ago, and twenty years later again, I saw it a third
time, and it had exactly the same impact. But this time I discovered in it something new and essential.

Apart from the atmosphere, the marvellous performances, the superb camera-work, the fascinating *mise-en-scène* with its brilliantly effective composi-
tions and depth of field, what struck me unconsciously and no doubt more
profoundly was the story of a fugitive. During the war I was a fugitive from
the ghetto. Twenty years later, in London, I was a fugitive from Stalinism. And
today I still am a fugitive!

During my childhood I no doubt identified with this man no one wants,
whom people would like to help but who frightens them because he's on the
run. At the time, the policeman's resemblance to a Nazi must have struck me
too.

I was sensitive to the development of the story. In the first scene Johnny,
who's preparing a hold-up with Irish terrorists, says it's going to snow. At the
beginning of the film the weather's clear and bright; then it starts raining,
snowflakes fall, and then it freezes. This touched me because it was the landscape of my childhood.

I remember, in Cracow, streets covered in snow becoming slippery underfoot.

When I dreamed of directing, I thought of the atmosphere which had so bewitched me in *Odd Man Out*. I remember an extraordinary scene where the hero finds himself in an old bathtub in a warehouse in the middle of a wasteland. There's also a moment when we switch to his accomplices without the slightest interruption in the narrative.

The unity of time is expressed by several clocks, including the town clock we see at the beginning of the film. This clock accompanies the odyssey of this wounded man, a man more and more prone to hallucinations. It's terribly moving. There's also a surreal touch to certain scenes, such as those with Robert Newton as the painter who wants to paint the hero's portrait.

And of course James Mason is fabulous. He's never been more moving. He's feverish, he can hardly walk. And he plays this with such truth and naturalness! There isn't a trace of showmanship: it's all organic.

We hardly hear him speak in the film. But when he does, it's incredibly moving.

For me, Carol Reed's film is the quintessence of post-war English cinema.

It was a fantastic period: Lean's *Great Expectations*, Olivier's *Hamlet*, which I saw twenty-four times before joining the film school, and *The Third Man* by the same director, Carol Reed.

James Mason in *Odd Man Out*.

Karel Reisz

Stroheim revisited

If you wanted to see Erich von Stroheim's *Greed* when it was last shown at the National Film Theatre, you had to book for a three o'clock double feature with *Treasure of the Sierra Madre* as the main attraction. The show was part of a season on the theme of Money, running concurrently with evening programmes of homage to 'Russ Meyer – American *auteur*'. The showing of *Greed* – the beautiful Museum of Modern Art print accompanied by an excellent pianist – was less than half full.

I curated a retrospective of Stroheim's films at the NFT forty years ago. It ran for three months, four nights a week. Lotte Eisner provided six long, impassioned programme notes (only three of which are now preserved in the archives). Stroheim was, with D.W. Griffith and Chaplin, one of the masters of American silent film; but his work is almost forgotten.

Erich von Stroheim was an immigrant from Vienna who directed nine films in Hollywood between 1918 and 1932. The films are savage comedies of sexual manners, fusing satire with melodrama; they make up, in effect, their own *genre*. (*Greed* is a special case.) Four have modern settings; the rest play in the pre-1914 court of Emperor Franz Josef's Austria. All revolve around a central love affair between a Prince or Seducer (usually Stroheim) and a Good Girl. The titles speak for themselves: *Blind Husbands, Foolish Wives, The Wedding March, Queen Kelly*.

The plot of *Foolish Wives*, Stroheim's third film, has the sexually insatiable Count Sergius (Stroheim), in cahoots with two criminal 'princesses', planning to seduce the American ambassador's wife in order to blackmail her into laundering his counterfeit banknotes in the casino at Monte Carlo. It involves a duel, a fire, a thunderstorm, an idiot girl with the face of an angel, a nosy monk, a spinster maid who gives Sergius her savings. And it ends with the maid's suicide, the princesses stripped of their wigs and arrested, and Sergius strangled and dumped into a sewer (Quentin Tarantino eat your heart out).

But the film is not made in fun. Stroheim learned his trade from D.W. Griffith, and absorbed his passion for reality. His inventions may be bizarre, but he sets them in the real world. Palaces and hovels are re-created in meticulous detail. A corner of the Monte Carlo casino is replicated in the studio with all its glitzy decay. The subject of *Foolish Wives* is decadent Europe, not Ruritania.

Stroheim has a way of making his characters both preposterous and recognizable that is unlike anyone else's; whatever their excesses, they carry inner conviction. The helpless little maid is seen as a victim, but Stroheim makes her ugly, a kind of crippled soul. And Sergius, for all his bravado, is a monster. In the seduction scene, Stroheim has him manicure his nails, then flex the nail-file like a whip. There is nothing here of Lubitsch's (or Ophuls') colluding charm. Stroheim may be dazzled by the rich, but he knows what they are like and what they can do to the poor. He is fascinated by declining Europe, but he also wants to expose it. We know where his feelings are: the scene of Sergius dumped into the sewer comes over with the force of a moral judgement. (It

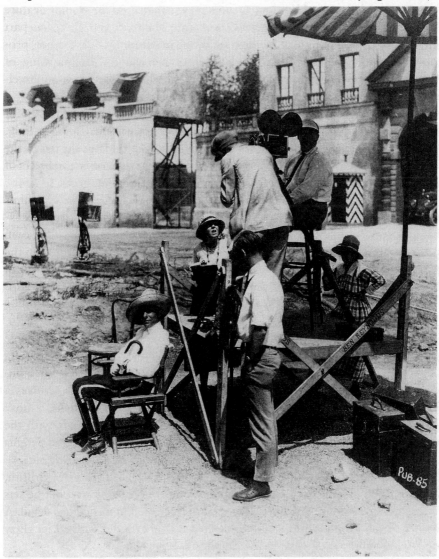

Stroheim on the set of *Foolish Wives*.

came as no surprise when a posthumous biographer tracked down his birth certificate, which proved that Stroheim did not stem from the aristocratic, military background he always claimed. He was a Jew.)

Foolish Wives went four times over budget and was advertised as a 'Million Dollar Movie'. *Photoplay* called it 'an Insult to the Ideals of American Womanhood'. And it made money. The films that followed became more extravagant and ambitious. *The Wedding March* even revealed a softer side, as did *Queen Kelly* (with Gloria Swanson), which was cut short by the arrival of sound. Every one of his films was in some way mangled by the studios or taken away from him. MGM reduced *Greed* from twenty-four reels to twelve. Stroheim never learnt to play by the rules of the industry.

It is tempting to see *Greed* as Stroheim's revenge on Hollywood, on America. Certainly, it stands quite apart from his other work. Based on Frank Norris's ambitious, naturalistic novel of contemporary San Francisco, *Greed* chronicles the disintegration of the 'normal' marriage of Trina and McTeague. The modern American society the film shows is, at first, middle class (McTeague is a dentist); then moves into the lower depths. But the centre of the film is Trina and her inner life. Stroheim presents us with a casebook of deprivation, leading ultimately to insanity. An all-destroying greed for gold

Greed.

takes over the actions and the fantasies of Trina's existence. Stroheim sees the story as one of sexual denial; at the same time, he makes it reverberate like a lament for the aspirations of the voiceless poor.

The climax of *Greed* has McTeague, the decent – now starving – husband, reduced to a despairing act of torture: he bites Trina's fingers to make her surrender her sack of gold. He succeeds, then murders her, and flees to Death Valley where, handcuffed to his wife's ex-suitor, he dies. The water from his canteen spills over the now useless gold.

It is a grand and formidable conception, supported by an extraordinary honesty of playing. Zasu Pitts's courageous, emotionally naked performance does not spare our feelings. Most remarkably, it doesn't court affection. Stroheim's aim is not sympathy, but the confrontation of a dreadful reality.

The same unsparing eye is brought to the settings. The hideous squalor of the couple's San Francisco dwelling – the mountain of unwashed crockery, the perpetually unmade bed, the bloody plasters on Trina's hands – the film is full of stinging detail. And it is not only of a descriptive kind. Stroheim knows how to use the great freedom of image-making which was one of the glories of silent cinema. The funeral glimpsed behind the wedding; Trina sleeping, covered by her precious gold; the repeated pictures of caged birds, echoing first the couple's affection, then their conflict, and finally released in the desert without a chance of survival; the vision of cadaverous hands grasping for gold as if in some ferocious ritual; finally, the vastness of Death Valley. The imagery creates a language, both real and surreal, grandiloquent and to-the-point, which is the perfect vehicle for Stroheim's dark, accusing vision. *Greed* still has the power to knock you over.

Stroheim's current neglect is as surprising as it is regrettable. In Europe, Jacques Becker and Jean Renoir have handsomely acknowledged their debt. So has Visconti. As for America, Gavin Lambert, on whose 1953 study of Stroheim I have drawn here, has proposed a convincing line of succession:

'The violent satire of *Foolish Wives* leads through to Lubitsch's elegant and cynical comedies, and finds a more recent echo in the ruthless upper class intrigues of Sturges's *The Lady Eve* and *The Palm Beach Story*, in the bizarre passions of Wilder's *Sunset Boulevard*. The cruel, declining aristocracies of *The Wedding March* are transferred to America at the turn of the century in Welles's *The Magnificent Ambersons*, in Wyler's *The Little Foxes* and *Carrie*; and the unaffectionate surface texture of American life in *Greed* in the numerous crime and gangster films of the last twenty years, in Lang's *Fury*, in Huston's *Treasure of the Sierra Madre*, in *Citizen Kane*. All these, like Stroheim's, are films of 'exposure', with an eloquent mistrust of society and of human motives.'

'An eloquent mistrust of society and of human motives.' Perhaps this explains why there is something so powerful about seeing *Greed* again after all these years. Perhaps it is because, beneath the satire and the fireworks, you can feel the source of that current of misanthropy that has been pulling at us ever since in so much of the best American cinema. And it is not only the films of the exiles – Lubitsch, Lang, Wilder – that I have in mind. You can still feel its chilling undertow in the work of Coppola and De Palma and Scorsese ... You make your own list.

Flashback to 1954

When Stroheim came to London for his retrospective season, he was sixty-eight years old and had not directed a film in twenty-five years. The attempt to complete his Viennese cycle *La Dame Blanche* had been stopped sixteen years earlier by the German *Anschluss* of Austria. He survived by acting, mostly arrogant Prussian officers – 'The Man You Love to Hate' – a job he despised and refused to discuss.

His personality seemed set behind a rigid and forbidding mask. The clicking of the heels, the curt bows, the absurd gallantry to women, and the boastful sexual asides to men – all this was played out as if giving you an option to smile (but heaven help you if you did). At a press reception an English woman critic, not without reason nervous of the great man, wanted to know something about the history of *Greed*. She spoke of MGM's vandalism ... art and commerce etc ... but Stroheim cut her short. 'Yes, yes, madam,' he said. 'I know, I know, but in Austria we have a saying: "If you put your finger in the shit"' – pause, regretful shrug – '"it smells".'

Later, asked about his fight with Louis B. Mayer over *Greed*, he was evasive: 'I tell you a story ... One day, on the set, I noticed one of my assistants, Irish McSomething (we had some kind of relationship, but *that* is another story) – she was speaking on the phone, obviously reporting to Louis B. – *spying*! I said to her, "Irish, I catch you doing that again and God help me! – I lift up your skirt, I pull down your knickers, and I slap you on your bare *caboose*."' All questions of substance were refused. The story of *Greed* was the story of defeat: something an officer doesn't dwell on. But he remembered the last meeting at MGM: 'When it was all over, Louis B. Mayer dismissed me. Just before I left the room he said, "That's a nice pair of gloves you're wearing."' It seemed an odd moment to recall, until you remembered that Louis B. Mayer started life as a glove salesman.

Lotte Eisner has recounted in moving terms sitting beside the anguished Stroheim in the Cinémathèque at the first post-war showing of *The Wedding March*. But by the time he came to London all that was far behind him. The years of exile lay heavy on him; only fond memories of D.W. Griffith could make him speak of the past. For the rest, he acknowledged whatever was offered by way of praise, but he didn't want to recall the triumphs and defeats of his Hollywood life any more, much less throw light on its enigmas. To get a little closer to him we must turn to earlier years. Here is Jean Renoir:

'At the beginning of the shooting of *La Grande Illusion* Stroheim behaved intolerably. We had an argument about the opening scene in the German living-quarters. He refused to understand why I had not brought some prostitutes of an obviously Viennese type into the scene. I was shattered. My intense admiration for the great man put me in an impossible position. It was partly because of my enthusiasm for his work that I was in film-business at all. *Greed* was for me the banner of my profession. And now here he was, my idol, acting in my film, and instead of the figure of truth that I had looked for, I found a being steeped in childish clichés. I was well aware that those same clichés, in his hands, became strokes of genius. Bad taste is often a source of inspiration to the greatest artists.'

My own last picture of Stroheim is at Victoria Station, in a carriage window, holding my hand and that of a colleague. He spoke slowly, the actor's tears coming into his eyes: 'Gentlemen ... before I return again to my anonymous life in Paris ... I want you to know ... that on the great ... running ... *syphilitic* wound that has been my career ... your homage to my work ... at your beautiful film theatre ... has been a small ... but, all the same, welcome plaster.'

Alain Resnais

Yes, I'll renew my subscription to *Positif*! The summary of its future issues is just too attractive.

Soon in *Positif*:

Crooning and Acting
Why do crooners make good actors? Frank Sinatra, Yves Montand, Dick Powell, Bing Crosby, Al Jolson, Gene Kelly, Gower Champion, Fred Astaire, Rudy Vallee, James Cagney, Jacques Dutronc, Eddy Mitchell, Bob Hope etc. By Bernard Chardère.

Television: Angel or Devil?
Television has saved fifty thousand films from the past, but will it destroy the films of the future? By Claude Beylie.

Tomorrow's World!
New technology has arrived. Each copy of a film can be changed *ad infinitum* and become as different from another as performances of plays in the theatre. By Jacques Rivette.

A Liberator
How Bob Hope was the first American actor to make fun of McCarthy. By Bertrand Tavernier.

The Matchstick Projector
Music-hall, the royal road to the screen. By Jean-Pierre Coursodon.

The Unanswered Question
Does the world change cinema, or does cinema change the world? By Bernadette Pluvier.

The Film of our Century
Special issue solely devoted to *The Tomb of Alexander* by Chris Marker. By the entire staff and Bertrand Tavernier.

The Road to Perdition
When Marcel L'Herbier moves the camera. By Michel Ciment.

A Liberator (2)
The days when Bob Hope stole Bing Crosby's lines during shooting. By Bertrand Tavernier.

Secret Liaisons
Grace Kelly and Bing Crosby. By Nicole Garcia.

The Gravity of Comics
The dramatic work of Bob Hope. By Walter Plinge.

Series
Conversations and controversy. By Bertrand Tavernier.

I duly enclose the sum of 370 francs.

Arturo Ripstein

Luis Buñuel and *Nazarin*

The poverty of cinema today has created a worship of technique. We no longer look for truth in cinema, we only see technical skill. The beauty of an anticipated poetry has given way to a strangely derogatory insolence. We think a film is bad if it doesn't contain either any shattering effects or surprises so slickly managed they seem to be the work of a computer. A kind of sordid instant gratification. The audience gives the impression of being in a constant hurry. Agitation is the order of the day. The beauty of time photographed and shaped is almost unbearable to us. A mechanism exclusively concerned with profits lies at the centre of film, rather than the heart, eyes and brains of those who could blow up the world. Compromise is the road to gratification and the well-being of all. The worship of technique is exacerbated by the even more dreadful worship of perfection. 'Perfect' films – films made by committees to

Nazarin.

prevent them from being altered by talent – are nothing more than still-born machinery. On the other hand, immortal works can encounter misunderstanding, insult, praise, indifference, commercial failure, all kinds of critical analysis, even terrible screenings with bad sound, and still survive intact. I don't believe in the virtues of a badly-made film, nor in badly-equipped, clumsy enthusiasts who let things happen in a trivial, unpleasant way, as if by pure chance, who make films the way other people scream. I don't like any kind of bad cinema, either the kind that 'lets it all hang out' or the kind based solely on technical expertise. Luis Buñuel was far from being a perfect film-maker. *Nazarin* is far from being a technically perfect film. But it's morally flawless, ethically perfect, and blessed with a poetic power that will always sing. It's a beautiful story with beautiful character and situations, beautifully told. *Nazarin* has never failed to move me. It's one of my favourite films and Buñuel one of the directors I admire most.

Nazarin.

Dino Risi

Is cinema bad for you?

We celebrate a hundred years of cinema and the *quatre cents coups* of *Positif*. I've been making films for more than forty years and I still don't know what cinema is, whether cinema shaped me, what I owe it, whether it's a good thing or bad; whether cinema is harmful, more harmful than alcohol, drugs and cigarettes; whether it should be banned because it shows life as it never is, the men brave, the women beautiful, whereas in life men are cowards and women ugly; whether cinema is responsible for corruption, aggression, envy, fear, neurosis; whether, since it has come into our houses via the small screen, it has corrupted childhood, tantalized the poor, and spoilt sex; or whether, on the contrary, it has inspired emulation, created role-models, modified behaviour, refined the intelligence, given strength to the weak, enriched existence, awakened love. I really don't know.

Stagecoach: Monument Valley.

M: Peter Lorre as the monster of Düsseldorf.

I only know that when I was eight my father took me by the hand into a darkened hall where a man on horseback rode across a white sheet, and a very beautiful blonde – Vilma Banky – kissed a chap with a moustache called Ronald Coleman, all to the strains of a piano being played below the screen by a white-haired lady wearing a velvet hat and veil. At that moment I discovered love and jealousy. I realized that on that white sheet was inscribed a life worth living. From that moment on, I led a double life. On the one hand, friends, school, family Sundays, first love, exams, a greedy aunt, the death of my father, an impoverished adolescence, brothels, my first disappointments. On the other hand, a waking dream: a frantic stagecoach race across Monument Valley; the terrifying close-up of Jean Gabin, dead by his own hand at the gates of the port of Algiers; the girl who regains her sight and recognizes poor Charlie Chaplin touching her hand and giving her a rose; Lola-Lola's garters; Fellini's voyages through childhood; Humphrey Bogart's mackintosh disappearing into the nocturnal fog of Casablanca airport; Erich von Stroheim saying 'Action!' and the demented star of the silent screen coming down the stairs; the Ziegfeld Follies kicking their perfect legs on the milk-and-honey stages of Broadway; the music of Cole Porter and Nino Rota; Toto's nonsensical jokes; Cary Grant kissing Grace Kelly in the doorway of an hotel on the Côte d'Azur; Billy Wilder's diabolical lovers in *Double Indemnity*; the terrible, heart-rending confession of the monster of Düsseldorf; Chaplin eating his boot; Marilyn Monroe's white dress blowing up in the draught from a subway ventilation grille; the fake rain, the fake snow, the fake loves so much more real than the real ones. As I tap at my typewriter while, outside, cars belch their poisonous gases – cars in which sit men and women who use up their lives without courage and imagination – I hear again the out-of-tune piano playing beneath the kiss of Ronald Coleman and Vilma Banky, and I feel again those first emotions bequeathed to me by the 'cinematograph', that angelic and demonic machine that has changed my life and the lives of millions of others, a machine which is now a hundred years old and which, according to the Lumière Brothers who invented it, never had, and never would have, any commercial future.

So is cinema bad for you? I think it is. Bad for those who make the films, good for those watch them. Or vice versa. Jack Nicholson was once asked why he was an actor: 'Because life rarely offers such powerful experiences.' You could ask the same question of an audience. And get the same answer. Except that in life, 'powerful experiences' are a bad thing.

Pierre Rissient

Other Men's Women: Mary Astor and Grant Withers.

A few brief, roundabout answers as the ink flows:

A film?

I'd hesitate between two: *Coeur de Lilas*, 1930. By Anatole Litvak. Anatole Litvak? Yes, Anatole Litvak. And *Von Samstag bis Sonntag*, also 1930. By Gustav Machaty. Nezval worked on the script.

Both 1930, therefore many months, three years even, before *La Chienne, M, Scarface, L'Atalante*, to cite only the well-known classics.

Amongst other lesser-known films from the beginning of the talkies: *The Yellow Ticket* by Raoul Walsh, *Ladies of Leisure* by Capra (with Barbara Stanwyck), *The Steel Highway (Other Men's Women)* by Wellman, *The Front Page* by Lewis Milestone (with Menjou).

Not forgetting the much better-known *Morocco*, of which, incidentally, Menjou is the pivot. But *Morocco* is also Furthman's dialogue.

The section of *Hello Sister* undoubtedly shot by Stroheim.

And what about Rowland Brown's *Quick Millions*?

And d'Abbadie d'Arrast's *Laughter*? 1929, co-written with Donald Ogden Stewart. Has the extraordinary suicide of the character played by Glenn Anders been sufficiently noticed?

A director?

Hanns Schwartz. How is it that this precursor of Max Ophuls disappeared immediately after having made *Nina Petrovna*, an absolute masterpiece?

At the same time, others sank into oblivion: Monta Belle, Clarence Badger, Malcolm St Clair, Elmer Clifton, William Beaudine and d'Abbadie d'Arrast whose talent, out of all of them, should have blossomed with the talkies.

And Robinson? Frejos? Capellani, for whom a retrospective would be welcome?

An actor or actress?

It could be Menjou, Dick Powell, John Garfield, Ida Lupino.

Nowadays I'd say Charles Boyer. I bumped into him at Cannes in 1964 with Fritz Lang but, although I liked him in *Madame de …* , I was so anti his image as 'the Gallic lover' that I didn't get much out of the meeting.

But once I'd seen him in *Love Affair* at Ledoux cinémathèque! In other films he can seem stiff, but how can I forget him in *Caravane, Tumultes, La Bataille,* and of course *Liliom*, a film whose intimacy I only recognized later, when it was shown on television a few nights after Lang's death? Neither can I forget Ellis St Joseph's skill in evoking his cultivation and civility, the charm of a sensibility both lively and sensitive.

Lighting?

(You didn't ask this question, but I want to answer it.)

Curt Courant's 'white' photography for Fedor Ozep's *Tarakanova*. A 'pre-response' to Musuraca and Alton.

Eric Rohmer

Dear Sirs,

You presumably want me to write about a film or a director I admire in the
way a film-maker might talk about a colleague and his work. I have written
about cinema in the past as a critic, even as a theoretician and I may still
have a few ideas under these latter headings – but not as a director. Seeing a
film has no greater significance for my present 'professional' activity – perhaps even less – than reading a book, going to a concert or visiting an exhi-
bition. As a film-maker, I have no ideas, tastes or preferences; I have no particular approach. In order to write these pages about Keaton's *The General*,
I had put myself back into the skin of the *Cahiers* critic I once was. If I
chose Buster Keaton, it was perhaps because I hadn't had the opportunity
of speaking about him before, except indirectly. Will this do?

Best wishes.

The General.

178

I'd choose, from so many other candidates, the film that made me laugh most the first time I saw it, a very long time ago, at Henri Langlois' Cinémathèque: Buster Keaton's *The General*.

I'd read an article in the old *Revue du cinéma* which, if I remember rightly, stated that Buster's best works were the shorts, that he didn't have the stamina for features. I hadn't seen the shorts, but I laughed without stopping for an hour and a half, as I had never done at any other film. I had never laughed like that at one of Chaplin's films, short or long, because apart from the moments of emotion they contain, the lead-up to the gag creates a state of tense expectation which makes you hold in your laughter until the crucial moment. By contrast, Keaton's comedy, which you could call 'visible' because it doesn't rely on surprise, operates all the time: his comedy relies on wonder, something quite different from Chaplin.

That said, I must admit that I didn't laugh at all the second time I saw the film, which may seem odd for a comedy that, as I have said, doesn't rely on surprise. In fact, I believe that surprise exists in every second of the story that unfolds before us. Does this mean that this kind of cinema cannot survive a 're-reading'? On the contrary; what I've said is not a reservation. The second, third or nth time I saw the film I didn't feel the embarrassment which can overtake you when watching a scene which, although trying to be funny, doesn't make you laugh. Laughter and comedy were present, no longer for my sake, but as a philosopher would say, 'in themselves for themselves', latent in the film, and had given way to an impression of epic grandeur I wanted to enjoy by itself; an impression I also had, and have never had since, when I saw the films of Griffith and Murnau. These were the three directors who revealed to me one of the most important secret principles of cinema: spatial organization.

But first let's talk about laughter. Laughter is born, it is said, out of a sense of superiority, either benevolent or malevolent. In the case of the silent comics, this feeling is in general benevolent towards them and malevolent towards their adversaries. One watches Chaplin as one would a naughty child whose pranks delight us; a fact which also doesn't prevent us from sympathising with his misfortunes.

By contrast, the laughter Keaton triggers is similar to that provoked by a small child solemnly attempting a task far beyond the competence of his years; a child trying to be a 'grown-up'. A certain amount of condescension, but also some genuine admiration, are present in this laughter. We're 'delighted', which means that, without diluting the laughter's intensity, it can be tinged with an admiring smile. It's the laughter provoked by someone pursuing his objective to its natural conclusion – an objective that is both naïve and effective. It's also the laughter one may experience when seeing an animal not 'aping' but evoking human behaviour in a deliberate and determined manner; or seeing a concrete object (in this case, a locomotive) seeming to have an intelligence of its own. We are far removed from Griffith, whose sentimentality is close to Chaplin's. We are nearer to Hawks and the aristocratic giraffes of *Hatari*.

In order to build, comedy needs space, a great deal of space. Space in Griffith is virtual, punctured by ellipses, and in Murnau it is more or less curved. Therefore they don't need such a vast field of action for the *mise-en-scène* to unfold; they can find their expression in tableaux with well-defined edges. In Keaton, however, space cannot be confined within a particular frame, because it defines itself as the field of operation of a movement possessed of three essential characteristics: *rectilinearity, uniformity* and *continuity*.

Rectilinearity

It doesn't matter that the journey of the General includes some curves. What matters is that it feels overall like a progress (and return) *straight ahead*. It doesn't matter that this journey is often filmed in depth. Once we have distinguished between the pictorial space of each individual shot and the cinematic space created by the montage, we imagine the journey – we could almost say we see it – as a transverse line from the left to the right on the screen. Logic would demand that the return journey be in the opposite direction, from right to left: but the crossing of the bridge is shot left to right, which bothers me a little, but only in retrospect.

Uniformity

This rectilinear movement results from the principle of inertia – a fundamental law of matter – which states that all matter not subject to a force is either at rest or animated by a uniform, rectilinear movement. There are therefore no accelerations, stops or pauses. The suspense is continuous and hence potentially self-destructive. You could say, to complete my opening remark, that the suspense springs not from surprise, but from an equally disconcerting expectation that goes beyond all hope, fear and credibility. Hawksian comedy operates in the same way.

Continuity

Continuity in space and also in time. Keaton's respect for real time endows the performance with great truth. He is the opposite of other comics, who stylize. His stylization is simply the result of his prodigious talents as an acrobat. It permits him to eliminate pauses without shattering the impression of truth or naturalness. Keaton has few of those expressive gestures that are the relics of traditional mime, nor is he affected by the Chaplinesque influence which jars in others. He performs only the movements demanded by the action, and the effectiveness of these movements is demonstrated at every moment. Buster is always at work. Chaplin, on the other hand, strains his wits trying to do nothing or to sabotage his own activities. Here Keaton has something else in common with Hawks, who also likes showing people at work: the most Keaton-like of his heroes is probably Sergeant York.

The logical result is that the values the character defends are those of the world in which he lives, values he would go one better than if he could. In the past the intelligentsia were alienated by this moralizing and the apparently mechanical performances, preferring Chaplin's non-conformism and nihilism. There is nothing corrosive in Keaton. There is no criticism of the established order. However, under the surface of this respect, the contradictions are just as apparent. The hero's belief in the purity of the chivalric ideal collides with the harshness of the world of men and things. There is, however, no sign of Quixote's folly and bitterness. One tends to think rather of Perceval – I already was in those distant days.

Francesco Rosi

From *The Kid* to *La Terra Trema*

I remember very clearly the first moving picture I saw: Charlie Chaplin and Jackie Coogan, *The Kid*. It was a Sunday afternoon in Naples, and I wasn't even three. The film was made in 1921 and I was born at the end of 1922. Taking into account the time that used to elapse between the American release of a film and its distribution in Europe, I don't think I'm mistaken about my age. My father used to take me to the movies; from my earliest years he communicated to me his passion for cinema. In fact, the images I remember, from even before I went to a movie theatre, were those projected at home on an 8 mm Pathé Baby with a central perforation – images filmed by my father with a clockwork hand-camera. With this camera he'd engage in his hobby like a real film-maker; he was cameraman, director, editor. The actor was mostly me. Therefore, what 'struck me most' was the cinematographic experience itself rather than a film: the mystery of shadows taking shape on the screen, the strange ritual of a theatre gradually filling up with people and becoming charged with a eager, febrile expectation, the lights going down, the violins and piano starting to play, and everyone, adults and children, feeling as if a miracle were about to take place. I think I've been very lucky to have grown up at the same time as the cinema, to have been able to feed my passion with images from the world over, images which crossed all borders, all nationalities and all social differences. One could become a down-and-out or a great lord, one could love or hate, one could take part – in the first person – in the miracle of identification, a phenomenon which, with cinema, could occur irrespective of one's level of culture and education.

I've gone this far back in order to point out that, after such early experiences, I could hardly have done better than to have my first experience of a film-set on Luchino Visconti's *La Terra Trema*. This was the film which 'struck me the most'. It was a film shot entirely on location, exteriors and interiors; without a pre-ordained scenario, but based on a script which Visconti developed from day by day, referring freely to a literary source (*I Malavoglia* by Verga). The cast was entirely amateur, chosen from the inhabitants of Aci Trezza, a village in Sicily, who thanks to Visconti's artistic conception, his mastery of his art and the rigour of his method, were as good as professionals. And it was made with a crew as small as that for a documentary, half-composed of people like me who had never worked on a film before.

To start with, Visconti wanted to make not one but three films, three documentaries: one about fishermen, one about peasants, and one about miners. Each was to be made in Sicily, each was to deal with some aspect of how disadvantaged people struggle against adversity. This was in 1947. Italy was emerging from the dramatic collapse of Fascism, from a war that had been fought all across its territory, a war which had left the country shattered by battles and bombed first by the Allies, then after the Italians had joined the war of liberation, by the Germans. The war ended in 1945, and since 1943, neo-realism, with its poetic and social agenda, its quest for truth, had been changing the way of making films. By 1947, therefore, the new Italian cinema was in full bloom. Already in 1942, with *Ossessione*, Visconti had signalled his break with the cinema of the regime. He would soon join Rossellini and De Sica in the pantheon.

Money was scarce, but the will to succeed was great. *La Terra Trema* was an inspiring, happy, though arduous, adventure, an extraordinary experience for those lucky enough to participate in it, and a fundamental work for the history of cinema.

How did Visconti organize a film such as this, which lacked a script? Each day's work was recorded in a large register, like a ship's log. In another register was the 'report', which recorded information about the lenses used for each shot, focal lengths, camera movements, height, footage used, plus the notes. These 'notes' were a precise record of what had happened around the camera: the weather, rain or sunshine, clouds or shadows ... also noises and sounds. Visconti wanted an authoritative written record to help him decide which takes to process later. There were rarely less than seven takes; usually twelve, fifteen, or even more. Another register was to contain the script, which would be written after the film was shot. Each image was to be described in it. Yet another register was devoted to sequences of shots and continuity. Each image would be drawn, its every detail minutely annotated, so that, were a sequence to be interrupted by say the weather, it could be picked up again weeks, even months, later. Continuity of course meant costumes, haircuts, beards and, most of all, actions and gestures. Polaroids, which were to become the salvation of continuity girls, didn't exist then. Anyway, Visconti would never have used them, because his method was also a form of apprenticeship. It was strictly forbidden for his assistants to check their doubts against the rushes; Visconti guarded them jealously, and only watched them himself. He had been Renoir's assistant in France and felt mystically linked to this period of apprenticeship. He handed on his experience to us. 'Us' meant me and Franco Zeffirelli, his assistants, both of us beginners. I was responsible for the registers just mentioned, for running the set, and for close-ups. Zeffirelli looked after the preparation of the actors, their costumes, the dialogue rehearsals in Sicilian – once Visconti had decided the dialogue with the actors – the decoration of the set, and the mid-shots. In addition, we constantly had to run around in all directions to set up the long shots that were decided and controlled by the director.

Respect your surroundings. Out of this method a style was born. Out of a respect for veracity arose a grave and rigorous form, a kind of classical realism quite different from 'neo-realism'.

Personally, I've never considered *La Terra Trema* to be a neo-realist film, but rather a realist work in the broadest sense. In *La Terra Trema* Visconti not only re-creates life as he sees it – like all neo-realists – but also, in his quest for a homogeneous style, he develops his interpretation of reality. His starting point is a cinematic method which, unlike neo-realism, leaves nothing to chance. The definition which best expresses my opinion is Georges Sadoul's: 'A great work of realism, constructed like a novel, and devoid of the sentimentality prevalent in other works of the period.'

The adventure of *La Terra Trema* was a turning-point for the professional development of many of the people who took part in it. For me this meant of course Sicily, which I grew to know and love, and which I'd often return to in my films. But the fact of having taken part in such a wondrous enterprise also allowed me to build my own entirely personal style, inspired by the idea that one must interpret reality with the eyes of reality. This was the fundamental significance of my apprenticeship.

Above and below: *La Terra Trema*

Alan Rudolph

The Boys

My family's first home was in a modest neighbourhood where there were plenty of kids my age. Yet it was Laurel and Hardy who reminded me that I was not alone. Television was fairly new then, with Stan and Ollie's fine messes influencing and comforting me each day, twice on Saturday. My life mentors became two brainless, optimistic Fools of God. Imagine my surprise on learning that one of them had moved into a small house down the block.

The real world has always been a confounding place for me. Societal atrocities aside, common details bewilder and frustrate me at deep levels. Nothing much has changed in my behaviour, except that now I make films concerned with the illogic of small treacheries. But from the beginning, negotiating through conspiracies of inanimate objects, impenetrable personalities and

Blockheads: Stan Laurel and Oliver Hardy.

unaccommodating places sent me searching for comrades in confusion. That's how I found The Boys.

I suppose I made profound connections with the Laurel and Hardy films long before knowing what directors do, who actors are, what stories mean. Defining these imprints is impossible at that age (maybe any age), but as years accumulate, it becomes apparent they are here to stay.

Although they vary in merit, I have no favourite Laurel and Hardy film. In fact, I had no idea that some of the best vignettes I'd seen separately on television were parts of a unified whole: *Blockheads*. This one-hour film contains for me some of the most hilarious and mysterious moments in all Laurel and Hardy.

Consider:

As an infantryman in France in 1917, Private Laurel is ordered to guard a trench until relieved from duty. The company is going over the top. 'Gee, I wish I was going with you,' says Stan. Ollie assures him, 'I'll be back, we'll all be back.' The battle begins and time passes, a lot of time. Years later, Stan finishes a can of beans and tosses it on to a small mountain of similar empty cans, two decades after the cessation of hostilities. When he is finally discovered by a passing plane (which he tries to shoot down), Stan admits that things have gone a little quiet lately.

At the Soldiers' Home, Stan, searching for a place to read his newspaper, sits down in a wheelchair with one leg doubled up under him. Ollie approaches, sees the truncated limb and becomes emotional, insisting Stan come home with him. 'But don't exert yourself, Stanley, I'll carry you.' To Stan's bemused wonder, Ollie lifts him, struggling, to his car. After they fall, *Stan* is the one helping them up. As he walks around the car, Ollie asks resentfully, 'Why didn't you tell me you had two legs?' Says Stan, 'Well, you didn't ask me.' Ollie's car is blocked by a dump truck. He tells Stan to move it. Stan climbs in and pulls a lever, and the entire load of sand is, of course, dumped on Ollie. All of this is telegraphed, we know it's coming. Maybe it's the inevitability that makes it so funny, so sublime.

There are various forms of white magic in this film: Stan pulling at the shadow of a window-shade silhouetted on a wall, and the shade snapping shut; Stan producing a glass of water from his pocket to drink, with Ollie asking sarcastically, 'Why don't you put some ice in it?' and Stan, thinking that a good idea, reaching into his pocket to get several ice cubes; Stan, after getting permission to smoke in Ollie's apartment, cupping his hand like a pipe, pouring tobacco into it, lighting it and puffing, even coughing a bit, with Ollie, as always, amazed to the point of rage.

Theirs was broad, low comedy, yet very subtle. And never reliant on jokes. Just two innocents in basic situations where something went wrong. I related to this. I still do. Some accuse my films of being unrealistic, inhabited by strange characters doing quirky things. I maintain that my films are closer to real behaviour than other, more natural ones. I read where someone asked Hardy how they ever dreamed up the characters and situations of their films. He said he simply watched people in hotel lobbies. I know what he means. I've stayed in that hotel.

As a child, you never imagine these marvellous characters being different from how they appear on the screen. They never age and seem indestructible, coming out of one sticky situation only to bump into another, surviving every conceivable calamity. So it was somewhat startling to discover that the quiet and kindly older man who stood with a cup of tea on his front steps each afternoon was none other than Stan Laurel. He would watch us play, sometimes offering encouragement. Once he asked a few of us inside his small and cluttered house to hear him sing an old English song while a woman played the piano. I remember thinking that he should be younger and more wealthy. One of the kids on the block heard that Laurel and Hardy weren't famous any more and didn't have any money. Abbot and Costello were famous and rich now, not these guys. I didn't know about such things then. That artists go under-appreciated, society is fickle, money fleeting. I only knew that their world was mine, and that their derbies, eye-blinks, camera-looks and tie-twiddles were the ludicrous physical language of our collective reality.

Raul Ruiz

This time, I want to talk about the affair of
The Black Cat

A few weeks ago I was taking a stroll in my neighbourhood, Ménilmontant, when a sudden downpour forced me to take refuge in a record and video store. Waiting for the rain to stop, I browsed through the shop without quite knowing what I was looking for, or what I would find.

It was then that I discovered, stuck between two porn films and an insignificant Italian comedy, a horror film by Edward G. Ulmer, *The Black Cat*.[1] I was sure I'd never seen it before, although I'd dreamt of it. It was the kind of film you think you know, because so many people have talked about it.

I watched it that night.

It rained in the film and it rained in Paris. The endless music furnished a running commentary to the alarm-bells, shouts and ambulance sirens coming from outside, and to the puzzling events which I shall now describe.

On the screen, a train animated by the play of lights and shadows, inhabited by faint, fleeting images as if shaped by the steam from the locomotive, accompanied by music fading in and out: Brahms (*Hungarian Rhapsodies*) and Liszt (the *Piano Sonata*, whose main theme becomes the leitmotiv underpinning the strange, disturbing world which appears in the very first minutes of the film).

Already, the Liszt had made me jump: it was the same music I had used in *Shadowplays*, a short I had made twelve years earlier between two features and which I had intended to be 'poetic'. Then Bela Lugosi appeared. The day before, I had had lunch in a Japanese restaurant with Martin Landau, who was playing Lugosi in Tim Burton's latest film. We had toyed with the idea of making a film in which Lugosi actually accepted the post of Hungarian Minister of Culture offered him by Janos Kádar (the anecdote was true) and returned to Hungary only to become a real Count Dracula and a dissident, dripping in blood.

Several times we discussed the extremely poetic character of the films of Ed Wood, Regy Le Borg, Ford Beebe etc: films shot in only a few days, whose faults and mishaps became the very substance of their energy and their poetry. My mind wandered again, leaping from one theory to another. I drew on the books I had with me, and especially on an article by Jakko Hintikka (that entertaining poet of logic) who, on the subject of theories of language, or

---

1 *The Black Cat* (1934), with Boris Karloff, Bela Lugosi and David Manners, based on a story by Edgar Allan Poe.

rather of general semantic constructs, makes fun of Noam Chomsky (his sworn enemy) by making a distinction between the recursive paradigm which states that 'language must be considered as a process governed by rules' and the strategic paradigm that 'language brings into operation strategic rules that govern a process analogous to a game.'

It seemed to me evident that, applying the same distinction to cinema, some films – Rossellini, Cassavetes – develop out of certain situations which are connected together according to the rules created by the situations themselves; while other films (the majority) present themselves as a completed game, with variations provided for by the rules that the game makes explicit (if they aren't so already) – films made in Hollywood, both now and in the past.

I've always believed that the two paradigms overlap: in a set of fragments of a game, each one potentially contains a film to be completed by the audience; also, the fragments behave from game to game in a generative sequence (according to the recursive paradigm).

In general, my films try to integrate both paradigms. They are made up of fragments of incomplete stories which, in an unpredictable manner, engender other stories about daily life, and lead to temporary conclusions. Each fragment wishes on the one hand to find its conclusion far away from the sequence we are watching, and on the other hand to 'beget' and link itself with other fragments, affiliating itself to them like a son is linked to his sires.

I've found very few examples of commercial films that illustrate my theory, apart from *The Black Cat*, which in its way is the best, the most drastic and irrefutable. It was what epistemologists call (but here I use the term in a mocking sense) a 'crucial experience'.

The film presents itself as a series of situations, each of which has an independent existence of its own: a game of chess, Bela Lugosi's cat phobia, allusions to an allegorical battle (Europe as a field of corpses), Bauhaus design. All these elements are stories that the film could do without, and which in the end stifle and obscure the central story. A bad critic would call these extraneous fragments 'decorative'.

Instead of gradually helping to reveal the narrative, as in a film which tells one single story, each of these stories dies outside the area of fiction that surrounds the narrative.

But the film held something far more disquieting for me. Several times I had been linked with Edgar G. Ulmer and I'd usually disagreed, one reason being because I'd only belatedly seen one of his films (in a double bill with *The Theory of the Missing Painting*). People as different as Jérôme Prieur, John Zorn and J. Rosenbaum had compared me to him. Now at last recognition came to me, and as in an old melodrama, I exclaimed: 'Father!' and he replied 'My son!'

For at least twenty of my films find their source in *The Black Cat*. Each scene in the film is transformed, and completed, into one of mine. The same goes for the fragments, which call on past or future films to complete them.

(By this I mean that these films will be composed of appetizing fragments.) Don't you believe me?

Another time, I'll give you some examples.

Valeria Sarmiento

The Red Shoes

When a film remains at the project stage in spite of all attempts to make it, I always say it's 'fallen in the water'. Since, in spite of myself, I often use this phrase, I started wondering where it came from.

I can still remember today the extraordinary impression my first visit to the cinema made on me. I was five, and the wait was endless; you had to reserve your seats, usually the day before.

Three tickets: row J, numbers 15, 16 and 17. My seat was number 17. The lights went down, the satin curtain went up, and the film began. Michael Powell's *The Red Shoes*. But because it had been shown so many times in Valparaíso, my native city, the copy was scratched.

'Mummy, mummy, why is it raining?'

'You have to look through the rain, mijita.'

Twenty years passed before I saw the film again. In the meantime, I had learnt to look at cinema through the rain: Lang, Sirk, Hitchcock, Curtiz, the Europeans in America, in other words my favourite film-makers.

The Red Shoes was subtitled (all foreign films were in my country). At the time, I couldn't yet read very well, but the images were so powerful that they stayed etched in my memory; the whole thing linked to a 'superimposition' of my own invention. I remembered the heroine in her costume (dirty and crumpled as the ballet demanded) jumping into the void with one leap from a balcony in Monte Carlo. Through the mists of time, the smoke of the train passing under the balcony and the smoke in the *Red Shoes* ballet fused into a single image. Was this leap into the void, connected with the dance, the image that symbolized the film? It did so for me, anyway, and for many years. But isn't a leap in the void during a ballet also an image that symbolizes our profession?

Twenty years later, at the start of my exile, I saw the film again, dubbed into German, in West Berlin. I went to see again the film which had given me a taste for cinema. I was profoundly moved, and the film certainly gave me an excuse to cry about other things. 'How can you be crying? You don't even understand German,' people asked. I didn't care. I was regaining the film of my childhood just at the moment when I seemed to have lost almost everything; but this time it wasn't through the rain, except perhaps that of my tears. So I continued to go to that same cinema. It was my way of recovering my wonderful country, my memory and my childhood. I saw *Mirage of Life* again, this time dubbed in German, and I cried again, even though I still didn't understand the language. The audience was laughing out loud. What was happening? I immediately felt

The Red Shoes.

alien to these Germans. How could they not cry when seeing this film, when they were able to cry listening to music or looking at a flower? Was this the absurd reason that made me leave Germany?

A year later, in France, I went to see *Algo para recordar*. It may not be a great film, but I cried and the audience cried with me. I felt this was my country. The French were capable of seeing cinema through the rain.

I have a video of *The Red Shoes*. I watch it occasionally and I think that, by chance, my life is linked to this film. Why did my parents choose this film when they first took me to the cinema? Why that one and not another? But does chance exist?

Claude Sautet

Le Jour se Lève

I was born in 1924. I only really liked going to the cinema of my own volition from 1945 onwards. I've never been a true film-buff: when a film moved me, I needed to see it several times to preserve the emotion it had stimulated within me. So several weeks would go by before I wanted to go to another film. At that time many films, from *Citizen Kane* to Renoir's masterpieces, over-whelmed me with their power, their mastery and their modernity, but one film I saw seventeen times in a month: *Le Jour se Lève*. The first day I saw it four times running, and left the theatre dazzled and crushed by a pain and a plea-sure I couldn't explain. Afterwards I couldn't stop taking friends and girl-friends to see it, one after another. I revelled in the sadistic pleasure of seeing them come out crushed and silent. One of them did however manage to put together some phrases, a few comments about the structure, the photography, the setting, the detail, and so on – words I would later hear at the ciné-club one evening, repeated by André Bazin as he dissected the film with tears in his eyes.

Years have passed. I've become a film-maker, and though the film has had no direct influence on my own work, it remains the decisive factor that made me tumble into that strange profession.

A year ago I saw it again. As is usual in these cases, I was afraid I might be disappointed. Would the mirage have evaporated? Was it mere youthful enthu-siasm? No. The twilight atmosphere was still there. Intact. And at its peak, in every sense of the word: historical, political, aesthetic. A peak. And therefore also a terminus. And that's perhaps why this 'perfect object' could not teach us anything, why film-makers who looked to it as a model were cruelly misled, while others rejected it as outdated. Dead. A sort of academic foil. The debate is endless, perfectly understandable and now irrelevant.

I've always been uncomfortable with the public and critical acclaim unstint-ingly given to *Le Quai des Brumes* and *Les Enfants du Paradis*; I've always considered *Le Jour se Lève*, which has been overshadowed by the others, to be the most accomplished work by the famous Carné-Prévert duo. Perhaps because it's their most 'dated' film ... It was shot in 1939, between the fall of the Front Populaire and the horrifying World War to come. In the fragile no man's land of a studio a group of sensitive, clever and inspired artists assem-bled. Their names will always be remembered: Jacques Viot, Jacques Prévert, Curt Courant, Alexandre Trauner, Maurice Jaubert, whose music for the film

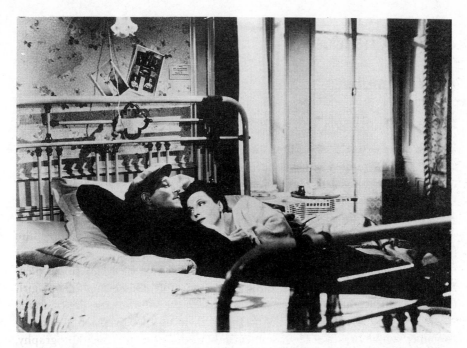

Le Jour se Lève.

was his least melodious but his most cinematic, and of course, Marcel Carné at his most refined and mature, the keystone of the project. And also Gabin, so handsome and sad, Arletty, never so 'true' and, above all, Jules Berry – the Jules Berry of *Le Crime de Monsieur Lange* – in his greatest role.

I shall never forget the first few minutes. Dawn over a small suburban apartment block, an ordinary door on to a landing, transfigured and disquieting, from behind which we hear gunshots ... then Gabin's tired voice, *'T'es bien avancé maintenant'* ... and the stifled reply *'Et toi!'* Then the door opens and Berry's corpse falls backwards down the stairs ... and soon after, the famous 'photo' of Gabin behind the window, and that intimate, fateful voice: *'Et pourtant, hier, souviens-toi ... '*, leading into that extraordinary flashback.

Fashions change, and *Le Jour se Lève* remains a masterpiece forever swathed in a twilit glory. That's how things are.

Jerry Schatzberg

Los Olvidados

What a difficult assignment! One director! One actor! One film! How do you choose one? Who do you leave out? It was quite a dilemma. And then I was fortunate enough to see a film on television that I had not seen in many years: Luis Buñuel's *Los Olvidados*.

Although this film was made in 1950, it deals with homelessness and delinquency as if it were a documentary shot today in Los Angeles, New York, or for that matter any other urban environment.

Buñuel opens the film with shots of New York City, the Eiffel Tower, Big Ben and Mexico City. He then shows the slums and desperation of Mexico City. Over this we hear:

> 'Concealed behind the impressive structures of our great modern cities are pits of misery which contain unwanted, hungry, dirty, and uneducated children ... Mexico City, a great modern city, is no exception to this universal truth ... and this film, based on real life, is not optimistic ... but leaves the solution of this problem in the hands of the progressive forces of our time.'

Unfortunately, the progressive forces were not able to accomplish too much, and the problems have not only remained, but have increased, adding epidemics of drugs and disease that not only affect the poor but the middle class as well.

Buñuel shows us how cruel we are, man's inhumanity to man. He's not making moral judgements; it's what he has seen, and he shows it to us. In one scene we see a youngster throw a stone at a blind man. It's appalling. How can a human being throw a stone at a blind man, or at anyone for that matter? Just recently, on television, I saw a young man drag another man out of a truck, beat him, stomp on him, and hit him on the head with a brick. He was so proud of himself, he laughed and did a little dance. He was arrested, tried, and convicted of a minor charge. He showed no remorse. He laughed and did a little dance. How much of this should we blame on him, and how much should we blame on ourselves? Our systems do not seem to favour the underprivileged. It's difficult for the underclass to find work, to find housing, to maintain a family, to have equal access to education, in short to maintain their dignity. In *Los Olvidados*, we see a young boy sitting by a fountain, waiting for his father to return for him – we know the father cannot afford to return. His family is struggling at home and this boy is being sacrificed. They hope he's strong enough to survive on his own.

Although so much of what Buñuel shows is without pity, there is a quality within human beings that is noble. Despite the pessimism in the film, you can see how accurately Buñuel cuts into the reality of their lives. At times you dislike these characters, but then you discover a look or a gesture that will turn you around and you will start to root for them. Buñuel is always showing us that there is some good in bad people, and vice versa.

I don't think Buñuel was interested in telling us how to solve the problem. It seems he wanted to expose it and raise our consciousness. Buñuel is able to find the humanity that is common ground between the characters and the viewer. He presents things as they are, without comment, sentimentality or moral overtones.

Los Olvidados.

Paul Schrader

Pickpocket

I can pin-point the moment my film sensibility was galvanized: April 1969, when I, as a film critic, saw Robert Bresson's *Pickpocket* (it had just been released in Los Angeles). I wrote about it for two consecutive issues, then went on to write a book about Bresson.

I had been drawn to films as a college student (film-going at the time was forbidden by my church). One never forgets one's first love, and my first love in the movies was the intellectual European cinema: Bergman, Resnais, Godard, Antonioni, Buñuel.

I 'studied' these films. They touched my mind more than my heart.

Pickpocket moved through my mind into my heart. It was as if my soul was deflowered. Strange to say, Bresson 'loosened me up'. A weight of High Art fell from my young shoulders. Films could be spiritual *and* profane. I was free to enjoy both.

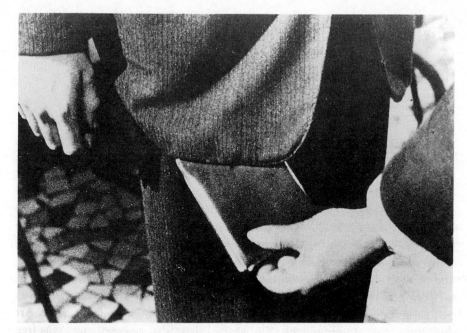

Pickpocket: the crime.

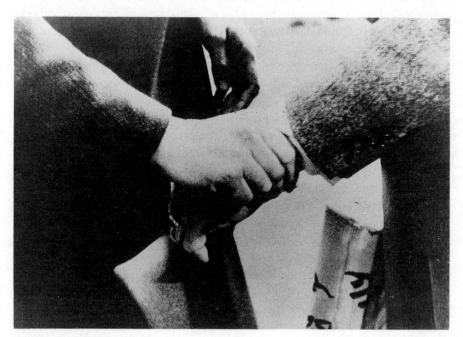

Pickpocket: capture.

Mrinal Sen

Revolt of the adolescents

(In response to *Positif*'s request to write on a film which impressed me particularly, I ransack my diary to find a list of my favourites. There are plenty of them, and as I recall, I liked them for different reasons. The late sixties and early seventies, which as an incorrigible Calcuttan I shall never forget, can be rightly characterized as a desperate period. Interestingly, such desperation was felt all over the world. It was a global phenomenon. There was contagion in the air. It was difficult for the average man to escape the contagion. Lindsay Anderson captured the period and made a film. He invested the film with wit and humour and, of course, with anger fermenting within. I pull out his *If ...* for *Positif*. In doing so, I relive the period left behind.)

If ... is the film of my choice – one that I saw for the second time in Delhi during the 1973 International Film Festival. My first viewing was at Venice where, unconnected with the festival programme, a very private screening was quickly organized in an exclusive theatre at the Hotel Excelsior.

At the Lido it was an after-dinner show. The fashionables, among others, visiting the festival and holidaying at the Riviera, hustled together, all in strictly formal dress, with all the customary how-do-you-do's. By contrast, the director of the film was violently informal in outfit, pacing up and down, squatting on the floor for brief moments, stretching his legs when he must, yawning without offering apologies and, by doing so, outraging the fashionables' sensibilities at every moment. A delicious thrill indeed!

Lindsay Anderson is the director, born in India and made in England; angry, intolerant, intense and yet endowed with an inimitable sense of humour.

In Delhi, four months later, the film was presented at the festival outside the competition, and under the conditions for all the festival showings, it was untouched by the then Censor Board.

In May 1968 the students at the Sorbonne made a big noise which soon grew into a national event – a kind of mini-revolution, drawing world attention. In May 1969 *If ...* got the Grand Prix at the Cannes Film Festival, where exactly a year before Godard and his colleagues had rushed on to the big stage of the festival theatre and created a 'militant' scene, chanting Mao Tse-Tung and succeeding in paralysing the traditional functioning of the festival. I can see a connection between the two: the ferment in 1968 and the verdict of the International Jury in 1969.

The script, I am told, was written before the May events in France. But

If ... : attacking the Establishment.

changes were made, so I suppose that made the connection more obvious. The story of the film, if it is to be called a story at all, is all about a juvenile attack on the Establishment.

From the beginning to the end, *If* ... is an outrageous protest film, absurdly funny on the surface and bitter to the core. In its overall structure, in its thematic exploration, in the application of its technique, and in the minutest details of its anatomy, *If …* defies all convention. It aims at times at the ludicrous, sometimes at the grotesque, but remains dangerously rebellious throughout. And nowhere in the film has anger said goodbye to humour, which to my mind gives Anderson's film a fascinating dimension.

The silent protest of the students, the ferment, the fun and violence of the inevitable sex-act among the adolescents, the ultimate resistance and crusade – all this is the story of *If …* A kind of wish-fulfilment: strange, youthful and vibrant, dreamlike in form and in content. The students at the public school dream a lovely dream, that of putting an end to the hateful business of 'licking the frigid fingers' of the custodians of the Establishment for the rest of its petrified life. While in essence the message of the film goes far beyond the boundaries of the school premises, it is interesting to note that the director, in order to find a 'model' school, did not have to cross the English Channel. The area of operation is a typical British public school.

A duty-bound, discipline-ridden inspector of the school lodgings walks into a room. He smells alcohol. The students feign innocence. Silence: awkward and amusing. Fuming within, the inspector walks out. With quiet defiance, the boys pull their bottles out from under the pillows and cushions.

'In Calcutta,' says one, an expert among the students, 'there is one death from starvation every few minutes.' Gulping beer, an inmate declares, 'War is the last creative act.'

And one sees a strange assembly of pictures and posters hung on the walls: Che and Mao, also images of Black Power – which, according to one of the boys, is 'fascinating' – not to mention the guerrillas and nudes, and, funnily enough, a familiar portrait of a Bengali girl who now is Aparna Sen.

In the gymnasium two boys play-act a sword fight, all so infantile. Suddenly, they see blood. So does the spectator. There follows an instant silence – a silence that is intense, profound and electrifying. Offering blood, the warring boys perform a ritual, pledging revolution. And thus 'through wisdom' the students 'get understanding'.

Charge-sheets are framed against a few boys for breaking the moral code of 'the house'. They are punished in a way that is distantly reminiscent of the horrors of the concentration camp. While law-breaking juveniles are being caned mercilessly, and the juveniles are steeling themselves for the blows, the camera surreptitiously captures another boy, in another room, looking through a microscope. The bacteria spreads. So does anger and violence.

The Establishment continues to function with efficiency and considerable tact. It projects a façade, promising to look after the well-being of the students. There is no end to the tall talk about the loyalty-bound public school, and tall promises about producing supermarket managers. But the boys refuse to be beguiled any more. In utter desperation, they rise in revolt. They take a pledge: death to the oppressors. Resistance, they say. Liberty, they promise.

Everything is now on a war footing. They call it a 'crusade', the visuals and aurals largely resembling modern warfare. And then, in the midst of sound and fury, the film ends abruptly, not with the customary 'The End' but with a big *If* ...

If ... is a funny film, a bitter allegory of an unusual kind, where the implications suggested through words and visuals, and indeed through its eloquent pauses, are as familiar – communicate as easily – to a Calcuttan as they do to a Parisian or a Briton or a New Yorker, or for that matter to anyone who lives and reacts in our contemporary climate.

If ... is a sharp note of defiance, a violation of the Anglo-Saxon understanding of the British code of ethics. It is by and large 'un-British'!

Even today, twenty years after my second viewing, *If* ... is a film close to my heart, and it stimulates my cerebral functioning. I love it for its flippancy, for the bitterness and defiance it playfully projects, and on a strictly formal plane, for its scintillating, non-conformist structure.

Slobodan Sijan

An image from *Rio Bravo*

There are films I'll always remember, and copies of certain films I'll never forget, but there are also screenings of films that will always stay with me as important events in my life, moments when everything conspired to make the experience perfect. Since I've spent a large part of my life in darkened cinemas, these moments have been particularly intense.

One of these moments occurred in a gloomy cinema in Belgrade at the beginning of the seventies during a screening of Howard Hawks's *Rio Bravo*, my favourite film. The cinema was part of a larger building called the Veselin Maslesha People's University, an institution typical of 'socialist progress'. Every district of a town had such a building. They were horribly ugly, built of

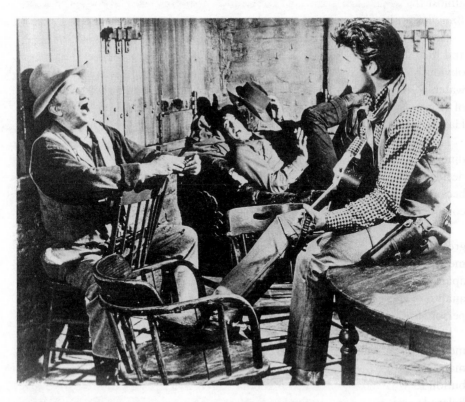

Rio Bravo: Walter Brennan, Dean Martin and Ricky Nelson.

concrete in the impersonal 'modern' style of socialism. They all bore the name of some Communist hero of the Second World War; some were also called 'workers' universities' or 'Houses of Culture'. Part of the building was usually a large auditorium with a stage that would be used for Communist Party meetings or various festivities, exhibitions of folk-dancing, amateur theatricals and so on. However, some of the money needed to subsidize these activities came from the screening of films, mostly reruns of old American films, on two nights a week.

This particular theatre had a large panoramic screen which descended right to the floor. If you sat where I usually did, in the first three rows, you'd be looking down on to the lower half of the screen. This wasn't a normal position to be in, given that most cinema screens are hung above you and you have to look up at them. This was an important factor in the great experience I had while watching my favourite film.

By then I'd already seen *Rio Bravo* several times, but something happened during that screening which completely transported me. I was 'sucked into' the Hawksian space. The axis linking my eyes with those of the characters was almost the same as that between Hawks's lens and his actors – I was 'in' *Rio Bravo*! The camera was in its famous position, 'a little below eye-level'.

The theatre was almost empty, or so it seemed to me. The sound was clear, and judging from the fact that the image was in focus, the projectionist was obviously sober (a rarity in those days; perhaps he liked Westerns and was watching from the booth). The screen was large enough to fill my entire angle of vision. From beginning to end, I was 'included' in the exceptional space of a Hawks film.

The way Hawks constructs a continuity of space is remarkable, and genuinely holds you 'inside' it. There is no possible way of escape, unless the film decides to provide you with one. My theory is that his films are captivating because they build a sense of continuity which is so strong that it allows the complete participation of the audience.

Howard Winchester Hawks is certainly the director who has made the greatest impression on me during my career as a film-maker. What fascinated me was that there was no single detail in a film of his which would impress me apart from the entire film itself. His style was so discreet, it was impossible to analyse. Yet if you've seen several of his other films, you discover the style and personality which, to this day, have made me a Hawks 'aficionado'.

I was introduced to Hawks by Tom Gotovac, a Yugoslav director of experimental films who nevertheless adored American popular cinema. Tom's minimalist, experimental works of the sixties were an important Yugoslav contribution to what was later called 'structuralist cinema'. It was autumn 1970 in Belgrade, my first year at film school, and Tom took me to the Yugoslav Cinémathèque to see *Land of the Pharaohs*. Annoyed by my interest in more 'artistic' films, Tom cried out, 'One image from *Rio Bravo* is worth all of Bergman!' The extremism of this statement – extreme like everything else in the Balkans – made a deep impression on my confused mind. I became a zealous student of Howard Hawks and his work. And I still am!

After having seen most of his films (apart from *The Cradle Snatchers* and *Air Circus*) several times, I felt I'd come to know the man. It felt a little as if I were someone's intimate friend. I could feel his pulse, appreciate how his mind worked – the intellectual process which informed the decisions he took in fashioning his films. A faultless logic underlies all his films. I've heard that certain mathematicians can be recognized by colleagues from the style of their formulae, whereas to the uninitiated, the formulae remain simply formulae.

In the same way, audiences will always find Hawks's films diverting without necessarily remembering anything else about them, or without finding anything that links them to the film, such as the suspense in Hitchcock or the sentimentality in Ford. For the initiated, however, his way of making films is always recognizable and intriguing, like the pictures of Mondrian and Malevitch.

Having seen most his films several times, I was struck above all by their crystal clarity, their fluid continuity. And I don't mean this just in terms of the story, but in terms of the visual continuity, the way the camera films the actors one shot after another as they move through space. The way Hawks shows space is for me the most distinctive characteristic of his style. I think it defines him much better than his themes, his characters or his pace. The flux of his films is characterised by a gentle fluidity of angles within the space of the set.

There is a scene in *Man's Favourite Sport*, somewhere near the beginning, where we see Rock Hudson driving a car, then in an ascending lift, then sitting at a circular bar in a restaurant on the top floor of a skyscraper. Suddenly one realizes: a horizontal, a vertical and a circle! 'So what?' you may say. But there's something exciting about seeing these things, which are purely aesthetic and have nothing to do with the story or the actors' performances: this is the way Hawks gives shape to an imaginary space.

This imaginary space exists in any film, and is no doubt different for each director, but it becomes the primary element in Hawks's style and a source of excitement and pleasure. What determines the special space of his films is always the change between where the camera is for one shot and where it is in the next. And this is always decided by the desire to show us (to tell us) what we need to see (to know).

I usually watch one of his films several times until the story fades from my mind. Only then does the dynamic of his art emerge. I start noticing what was hidden by the seductive envelope of the story, the dialogue and the characters.

The pace with which the spaces change, or the grace with which he moves the camera around his actors, shifting from one angle to another. Unusual orientations of space in his films always seem unforced and easy. But if you start to analyse, hundreds of small details begin to appear: the invisible way his shots cut together, the equally invisible movements of the camera, the simple but perfect choreography of the actors' bodies and their gaze ...

When you compare *Rio Bravo* with the cinema of today, it's almost shocking to see how much of the film is composed of master shots, and how little he uses the Hollywood techniques of today. But the film doesn't seem slow at all. Naturally, you have to see it on the big screen. And that is what makes me realize that the classical art of Hollywood cinema is dead, because films are now increasingly made with television in mind. As film editing evolves towards video, a tyranny of close-ups reigns on our screens. And this will go on. Huge talking heads are here to stay!

Jean-François Stévenin

An economy of energy (on *The Hustler*)

Cinema-escape

In winter 1961 I had escaped from the prison of my family only to enter another one: final exams. At the time, apart from Gabin's films, only American cinema really interested me. I had seen an incalculable number of westerns dubbed in French, but I didn't feel particularly destined for cinema. That year at Besançon the 'Building' showed Robert Rossen's *The Hustler* in English. The film was an incredible revelation. I didn't know whether the camera had been hand-held or foot-held. I didn't know anything except that Paul Newman was a great actor. I was *naïvely* impressed; and I discovered the world of shooting pool. Shooting pool then became a passion. It was one of my main occupations at college in Paris a few years later. My studies ended, life went on, and the memory faded.

Tele-visions

January 1994 and I'm snowed in, alone in my farmhouse in the Jura. The outside temperature is minus twenty. *The Hustler* is shown twice on satellite TV. A new revelation. Again I'm bewitched, to such an extent that I'm glued to the screen and the log fire goes out. Normally I should have detested such a film, because I much prefer a baroque, insane kind of cinema. So why did *The Hustler* give me such a shock?

Revelations

The Hustler is a film that knows a lot about me. How many times in a tricky situation have I made the same gestures as Minnesota Fats does during his first game against Eddie Felson! For example, during an important meeting on whose outcome depended the fate of one of my two films, I went to wash my hands and drink a glass of water. I didn't do this out of a sense of imitation: it was unconscious, instinctive. And sometimes images from *The Hustler* would come back to me. There are films which accompany you for your whole life, even in simple day-to-day gestures. For me, *The Hustler* is such a film.

The theme of the film is that of 'coaching': a philosophical, existentialist theme that's about liberty. Talent is not enough for success; one must be accompanied and instructed. Eddie Felson (Paul Newman) is a young, brilliant and refractory player. He is better than the champion. Yet he loses. He hasn't the discipline to know when to stop playing. Eddie symbolizes the man of pure energy, the man who gives everything. He's a likeable show-off who needs the admiration and reassurance of others in order to exist. But he is fast expending his capital. Fats, by contrast, is a measured man: he never wastes his capital, he only spends the interest. Because he has an accomplice, a man watching over him: Charlie Burns (George C. Scott) the coach is hardly sympathetic, but he fulfils a vital need. He shares in the risk. He watches over the player. He sends him into a highly-organized battle. And after the battle he picks him up again.

The young player Eddie Felson reveals me cruelly to myself. We share the same desire for extinction.

I thus experienced my two films as a complete dispersal of energy. Their end wasn't planned: it was simply due to the limits of my physical strength. It's a fault linked to my lack of a coach. I'm more and more aware that the success of a film depends on the control of all one's energies. I would have liked to have made more, but the accomplice, the man who guides and limits one's energies by imposing rules, has always been missing. And he still is.

Jubilation

At the second viewing, I discover a film which is totally anti-realist. The whole thing is shot in the studio, rigorously controlled and stylized. When Newman goes walking in New York with Piper Laurie, we only hear the sound of their steps and a vague blues in the background. Nothing else: neither the footsteps of passers-by nor the sound of the traffic. When we enter the pool hall, we hear a minimum of sounds. The lack of noise immediately concentrates the audience on the game.

The light in the central scene of the film is equally anti-realist. It's the moment when the young player first properly meets his coach. Eddie is standing facing the bar. Burns (the coach) is sitting behind him. The camera focuses on both men from behind, thanks to the mirror behind the counter. The film is black and white, the light subdued.

It must have been 70°C on the set. The result: a rather dirty light which endows the scene with a totally anti-realist atmosphere. This light has a meaning in the film: Eddie, the pure, encounters the impurity of compromise and double-dealing.

The actors are always on the move. At no time does Newman's technique have to fill out a deficiency in the *mise-en-scène*. There isn't a single blink which hasn't been directed. The actors' performances are controlled, created and stylized by the direction of their gaze.

When Eddie and Bert (Piper Laurie) first sleep together, the camera at the start of the scene is outside the shutters. The two characters exchange a few words; then, as Eddie kisses her, he pulls the shutters to. You only see such tacky scenes in telefilms. But *The Hustler* has grace, in the sense that the whole is greater than the sum of the efforts made to create it. But grace can only be attained through hard work and control at every level.

Simplicity is evident right from the start of the film. Eddie enters the pool hall, accompanied by a friend who looks like a loser. He asks the cashier for a table. We only see the set behind when Eddie asks him some questions. It is almost deserted. The cashier replies that there is no bar and no cigarettes: 'You're in Adams's.' Everything immediately becomes clear for the audience. This is *the* pool hall in the USA, and the champ arrives when he wants, according to a well-established ritual. Time accelerates according to a basic and totally classical cinematic language.

Effectiveness is guaranteed. Although we are told nothing about it, we are made to think we have always shot pool, that we know all the rules. The simplicity of the scene camouflages considerable technique and artistry. It makes the film immediately accessible to the audience.

The Hustler makes us really understand the pleasure as well as the manufacture of a fictional film. Joy and work combined.

Bertrand Tavernier

Sound of the Mountain

Sound of the Mountain.

Recalling in a few words a film, an *auteur,* that has impressed you, marked your life (or branded it as the cattle are branded in Anthony Mann's Westerns), while desperately trying to finish your own film (and, as luck would have it, simultaneously preparing the next one) is a tiring and difficult task. You don't want to think about other film-makers, or see other images. Words don't appear easily on the computer screen. They rebel, desert you in droves, or remind you that you have something else to do. The time spent choosing an adjective or changing a phrase seems shamefully stolen from one's other preoccupations.

What should be a pause and a rest becomes an escape, a dilettante's betrayal, a test of his strength. You are in a state of urgency, working at full tilt, and someone asks you to rummage through your past, to summon up the ghosts that haunt you – often amicably and warmly – but which you try to keep at arm's length during the weeks of incandescence called a shoot.

I must press on and pass this new test. Because I'm making a cloak and dagger story, I thought of one of the films that lit up my adolescence, works which seem to illustrate the advice an old Hindu story-teller gave to Kipling: 'Since man is your subject, speak to him of kings, elephants, battles and horses.' Shakespeare, for example, or *The Life of a Bengal Lancer, Distant Drums.* Stories full of mysterious forests, fires, secret hideaways where kings can become beggars, island kingdoms of white sand, elephants turning into octopuses, crocodiles or, best of all, royal eagles, like the eagles in *Wyatt* that Gary Cooper feeds poison to. In any case, as Alexandre Vialatte remarked, 'Not being able to see the elephant doesn't mean there isn't one there. The sensible man must always beware of the invisible elephant … ' Policemen say *'Cherchez la femme'* when there's a crime. When there's a man, I say *'Cherchez l'éléphant'.* He's always there, even though invisible, unless the situation's so awful there's nothing further to look for. The elephant means vastness and grandioseness, reinforced by fantasy.

Suddenly last night there came other images, other emotions, far removed – or so it seemed – from the film I was trying to make. Images from films by Naruse, from *Sound of the Mountain* most of all; tranquil, sharp images, at once serene and piercing, like needles stuck in a doll. There are crimes, of course: a young girl forced to take a husband, a humiliated woman, an old man who fears time is flying past him. And there are also elephants, almost invisible, transparent, divined in the shape of a cloud, in the calligraphy of a *kanji* hidden in the folds of a kimono, in the dream of the old man, who yearns to see the first maple leaves or the first red blooms of the bitter apple.

There are in this extraordinary film – adapted, like several of Naruse's masterpieces, from an extraordinary novel – several unforgettably-filmed sets; sets which, like the *basso continuo* in baroque music, sustain the breath of the film. Most importantly, the narrow, suburban alleys, sandy or muddy and full

212

of obstacles, lined by low houses, the houses of the poor, most of them wooden, fragile but welcoming like the alleys themselves, which merely seem a secret extension of them. Naruse minutely describes each journey, the return from work, the departure for a visit whose outcome is uncertain, or the setting-out on a search you know to be hopeless. Bicycles, children playing. In the distance, we see or hear the express train or the tram connecting this microcosm to the modern buildings of Shinjuku, to the heart of towns full of American soldiers and images of the world to come. In this infinite chaos, such comings and goings represent uncertain yet reassuring transitions: they are a way of taking stock, of defining a feeling, of asking a question one cannot ask in public or within the family. Walking through these sets allows the characters to avoid the eyes of others; they favour uncertainty and murmured confidences. Movement, so much better than the static confrontation on a *tatami*, also affords hope.

Admirable shots, sometimes static, sometimes moving, allow Naruse, the painter of day-to-day determination, of gestures repeated a thousand times, to root his characters in sets which, though simple, endow them with the weight and the past of an entire civilization. With serenity and a heart-rending courtesy, he makes us feel, as Jean Pérol says in his wonderful book *Tokyo*, that 'the alleys are the being of Old Japan, an Old Japan of habit subsisting amid the motorway grid, like truth amid chaos.'

Naruse also uses these incessant comings and goings to break up the dramatic rhythm and loosen the grip of the plot (in spite of the meditative nature of Kawabata's novel, Naruse left out, with the author's agreement, some of the narrative). He thereby heightens that atmosphere of hesitation and indecision from which he constructs all his films, chronicles of flux and doubt ... The characters, especially the brilliantly-described and ever-present old men, seem to be floating between two worlds, two clans, two emotions. Like the clouds that play such an important role throughout, they either cannot or will not stay still. Not out of a spirit of rebellion, but simply because, if they did stop, they would feel that they were dead.

Naruse suddenly contrasts this emotional flux with irreversible movement. This brings in another strong point of his work: the scenes in trams, cars (rarer these) or trains, notably the sublime train-ride which concludes *Repast*, and the letter falling out of a window which we hear, in voice-over, to be a calm, terrifying and lucid acceptance of despair.

Or there is an absolute stillness. The stillness of the park with its vast avenues, the gigantic lawn of *Sound of the Mountain* where an old man and a young girl go for a walk, the fragility of their feelings contrasted with the perishable yet eternal workings of nature. Naruse alternates lyrical wide angles with mid-shots devoid of drama. In the calm silence of the garden, the two characters experience at the same time closeness and distance, acceptance and loss: '"So I'm free?" she says, tears in her voice, looking at the pigeons flying away.'

Naruse could include that phrase of Kawabata's in all his films. The tears, the unconquered yet reluctantly-accepted freedom, the birds flying across the sky, the feeling of eternity, the way of filming with an infinite variety of close situations. Kawabata wrote about haikus: 'For trout there are all kinds of useful expressions: the autumn trout, the plunging trout, the rusty trout ... The autumn trout drifting with the current. The trout in shallow waters not knowing death awaits him.' Those lines could apply to me.

Paolo and Vittorio Taviani

Memories of Pasolini

We were driving along the road from Rome to Viterbo when, on the top of a hill, we noticed a kind of ruin, half-ancient and half-modern. With a feeling of pain and anxiety we recognized the little medieval castle Pasolini had once bought and had asked Dante Ferretti to restore as a place of retreat. Now, with Pasolini dead, the house has been taken over by weeds.

We both remembered the last night of 1974, when Pasolini invited us and a group of friends to celebrate New Year's Eve. A group of friends, we say. But we were not strictly speaking his friends. Our relationship stretched to a few meetings, the kind of encounters common among film-makers exercising the same profession, as we had been for fifteen years.

Our hostess was, of course, Laura Betti, who demonstrated her imagination even on this domestic occasion. Welcoming us at the door was Tonino delli Colli. The master of the house, Pasolini, could hardly hide a certain self-mocking complacency when showing us around his new home, perhaps because the house, with its contrast between ancient red walls and Ferretti's modern glass partitions, was an extension of himself. We both admired his films for precisely these contrasts.

The heating system wasn't working properly and we all moved about in a bluish cloud. The host and his guests, perhaps unconsciously, took advantage of this problem, and the attempts to remedy it, to dissipate the kind of embarrassment caused by such gatherings, where people with only a little in common feel obliged to celebrate.

Pasolini had decided to follow the traditional ritual with an almost melancholy docility, and in this we were his accomplices. We thought of another meeting, at the house Pasolini lived in at the EUR. That time, we were struck on our arrival by another obvious contrast: between the sunny, tranquil bourgeois interior Pasolini shared with his mother, and the frantic abandon of his nights. We had come to offer him a part in a film we were preparing, *I sovversivi*. All his works told us of his need to expose himself without mediation, to exhibit himself even to the point of courting disaster. Acting attracted him because it trod a fine line between glory and opprobrium. For our character Ludovico we needed Pasolini's face, his fierce yet Franciscan gaze, the same gaze which created our favourite films of his, *Accatone*, *Il vangelo (The Gospel according to St Matthew)*, *La ricotta*. We weren't wrong: the project interested him at once. We talked of dates. He smiled at the idea of finding himself on the other side of the camera. But there was one condition: the character should not be, as we had imagined, a director. Certainly, he should be a man who had devoted his life to art, and who now suddenly, anxiously, had to face death. But he couldn't be a director, or the parallel between the character and Pasolini himself would be misleading, if not embarrassing. 'Why not make him a musician,' he asked us, 'or an architect?' But his objections were countered by ours: we wanted to give the director Ludovico, a character we had lived with for quite some time, a face and a voice. That time we didn't get Pasolini on to the set. But we met again, with our respective films, in the street where, along with millions of others, Communists, we followed Togliatti's funeral. Pasolini admired *I sovversivi* and we admired *Uccellacci e uccellini*.

Meanwhile, back at the castle, midnight was approaching, and as we waited, we followed each stage of the ritual with good-natured determination. A tombola was set up and the guests crowded around the table. But where was our host? We found him in the most medieval part of the house. He hesitated, then told us quietly about a film he was preparing: a project Sergio Citti had brought him, Sade's *The 120 Days of Sodom*, but which he would set in Salò during the last days of Fascism. His tone of voice reminded us of yet another meeting that had occurred some time before and which counted for much in our subsequent relationship. Pasolini had come to a private screening of *San Michele aveva un gallo*. At the end of the film, unlike Rocha and Bellochio, the other guests, he said nothing and left, looking tense and withdrawn. We thought he didn't like the film. But it wasn't that at all. We met him again at Laura's. He arrived late for dinner and apologized. He'd come on foot, but had had to keep his eyes glued to the pavement because it was impossible, unbearable for him to look at the faces of passers-by, a procession of monsters. This was another reason why we had felt the need to meet together: he had become convinced that the future was already dead, while we felt that we had been engulfed in a period of chaos through which we were stubbornly trying to find a way and a meaning. Sitting apart from the others, who'd started to eat, we spoke to him with a brutal frankness arising out of mutual respect. And his conclusion was equally brutal: 'Your optimism,' he murmured, 'is more tragic than my pessimism.'

At the castle, midnight finally came, and the champagne was opened. The noise seemed to cheer Pasolini up, and bring him back from the faraway place he'd travelled to. Enough! We should all go out. Bring the cars! He drove us through the night to a village dance a few miles away. The dance was almost over, the lights were about to be put out, and the last couples only had eyes for each other and their love. Pasolini wanted, demanded music. And he danced, with Gisella, with Ninetto and all the others. He danced with joy, strength and grace. We watched him concentrating on the steps of the tango and flying lightly through a waltz. We watched this poet who, a little later with *Salò*, would look Evil straight in the eye, and we remembered that he had once said, with his desperate candour: ' ... But I'm a joyful man!'

Accattone: Pasolini with Franco Citti.

Agnès Varda

Buñuel in fourth gear

Some notable numbers (and positive ones, if quantity makes for strength):

Forty (40) years of cinema since my first long film in 1954 (*La Pointe Courte*); four hundred (400) numbers of *Positif* in forty (40) years; and forty (40) days since I agreed to write for them an article of four (4) pages, interrupting the writing of a script that is giving me a little difficulty but a lot of pleasure.

So let's get straight to the point. *Buñuel's films are magical,* in that the effect they produce goes beyond the visual impression and the other periods of satisfaction that stay with us after a film ends, either as one leaves the cinema or – for we live in the present – when we switch off the video and the machine ejects out the cassette. Exit Buñuel's *L'Age d'Or* and let the pleasure continue!

Others have written about Buñuel, and when *L'Age d'Or* was restored, Buñuel himself told some anecdotes; Carrière has collected his memories into a book. But it's his films which speak the most, which promise the most and deliver it.

I only have to think about Colonel Piéplu interrupting the meal that a group of bourgeois friends never manage to finish, and I start laughing. Stéphane Audran sends the bishop to find some chairs. Piéplu smokes a joint. Delphine Seyrig simpers. And before the soldiers leave on manoeuvres, a sergeant tells them his dream. What a feast!

I delight in these blunders, which are the quintessence of Buñuel's cinema. They try to eat together and they fail every time. They get the wrong day or the wrong place, and they have to leave. They believe themselves to be in private, but they're on stage, booed by an audience. Another meal turns out to be a dream.

They walk along the road, and here they are again at supper. I remember Audran and Cassel escaping into the garden to make love, and when they come back, they crouch under the dining-room windows so as not to be seen by the other guests – who have already left!

Later, the gardener is dying. The priest takes his confession, and discovers that the man had murdered his own parents. No time to lose. The priest gives him the last sacrament, takes a gun, and shoots the erstwhile assassin. Is there any better way to wield the gun and the aspergillum, revenge and absolution?

No. No other film-maker could so stylishly contradict and mock hypocrisy.

He was naughty to the end, Buñuel. I remember seeing him once when he

L'Age d'Or.

was shooting in France. Sitting in a wheelchair, with his hearing-aid, he looked like an old man cut off from the world. But I suspect he heard what he wanted to hear; his eyes shone with malice.

This brings back more distant memories. Mexico, 1965. I'm copying out some words from the book I've recently published. They're still on the hard disk of my Apple Mac: 'Arrow – book. Click! – index. Click! – B. Click – arrow – Buñuel – cut. Click! – mouse, arrow, paste. Click! – T as in Typhus.'

'I had a mild bout,' said Murin one evening when Jacques and I were having supper with Buñuel in Acapulco. Was it the exhilaration of having met this special man? The fever struck at the end of the meal. All night, during my delirium, I saw Buñuel struggling amongst coloured fabrics and I felt it was my duty was to protect him: 'Father, watch out! On the right! On the left!' Jacques called a doctor. My temperature was 41°C. I was flown home.

I spent a month in bed, delighted that Buñuel was responsible for this long rest.

I'll add a few details. The meal took place on one of the terraces overlooking the sea at Acapulco. The menu: raw fish marinated in lemon and tomatoes. Delicious. I don't remember the rest.

Having suggested we brush our teeth in mineral water to avoid catching anything, Luis Buñuel talked to me about my film *Le Bonheur*, which he'd just seen at the festival. He liked the colours, the cruelty, the dangerous suavity etc.

I was delighted, but also scarlet with embarrassment. Jacques smiled at my discomfort, and I managed to interrupt Buñuel and ask him about his films. Having read and liked the Surrealists well before I (belatedly) started going to the cinema, *Un Chien Andalou* and *L'Age d'Or* had the effect of a time-bomb on me. I told him this. It still amuses me to think back to this dinner, to my sudden fever, my Buñuelesque delirium, and to the stories I've just paraphrased. Anything goes when it comes to thinking about Buñuel.

The exaggeration – to my eyes – of Gaston Modot's revolted gaze (eyes raised to heaven when he feels desire), the sensation of Lya Lys sucking the toe of a statue (do M. and Mme Ussé have a son? What's his name? James), the clumsiness of the couple trying to kiss on a park bench and falling on to the gravel, the girl slapping the lubricious old man (between two bars of music) ... The pallor, the semi-staccato rhythm and the light vagueness all help me tackle *A Thousand and One Nights*, my next film. Monsieur Cinéma, whom I've invented and am now describing, is nearly a hundred years old. But when one asks his age, he always replies: '*L'âge d'or*'.

And I shall quickly return to him, leaving without further ado the writers, artisans and technicians of *Positif*, to whom I address a smiling farewell – like Buster Keaton raising his hand to say goodbye and immediately coming a cropper off-screen (now *there's* another sublime film-maker whose appeal never fades!).

Billy Wilder

I have bad news, I'm afraid. I can't do the piece for you like I promised. Suddenly last Tuesday my roof fell in. No, it was not the earthquake. Worse than that. I have to rewrite about sixty pages of my script. I must do it by 6 May. That means working sixteen hours a day. No sleep. I'll be dead on my feet. Please remember that your good friend Wilder is about sixteen years older than the Pope.

Edward Yang

On Films

I positively belong to the film generation. I am of the first generation of Chinese who were brought up watching movies. Many films throughout my life have had a very powerful impact on me, have somehow influenced its course. From the first movie, *Escape From Fort Bravo*, which suddenly seemed to cure my fear of movies at the age of six, to Fellini's *8½* (after watching it four times I recognized how overwhelming the power of a film can be), I don't believe I am able to pick one single film and say this is the one that impressed me the most. Two major currents have made the strongest impression on me: Japanese film in the sixties and the German New Wave of the seventies. Out of all these, it was Werner Herzog's series of films in the mid-seventies that has inspired me the most. I was giving up on my attempt to become a film-maker at the time. His simplicity and the direct power of his images that articulated the deepest sensations of our soul quickly resuscitated my heartbeat. Best of all, his independent perseverance made me deeply believe, even to this day, that a film is made by one man's power alone. The first Herzog film I saw: *Aguirre, Wrath of God*.

On Directors

To rate a director is a tough task, to undertake a process of elimination in order to arrive at a single choice is even tougher. There are role-models of the past and there are peers in the present. It is not a sporting event where a won-lost record can easily justify a selection, or a championship game can finally decide a winner.

Many directors perform admirably with one particular film, fewer can maintain a body of impressive work. There are ones who apparently became corrupt after a certain career accomplishment. And there are ones who became clowns in their effort to appease after a failed noble attempt. Since it is a personal choice, the rating process I would apply is very much like the one used for rating professional heavyweight boxers or racehorses – by their track record. Very few directors, to my mind, have a perfect record without one disappointing work. The few I can think of are Maurice Pialat, Alain Resnais, Andrei

Tarkovsky. This does not mean that I have any the less admiration for Fellini, Woody Allen and Kubrick, not to mention Mikio Naruse and Werner Herzog.

On Actors

The most simple, singular similarity between a film-maker and an actor is that they both attempt to create a falsified reality with truth. No matter which school the actor comes from, once the camera starts to roll he or she goes through the process of pretence or make-believe. As among film-makers, the difference between a good actor and a great one lies in the ability to be truthful to oneself while performing the most demanding functions of one's profession. It takes a kind of courage very few would dare, for the risk is too great between the reward of a personal triumph and the punishment of a nervous breakdown. The impression of untruthful pretence is also one major reason why those who are not in the business often mistake our profession as being made up of a bunch of liars and prostitutes. Unfortunately, the great ones are so few in number to outweigh this prejudice.

In making feature-length films, actors are like players in a team sport carrying

Klaus Kinski (left) as Herzog's Aguirre.

223

out the strategy and plan of the team under the direction of the coach, the film-maker. The technical polish of an individual player can only contribute to a certain limited extent; the rest is courage, confidence, trust in others, understanding, unselfishness, and the belief that the reward of team accomplishment can be many times greater than all the personal accomplishments combined. I am fortunate enough to have worked with a great number of actors, young and old, and together we have produced memorable results. Unlike other people, a film-maker has to have a few actors at the top of his list as the most favourite to work with, not just to admire. Most often, these actors may not be the ones ordinary folk read about in the papers. At the top of my list is Ni Shujun, who is playing one of the leading roles in my current project. She has all the qualities of an actor mentioned above and, hold your breath, she will show them to the world in due time.

Krzysztof Zanussi

My first visit to the cinema

Most of an individual's life follows a universally-shared timetable: at roughly the same age we have our first communion, our first date, our first exams. In general, we all do our military service at the same age as well. More often than not, school determines the rate at which we make literary discoveries. The same applies to philosophy. If someone were to ask me when I first heard of Socrates, or read Pascal and Nietzsche, I'd simply refer them to my school syllabus. Having begun to read earlier than expected, I was rarely less than a year or eighteen months ahead of the school reading programme. On the other hand, I would also skip certain set books, and I only read them when I was much older (I can now admit that, influenced by the film, I have just read *Germinal* – fifty years after it was first prescribed for me!).

By contrast, one's relationship with cinema does not follow such a precise timetable. Time is merciless to our art, which is more vulnerable to forgetfulness than any other. In the cinema one most often sees what is new. The life of a film resembles that of a butterfly, dying after the season's over; everyone sees a film at the same time, then forgets it. For modernity means an absence of memory. My Latin teacher lived as if Caesar were her contemporary; she seemed to know Virgil personally. She could bear the barbarity of her age only by pitching her tent as far away from it as possible, at least that was my impression. She had survived Auschwitz, but in reality had never left Antiquity. She was part of it and had the air of someone belonging in a museum.

Cinema is not yet a museum piece, although it's slowly making its way there. Cinema lives in the present moment, like the audience. It only exists in the today. And yet you ask me about my first and distant encounter with it!

It happened nearly fifty years ago. I'm now fifty-five. I imagine I first went to the cinema just after the war. I didn't go before because, in German-occupied Poland, going to the cinema – even for children's films – was considered a betrayal. So I didn't see any of Disney's cartoons (something I don't regret). I knew the music of *Snow White*, but I only saw the film much later at the Cinémathèque. The Resistance had a slogan, 'Only pigs go to the movies', which rhymes in Polish, and my parents respected the ban. They never went to the cinema, ate meat only on Fridays, and belonged to the Resistance. So for me, cinema began after the war.

Warsaw was in ruins and only a few cinemas were left standing. To see a film, one had to queue for hours – the fantasy of all directors, the long queue in front of the cinema. Before the advent of Stalinism, everything was shown: French, American, Italian films. Nowadays I laugh about it, but it would never have occurred to my parents to go and see an American film: they considered American films to be the province of our cleaner or the chauffeur who drove my father to the works where he was an engineer. My parents only saw French, Italian and English films. These films became rarer in the fifties and were replaced by Soviet films, for which no one queued, and which workers would be ordered to go and see by their managers, who'd hand out cut-price tickets.

Since French, Italian and English films were disappearing, they were highly sought-after, and the queues for them bigger than ever. Often one wouldn't know when one would get in: once the theatre was full, one would carry on queuing for the next showing. Every two hours another crowd of spectators would disappear inside.

And now for a more personal memory.

My first film – not the first I ever saw, but the one which first struck me – I remember very well. I have no difficulty in remembering the title. I also remember the circumstances of my getting in. Because it dealt with love, only adults were allowed to see it. I couldn't have got in without cheating. The usherette at the entrance was asking for school identity cards, on which were written one's date of birth. One could make the date illegible with an ink-stain, but that was too obvious. One could also assume a disguise. Which is what I did. I was about twelve or thirteen, but tall for my age. I put on my father's hat and darkened my upper lip and cheeks to give the impression of a badly-shaven, darker man (I was blond and beardless). And I got in. The usherette didn't even ask me for my card. The film was *Les Enfants du Paradis*.

I've rarely seen a more beautiful film since.

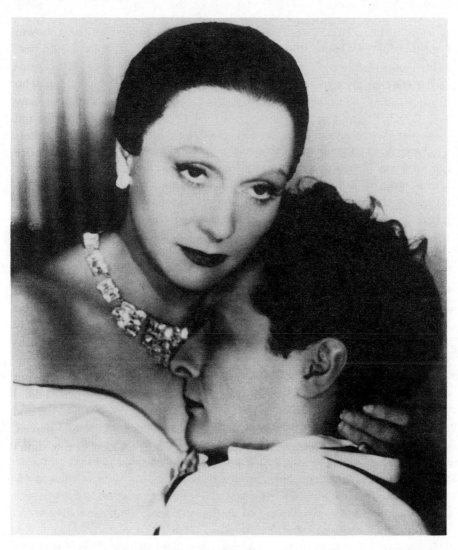

Les Enfants du Paradis: Arletty and Barrault.

Andrzej Zulawski

'The ghost of cinema'

I've long been of the opinion that one should never see again the films that one cannot tame. Watching television, for example, is like chewing gum, and therefore suitable for taming films, no doubt because we always see the same films on it – or perhaps it's the films which have all become the same. Paradoxically, it is only the untameable films that have the power to make us love cinema. I remember those films because of the shock they caused. I cried while watching them, but they were not tears of sentiment. I suffered because my heart was expanding, tearing its way out. I was dazzled by the spirit of those who made these films. I would happily recommend young people to go and see such films. But I know that what they'll see through the screen is themselves, something I can no longer do.

Therefore, since I have not seen again the films that gave me everything, I retain a memory of them which must be rather inexact. These films would probably be irritated to learn what they have become in my head. I'm often asked to draw up a list of the ten best, the fifteen greatest, the three most astounding, the hundred most eternal. The list changes every time. The self that one brings to cinema is more directly affected than it is by the touch of other ephemeral art forms, and the vast mass of cinematic masterpieces more vulnerable to the relativism of conditioning. Some films do, however, spring to mind. For example, bumptious, frenetic, minor and kitschy films such as *Mr Arkadin* or *The Criminal* by Orson Welles – whose reputation in Europe was based entirely on *Citizen Kane* – films that are more understandable when viewed through the kitsch of the eighties.

Since I lack a canonical film, and can only refer to old films in terms of which age-bracket they appeal to, because I still know what effect a work may have and on whom, I live in a kind of no man's land, more paradisal than purgatorial, and I can still conclude that Gary Cooper, a charming but terrible actor, is an actor of genius, and that I could watch him again in something passable – that is, on television.

That said, I thought I'd remind you of a film about which I have an even vaguer memory than most; and here we're talking about films that have done something for us that other things could not do. It was by Jean Eustache and not very long. A short or medium-length film. It's a film I often think about. I remember it, even through the mists of my forgetfulness, with greater clarity than films I know better, and would therefore not be able to talk about.

It's set in the country, somewhere hot, perhaps a holiday resort. It was about a little boy and a woman looking at some photographs.

Looking back, I think the woman was the mistress of the boy's father. And wasn't looking at the photos – family photos, I think – a way for the woman to bond with the boy, to approach him, to tame him in fact?

So we look at the photos and the young woman comments on what we see. People, landscapes, moments. Gradually, and without us noticing it – the story-line not having much significance for the moment – the commentary begins to dissociate itself from the pictures. A finger indicates a tree, and the voice says: 'A worm'. We see a window, and we hear: 'Shoes'. Day turns to night, closed becomes open, a tragic dullness becomes a cheerful obscurity.

Is it the woman talking or the little boy? Are we slowly plunging into the madness of a character, a life or a situation? Of reality itself? Of cinema?

I don't know how the film ends. I don't even know whether what I'm describing is exactly what Eustache filmed. After several minutes of the film, I was 'in' cinema and therefore 'in' myself, my eyes wide, ensnared and exhilarated at the same time. I was witnessing a mystery. One doesn't remember mysteries.

I hope the young woman never tamed the little boy. I know that I shall never tame that film. Eustache died from a lack of filming, Fellini too. Federico's death closed a chapter in which cinema, at its best, believed it could describe simplicity with the help of the extraordinary, because directors existed to make a spectacle out of everything. The new chapter opens with the fantastic described in a formal way.

Intelligence will always find a place to hide where the layers are coming unstuck, where to look is to become clairvoyant. The ghost that I glimpsed will come to haunt me in both my greatest excitements and my smallest certainties.

In Addition ...

Inspired by *Positif,* we extended an invitation to an additional group of film-makers to answer the question.

The response was as follows ...

Michael Almereyda

Notes on Derek Jarman

Watching *The Last of England* for the first time felt something like being caught in a lightning storm. The film moved in bursts, surges and jolts, leaping from one inspiration to the next. At least half the scenes featured bonfires and flares, and the whole picture unspooled with a continuous flickering, flashing and hissing quality.

As a portrait of a ruined empire, an anguished political cartoon, a howl of conscience and rage, the film invited its viewers to feel fairly grim, but you couldn't doubt that the director was furiously in love with the world, and Jarman's ecstatic formal energy outshouted the declaration of doom. I was amazed to see such momentum, emotion and life sustained in a film that turned its back on conventional story-telling. I left the theatre feeling exhilarated.

Someone from the New York Film Festival supplied me with Jarman's number and I called him a few days later. I was back in Los Angeles, in post-production on my first feature, fighting with the producer and editor, men fifteen years older than me who found my intentions incomprehensible. I could see I was in for a rough ride, I was looking for guidance, and I wanted to make another movie, fast and cheap. Jarman, of course, was the same age as my unhappy collaborators, but I sensed a kindred spirit. His work had opened a window in my head.

He called back without having any idea who I was. I told him I liked *The Last of England* – that seemed to be enough to warrant his goodwill, and we talked for more than twenty minutes. He explained he'd made the film with three or four Nizo 8 mm cameras, venturing out on weekends with friends for improvised shooting sprees. He was patient and specific, detailing his technical processes and decisions, and at the end of this he invited me to London to visit and possibly work on his impending *War Requiem*. I got the impression, later, that such off-hand openness and generosity were characteristic of him, and I came to feel a lingering regret that I wasn't quite foolhardy enough to leap at his invitation. But I did buy two 8 mm cameras – a handsome old Nizo (a product of West Germany, as sturdy as a Volkswagen Beetle and just as defunct) and an expensive Beaulieu with multiple lenses – though it shouldn't have taken much thought to recognize the simple differences between Jarman's situation and my own. He was shooting without scripts, without dialogue, without sync sound, using slow, rich Kodachrome film in natural sunlight. The

Derek Jarman with Richard Heslop, Christopher Hughes, and Cerith Wyn
Evans.

movies I wanted to make involved scripted stories with night scenes and tor-
rents of talk.

All the same, in the ensuing year, working with friends in New York, I shot
a series of Super 8 tests before someone, late one winter night, broke into my
apartment and made off with every camera I owned. It took a while for me to
get back to work, but Jarman's voice was still in my ear when I took up a
Fisher-Price Pixelvision camera and managed more completely to follow his
lead.

*

Jarman was original and wilful enough to make films that were intrinsically uneven, unclassifiable, imperfect. He had his overbearing obsessions, and could be counted on to toss in at least one stridently kitschy dance number per picture. But you didn't have to share his passionate interest in flowers, crucifixes or half-dressed young men to feel shaken and moved by his work, to receive these images as gifts. And all his films reliably lift off the ground for long stretches, usually when Tilda Swinton shows up and when Jarman flings in footage of water and sky, his speciality being Turneresque red and yellow sunsets, radioactive clouds rushing in reverse at high speed.

As his health became more embattled, the emotions in his films, it seems to me, became sharper, increasingly pressurized, and his description of the world became both more convincing and more private, moving from the apocalyptic commotion of *The Last of England* and *War Requiem* to a quieter, more piercing turmoil in *The Garden*. In that film, as in the others, depictions of innocence and wholeness jostle against scenes of humiliation and horror, but Jarman was now literally bringing it all home, filming in and around his cottage on the coast of Kent, peeling back his sense of allegory to a diaristic core.

What he conjured there, in his own back yard, was often blazingly simple. Tilda Swinton, looking like a ghost haunting her own life, lights a candle, watches the flame, and abruptly screams. Jarman himself lies curled naked in bed. The bed's on the beach, ringed by men and women carrying flares. By the

Tilda Swinton.

Rupert Audley.

film's end, all panic and rage seem to have burned away. Swinton and a young boy and a pair of apotheosized young men sit together at a table and raptly watch burning paper lift and float in the air like disembodied spirits.

Clearly enough these images are about AIDS, mortality, mourning and loss. Also about yearning, acceptance, transcendence. But this doesn't say enough; or rather, it says too much. You just have to experience them.

I met him once, four months before he died. Sat through a meal in a New York coffee shop. He was in town for *Blue*, riding the last festival wave. He had an impressive, oracular voice. He was unguarded, theatrical in a dry, dapper way, advising me to take a walking tour of the British countryside, then discussing, with the same fervour, the virtues of home fries versus French fries. The ravages of his illness registered on his face like a sort of irrelevant horror movie make-up, but I thought I could recognize, outside my own feelings of sentimental awe, that he was at peace and unafraid.

Back at his room in the Chelsea Hotel, amidst an entourage of old friends, he took off his shoes – revealing bright blue socks! – and sat on the edge of the bed, ignoring a sitcom on TV. 'I've become an invalid,' he said calmly. 'Old before my time.'

'At least you can get round on your own,' somebody said.

'That's true. At least I'm not like – ' He named a friend's mother. 'She calls him *Doris*. Her mind's gone and as far as I can tell mine's not.'

Adam Elliott and Rod Laye.

He lay on his back, fully dressed, knees up, hands on his chest. We variously said goodnight, goodbye, but hovered another half-hour, mostly listening as Derek held forth, focused and funny, his voice creating a slow aural whirlpool of declamation and gossip.

Earlier, like a dutiful acolyte, I had presented him with a handful of gifts gathered from my apartment before I rushed out the door. Postcards of paintings, and a box of Chinese sparklers. 'These,' I said of the sparklers, 'are for the plane ride back.'

He took them solemnly and looked at me, it seemed, for the first time.

'I love sparklers,' Derek Jarman said.

Home movie footage: Derek Jarman with sister Gaye and mother Elizabeth.

His films remain, among other things, anthems for freedom of all kinds. They refuse to settle down in my mind. As a routinely impoverished film-maker, watching Jarman's work, glimpsing his life, I read an immensely basic message, sharp as a shout: the world is open. Don't let your life escape you, or allow your work to detach itself from your deepest feelings. Get on with it. Hurry. *Now*.

André de Toth

Gary Cooper

Springfield Rifle: André de Toth with Fess Parker and Gary Cooper.

You asked me to talk about actors I worked with, 'specially Gary Cooper.

It wouldn't make sense to me to mention Gary Cooper and actors in the same breath.

You know I don't like actors.

Hitchcock called actors 'cows'.

I don't like Hitchcock either.

I won't write anything about 'Actooors'. It's bad enough punishment to be an 'Actooor'. Now, Gary Cooper was different. About Coop I could write volumes.

But – as Gary Cooper was not an Actooor, he never Acted. Coop was as real as his horse's hair stuck to the seat of his pants or the horse-shit clinging to the heels of his boots.

Whatever he did, Gary Cooper was the truth.

According to Webster's, Roget's and the *American Thesaurus of Slang*:

An ACTOR is a theatrical performer, one who takes part, a participant, one who represents a character, one who ACTS, one who BEHAVES as *ACTING a part*, a role-player, SIMULATOR, player, performer, mummer, mime, scenery-chewer, ham, hambone, thespian, PERSONATOR, DECEIVER, PRETENDER, a *PHONY!*

Gary Cooper a phony??? And he didn't fit any of the rest of the definitions either. I don't believe he even heard the word 'pretend', he never performed, he *WAS* THE CHARACTER whose life he believed he lived.

It's a pity that nowadays the image of him and some other giants of the screen is fading due to the fodder, the sparkling PR bullshit fed to the mindless public by those who should be grateful to these giants for the magnificent heritage they have bestowed on us.

Lodge Kerrigan

Taxi Driver

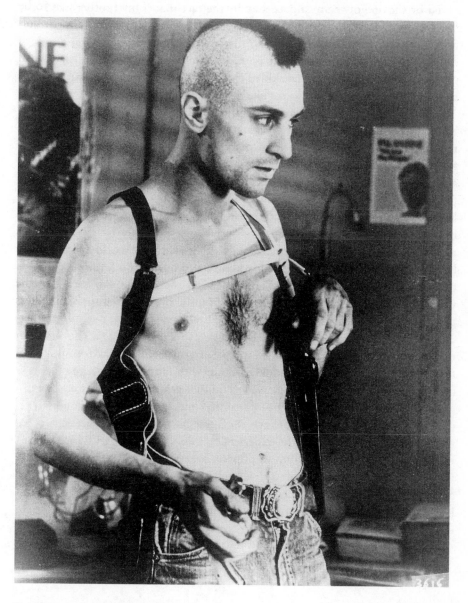

Taxi Driver: Robert De Niro.

When I was a boy, at dinner-time, my father would ask my brother and myself what our favourite things were. The categories would change nightly, from books to pieces of music to favourite meals. We would have to come up with our top ten, five or sometimes three items, in the event that one day we might get stranded on a desert island and have to live the rest of our lives with a limited, but pre-chosen, access. Sort of like packing for disaster. Invariably, I was saved by the end of the meal (speeded by the fact that if my brother liked the food, he would eat the entire meal without breaking for conversation), but my father would always smile, knowing that the next day would bring another dinner and another category. Here I am, years later, faced with the task of singling out one film from the truckload that continue to make a lasting impression upon me. In the end, it looks like my dad has won.

I first saw *Taxi Driver* when I was fourteen. I remember that when I left the theatre, I felt completely devastated; I had difficulty instantaneously reintegrating myself into my immediate environment. I have watched the film again many times. To this day, I am continuously mesmerized by a character who is riddled with so many internal contradictions and who is so painfully at odds with himself – without holding any of the answers – that he somehow transcends characterization and becomes a real person captured on film. I find myself repeatedly seduced, not only by the romantic notion of the 'heroic' loner, isolated and at odds with the world around him, but also by Travis's innocence, vulnerability and desperation, the very qualities which turned on their heads simultaneously repulse me. For better or for worse, here is a person who reveals himself fully, in a way that perhaps only people who are rejected by society can.

In November 1994 I saw Michael Haneke's *71 Fragments of a Chronology of Chance* at the London Film Festival. After the film, Haneke spoke at length and touched upon his dissatisfaction with current American cinema's obsession with plot-driven movies. He said that a film driven by a constructed, manipulated plot that does not take into consideration the random nature of life is a lie. Although I believe that cinema should not necessarily be restricted to reflecting 'real life' experiences, I do sympathize with his frustration. There is a poverty of films in present American cinema that are character-driven and reflect not only the complexities and ambiguities of life, but also the beauty and grotesqueness of human beings. The days of Travis are long gone from American cinema, but fortunately Mike Leigh and Ken Loach are filling the void.

Richard Linklater

L'Argent

Summer 1985. Robert Bresson's *L'Argent* is playing Friday, Saturday and Sunday at a campus theatre near where I live. I've never seen a Bresson film before, and go knowing only what I've read: that Bresson is an older, highly distinguished French master, that the film is based on a Tolstoy story, and that it won an award at Cannes in 1983.

I return to the cinema each evening this weekend, drawn back by something I can't quite fathom. I only know I like the transformation that's going on in my mind as I watch the film. It seems that something that is meant to be is occurring – some higher function in my film consciousness is being fulfilled. By the end of the weekend I've witnessed and fully experienced a different cinematic language, and this redefines my acceptance of what a film can, or should, be.

What I judge on the first night to be strange or not very convincing acting becomes by the final showing a complete transcendence of acting altogether. What's on the screen is pure human form – a direct communication. From the first to the last screening, what I think is almost like a non-narrative becomes the most perfectly refined narrative imaginable. The leanest film possible – not a superfluous frame. Watching *L'Argent* is to be in the hands of a master.

From the opening image of a money machine closing, we are whisked through a modern, mechanized world as seen through an elegant and fragmented gaze. Through a deliberate and precise flurry of hands (passing money, planning robberies, washing blood off a knife), doors (constantly entering and exiting), and confined spaces (rooms, shops, prison cells), Bresson contemplates mortality, gravity and faith. This world is inhabited by many determined people who want to live, who know, as Yvon's cell-mate describes, 'the absurdity of modern society and the impossibility of change'. The characters all seem to be exercising a determined free will in a world of none.

L'Argent unfolds in a fashion as mysterious as life itself. It is impossible to predict or even anticipate what might happen next – a new scene is simply a leap into a new unknown. And yet, all in a seemingly fated, fully predestined universe. In Bresson's rigorously-structured universe, each event follows the previous one in the only way it could. Greed is followed by debt, which is followed by dishonesty, which leads to desperation, and finally to murder. The innocent, Yvon, after being wrongly accused of knowingly passing the counterfeit notes, goes back to the shop where he received them. Lucien, the

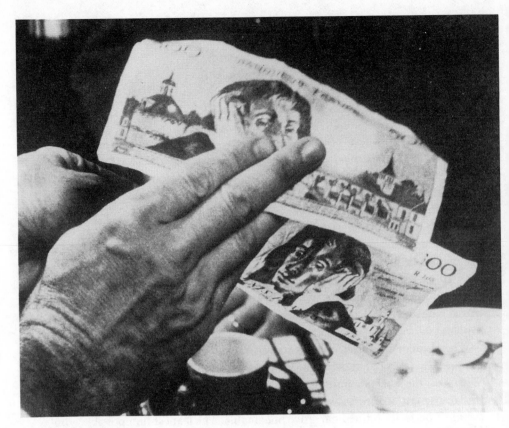

L'Argent: the crime.

employee, after some coaching, claims never to have seen him. Being led away by the authorities, Yvon offers no resistance, looking straight ahead and stating simply, 'They're crazy.' A shiver goes through me – if he's not going to be outraged, I am. All the wrongs of humanity, our corruption, our failure, come together in this one moment of a lamb being led to slaughter with the serene assumption of agony and grace.

Before the final screening that weekend, I read Tolstoy's story, translated into English as *The Forged Coupon*. It has a second half not included in Bresson's film. Yvon's character (Stepan), after participating in this circle of evil, eventually puts forth a contagion of goodness and redemption from evil. I think both Tolstoy and Bresson would have us believe our most trivial actions can have the most profound consequences, for good or bad. This is a responsibility so few of us even want to think about. 'If I were God, I'd forgive the whole world,' says the saintly woman who takes Yvon in. Is Yvon's confession of murder at the café at the end of the movie his initial step towards sainthood? Bresson isn't telling, but the silhouetted crowd gathered, watching Yvon

L'Argent: capture.

being led away by the police, ultimately stares back at *us*, the audience, in horror, in wonderment, in mystery. The closing of a perfect film and most likely this ultimate master's final cinematic image.

Richard Lowenstein

Elvis and the Aboriginals

A battered sign by the side of the road read 'Last petrol for 300 miles'. Pressed up hard against the grease-smeared window of a desolate petrol station, baking in the harsh overhead sun, I stared into the inky darkness at a glowing black-and-white TV sitting on the counter. The blurry white blob of Neil Armstrong in an unwieldy spacesuit was taking gigantic bunny hops on something that resembled the endless miles of landscape we'd been driving on for the past few weeks.

I wasn't impressed with the image quality. It wasn't anywhere near the clarity of the opening of *Planet of the Apes*, seen the year before in the air-conditioned comfort of a Melbourne inner suburban cinema. They were gonna have to improve the quality of interplanetary picture transmission if I was gonna be impressed.

We were soon back in the Toyota Land Cruiser, being bounced around in more than hundred-degree heat across hundreds of miles of rock-hard corrugations on the dirt road that was called a national highway in 1969. I was in the back seat vainly trying to steady a second-hand Superman comic, staring at it determinedly whenever the matriarch told me to stop reading and look out the window.

As she began ranting about putting us all in boarding school so she could travel around Australia by herself, the sudden, velvet-like relief of a sealed road hit like a blanket of feathers after days of bone-juddering vibrations. This was a signal for the encapsulated nuclear family to burst exuberantly into song, the lyrics of which extolled the merits of 'the bitch', otherwise known as bitumen, and what a wonderful surface it was to drive on. 'The bitch' was also a sign of impending civilization.

Civilization in this case happened to consist of a petrol station, a general store, and a caravan park. A few ramshackle dwellings were sprinkled around, and one very strange structure jutted up from the red desert floor. The structure was a large rectangle of dilapidated corrugated iron, painted on the outside with faded palm trees in an attempt to emulate a beach resort in the South Pacific. Where there is usually a roof, there was nothing. Empty. Open to the sky.

An open door banged loosely next to a cracked box-office window. Off to one side, a faded poster for an Elvis Presley movie peeled off the wall. I think it was *Clambake*. Elvis was holding a guitar.

Once our caravanette was erected and all my duties performed, I explored. Inside the corrugated iron and past the box-office, a pre-war ice chest sat empty of all goodies. Ratty deck chairs were piled up against the painted palms that lined the interior. A square hole cut into the wall above the box-office was the only indication that there was a bio-box. The place looked like it hadn't been used for years.

After nightfall, it was time to celebrate mankind's conquering of the moon. Clutching my hard-stolen pocket money, I ventured out.

The theatre was unrecognizable when I got to it. A string of bulbs lit up the top of the four walls, a light illuminated the poster, the owner was in the box-office window selling tickets. Trucks full of exuberant Kooris from the outlying areas were pulling up out front. It was a wonderland transformed.

Passing by the box-office, I found the candy bar had come to life; now fully-stocked, it looked like a treasure-chest of sweets and ice-creams. After purchasing my Peter's Choc Wedge, I moved in to find my deck chair.

The atmosphere inside was electric. The auditorium was cram-packed with Kooris, all driven in twenty to a ute from the outlying cattle stations and camps. The kids all sat on the ground down the front, pulling and pushing each other, giggling with excitement. The teenagers and adults sat back in the deck chairs, reprimanding, encouraging, chastising and just waiting. There was a giddiness in the air. A sense of excitement, euphoria and intimacy, even though most were seeing the film for the tenth time. It was as if they were revisiting an old friend.

The lights went down and the projector flickered on. The stars and moon shone down as the film unfolded with the usual array of girls, songs, cars, songs, romance, and more songs. Wolf-whistles and shouts of encouragement greeted the girls, oral engine noises greeted the cars, more wolf-whistles and shouts met the kissing scenes. Men were walking about on the moon above us, oblivious to this momentous occasion happening beneath them in the Australian outback.

It was during the songs when things really got moving. Whenever Elvis picked up his guitar and started crooning, the entire audience began to cheer and clap. Then they would begin to sing along, knowing every word of the song off by heart. The song would finish to more clapping and cheering, the ensuing dialogue getting lost as the audience settled down, biding their time through the necessary dialogue until the next song. The film and audience went on like this to the end of the show, except for one notable exception.

There was a recurring gag in the film between two young brothers, one bigger than the other. Elvis would break a candy bar and give half to each boy. The trouble was that one bit was always bigger than the other, creating a conflict. The dilemma would be resolved by the bigger boy biting the end off the larger piece of candy bar until they were both the same size. This seemed to keep both brothers happy and was greeted with hoots of enthusiastic laughter each time.

These two momentous cinematic experiences happening on the same day seemed to be trying to tell me something. Was this to be the *Cinema Paradiso* of my childhood? A future flashback sequence in my eventual remake of *Day for Night* with Elvis replacing the stills of Orson Welles stolen from the cinema foyer? Or was Elvis to be the Cardinal in a future version of $8\frac{1}{2}$, unevenly breaking my candy bar in half?

Man was walking on the moon thousands of miles above our little open-air cinema, but future flashback sequences were being created here. Forget *Citizen Kane*. Forget *La Grande Illusion*. Forget Kurosawa. It was to be Elvis in *Clambake* and an open-air cinema full of Aborigines revisiting an old friend, while man walked on the moon many miles above them.

Sally Potter

Bicycle Thieves

The story of *Bicycle Thieves* is a simple one. A man desperate for a job is offered one that requires a bicycle. With great difficulty, he and his wife manage to retrieve his bicycle from the pawnbrokers. But on his first day at work the bicycle is stolen. He and his small son search the city in an attempt to find it. But in the end it seems the only solution is to steal one himself.

The story rests within a complex structure of understanding of the economic conditions of the time and of the effect of poverty in general on the lives of individuals. The poverty of the protagonist is never romanticized or exaggerated. It is simply made visible. And it becomes clear through the story that poverty may degrade and even break a man's body, but it does not need to destroy his spirit or his relationship with others. In fact, the central relationship between father and son is strengthened through their struggle to find the stolen bicycle and catch the thief.

The story is ostensibly a moral tale based on a humanist, socialist perspective: the moral being that, if a man is stolen from, he will become a thief – and the socialist perspective being that the real thief in this context is the capitalist economy, which exploits its workers and creates an environment in which desperate individuals will steal from each other. But the manner in which the story is told is neither didactic nor moralistic. It is poetic.

The images condense layers of information in such a way that there seems to be a distillation of meaning into an essence of experience. Reality is described, but a meta-reality is invoked. An existential, mysterious, lyrical journey of inevitability, in which the hero is doomed to become that which he most despises and fears.

There is no happy ending to redeem the story neatly. But the ending is soft, and tender even, in its sadness. Our hero, the would-be thief, is caught but released. It is his son's small, bewildered, tear-stained face which saves him from arrest. The son who admires and loves his father above all else, and who has witnessed his desperation, his degradation, and his final humiliation.

This scene tells us – as a poem might – of the complex relationship between father and son, taking on the world together, dealing with responsibility; loving each other and fearing other men. And bearing witness to each other's struggles. You feel the meaning of male pride, not as *machismo*, but as love in the face of danger, survival in the face of possible annihilation.

The poetic form of the film also comes from its quality of observation of the

Bicycle Thieves.

simple, unremarked details of every day existence. The *feeling* of riding a bicycle, of walking the streets; the intersection of the lives of working people everywhere engaged in servicing the life of a big city.

And yet realism, even social realism, feels like a misnomer for how the film functions. Through the understated depiction of 'real life' one is led to experience other, less tangible, aspects of human existence. Somehow, what is evoked is a feeling of infinity. By concentrating on a very specific and personal story, we sense that 'society' consists of millions upon millions of individual, rich, complex, complicated, suffering lives. And that ultimately, whilst there may be no justice for many, there is at least the mysterious fact of the power of love.

When I discovered *Bicycle Thieves*, relatively late in my viewing experience, it was a revelation. My love of 'magical realism', of formal experiment, was tempered by the modesty of the film and its acceptance of its own conventions. Far from being a limitation, this seemed to create certain freedoms for its makers.

The sentiment in the film is expressed overtly. The feelings evoked are a natural consequence of the themes of the story and the point of view it is told from. It is a politically committed film, fuelled by a quiet but burning passion. But it never lectures. It observes rather than explains.

And then there is the music.

Haunting, shamelessly emotional, orchestral – as stated as the images are understated.

The total effect is to say: yes, this is how we are. Apparently separated from each other by class, age, gender and any number of other differences and divisions, but we spring from the same source. We *are* linked. In *reality* it is one for all and all for one. Ultimately, that is the only perspective that makes sense.

Philip Ridley

Alien Heart

Close Encounters of the Third Kind.

252

I was looking in a mirror, combing my hair and thinking of aliens, when the bedroom door opened and Mum walked in.

'Turn that music down,' she said, then added in the same breath, 'You're not wearing that tonight, are you?'

'Don't bother to knock,' I muttered. 'And what's wrong with what I'm wearing? Or the music?'

'They're both morbid,' she replied, picking fluff from my jacket. 'When I was seventeen I played dance records and wore party clothes on Saturday night.'

'We're not going to a party.' I sat on the edge of the bed and put my shoes on. 'We're going to see a film. A film with this morbid music.'

'Sounds like a bundle of laughs,' she commented, running her hand down the back of my head. 'Who you going with?'

'Don't mess my hair up,' I complained, pulling away. 'Why do people have to keep touching?' I stood up. 'How do I look?'

'Like you're going to a funeral. Why do people have to wear black all the time?'

'It makes my eyes look bluer, my teeth whiter, my skin smoother, and, oh yes, I like it. Next question.'

'Why's the music so loud?'

'Oh, just listen to it, Mum,' I pleaded, turning the volume up even more as the chorus came in. 'Isn't that wonderful?'

Mum looked unconvinced. 'What's the film about?' she asked. 'Nuns?'

'Aliens,' I replied. 'They come down to earth and kidnap a child or something. It's just incredible.'

'How do you know? You haven't seen the film yet.'

'I just *know*,' I told her. 'I've loved everything about it so far. Just the title alone is magic, *Close Encounters of the Third Kind*. What words! And the poster. The light at the end of the dark road. Not to mention this music.' I turned the record off, pushed past mum and out of the bedroom.

My younger brother was in his room with his girlfriend. His door, as usual, was wide open. They were knotted together, feeling each other's fingers.

'I'm going,' I said.

'Your music makes the walls shake!' my brother shouted. 'Why does the whole house have to hear your shit?'

'Why do I have to *see* yours?' I yelled back. 'You should close your door. Snogging in front of everyone. It's disgusting.'

My brother was getting to his feet, his fists clenched, eyes glaring.

'No fighting,' Mum said, shutting his door. 'Don't deliberately provoke. They're in love.'

'He started it,' I insisted, going downstairs.

Mum followed, still picking fluff off my clothes. 'You got your inhaler?' she asked.

'There's no room for my inhaler,' I replied. 'It makes my pockets bulge.'

'What if you have an asthma attack?'

'Then I'll die,' I said, giving myself one last look in the hallway mirror. 'At least I'll be dressed for it.'

'Don't joke about things like that,' Mum warned. Then added, 'You still haven't told me who you're going with.'

'A girl.'

'What girl?'

'Beth.'

'Oh, the one who's ringing so much. She sounds nice. I had a long chat with her.'

'When?' I demanded.

'When she phoned the other day.'

'What did she talk about?'

'You.'

'What did you tell her?'

'What a loving boy you were.'

'I don't want her to know things about me,' I said. 'I've only known her a month.'

'I think she loves you.'

'Even more reason,' I insisted. A hooter sounded outside. 'That'll be her. 'Bye, Mum.' I kissed her on the cheek, then poked my head round the living-room door. Dad was sitting in front of the television. He was asleep.

'Tell Dad I said goodbye,' I said, opening the street door.

Beth was in a red car. She wound down her window and said hello. Not to me, but to my mum, who was rushing over to further the conversation. I got in the car as quickly as possible and waved the cinema tickets in the air. 'We'll be late,' I warned. 'The doors open at half past eight.'

'Then the film won't start till nine,' Beth said.

'But I have to see the trailers!'

Beth looked up at Mum. 'Everything has to be done his way,' she said.

'Always been the same,' Mum told her.

'Of all the boys to have as a boyfriend – '

'Hurry up!' I demanded.

The car pulled away.

'I wanted to talk to your Mum,' Beth moaned.

'Why?' I asked. 'You're going out with me, not her. And don't call me your boyfriend. I hate all those labels and things.'

'What are you afraid of?'

'I'm not afraid of anything.' I calmed down a little. 'I'm really looking forward to the film.'

'Yes, so am I,' Beth said. 'And now for the good news. Mum and Dad are out all night. So, after the film, we can just have a quick drink and go back. You can spend the whole night not being my boyfriend if you like.'

'Fine,' I said. 'Just hope you've got some chocolate biscuits in the fridge, that's all.'

'That's all you want me for. Chocolate biscuits. Oh, and my car of course.'

It took about half an hour to get from Bethnal Green to the West End of London. We managed to find a parking space in Beak Street and walked to Leicester Square.

The film was showing at the Odeon. The poster image was huge above the cinema entrance. I prickled all over when I saw it. I had to stand there for a while, just staring. The crowd bustled round me. Beth tugged at my sleeve. 'We going in or what?' she asked.

'Just look at that!' I exclaimed. 'What an image!'

'Forget the image,' she said. 'I'm still trying to work out what the title means.'

We went into the foyer. I bought a programme. Beth put her hand in my jacket pocket. 'What do you want?' I asked.

'Money,' she replied. 'I want some popcorn.'

'You're going to *eat*!' I cried, pulling away. 'You're going to *eat* during the *film*!'

'But I always have nibbles in the back row.'

'We're not sitting in the back row,' I told her.

She stared at me. There were tears in her eyes now. I would have comforted her, but I could hear the trailers beginning.

'Get your nibbles,' I said flatly.

She did so, and we went into the auditorium. Beth clutched my arm. The closer we got to the screen, the tighter her grip became. 'We're not sitting near the front, are we?' she asked.

'No,' I replied. 'We're sitting *at* the front. Right in the middle. It's the only way to see a film. It's got to overwhelm you. Fill your vision.'

We found our places and sat down.

'It's much too close,' complained Beth. 'All I can see are fuzzy dots.'

The trailers and adverts over, my stomach started to flutter in anticipation. As the light dimmed for the start of the film, I glanced at Beth to share the moment. She was squinting into her popcorn.

The curtain parted in front of us.

A dark screen.

Silence.

The titles began. White on black. Fading up, then down with majestic leisure. My heart was beating so hard my lapels were twitching.

Beth nudged my arm. 'The soundtrack must have broken,' she whispered.

'What?' I hissed, irritably.

'No music.'

'It hasn't started yet.'

'How do you know?'

At that moment, the music began. That ethereal, shimmering sound, as if the air itself was buzzing into life.

'Not much tune,' moaned Beth.

The music grew louder and louder. Closing in on all sides in delicious ambush. And then a thunder-blow of sound!

An explosion of light!

It was the best beginning to any film I had ever seen. This was pure cinema. A light and sound show. Light as bright as sand in your eyes. Music so loud you felt it in your lips. I heard the audience gasp behind me. A few laughed. Not in amusement, but in the spontaneous delight of experiencing perfection.

Beside me, Beth had dropped her popcorn.

'Made me fucking jump,' she said, brushing herself down.

'Shhh,' I demanded.

As the film unfolded I felt things unravel inside me. Every cut, every composition, every colour, the acting, the music, everything combined to produce one complete vision. A vision so beautiful it was terrifying.

And then the moment at Devil's Tower when, after all the smaller spacecraft have disappeared, everything goes completely quiet. I could feel the audience behind me hold its collective breath. We were there. At Devil's Tower. And something was about to happen.

I reached for Beth's hand. Yes, I did love her. The past month had been a joy. Her late-night phone-calls, her kisses, the way she tickled my back. Call me boyfriend, I thought. Make me belong. Untie the knot of my heart and lasso us together.

I threaded my fingers between hers and squeezed. She did not respond. I looked at her. She was asleep. I felt a betrayal so intense I wanted to continue squeezing until I heard bones snap and knuckles pop. But I merely let go and continued watching the screen.

A gentle rumbling was heard coming from the back of the cinema.

Someone in the film was saying, 'Oh, my God!' People in the audience were saying it too.

And then it appeared!

One of the greatest moments in cinema: the appearance of the Mother Ship. Two men behind me started talking. I spun round. 'Shut the fuck up!' I said.

'Free country,' whined one.

'Just shut up!'

'Paid me money,' whined the other.

Beth tugged at my sleeve. The argument must have woken her. 'Don't get in a state,' she said. 'You'll only cause more trouble.'

Relax, I thought. For the sake of the film. Relax.

On screen, aliens were appearing. The sight of them made me want to weep. Held in a crucifix pose, Richard Dreyfuss was taken into the Mother Ship.

Take me, I thought. Take me to your world. A world where you can play music as loud as you want, where people knock on your door and don't ask questions. A world where you don't have to be a boyfriend or girlfriend. A world where you hear in Dolby stereo and see in Technicolor. A world where they know how to go to the cinema. Where they sit in the front row and don't eat or talk or sleep. Take me to your heaven, I thought. Save me.

The Mother Ship began to rise. A cathedral ascending to starlight, becoming a star.

When Steven Spielberg's name appeared I clapped until my palms were sore. The credits started to roll.

Beth stood up. 'Come on,' she replied. 'I'm gasping.'

'The film's not over yet,' I insisted.

'It's only the credits.'

I didn't budge. Beth continued to stand. I waited until the last credit had gone and the curtains had closed. Only then did I get to my feet and start to leave the cinema.

I felt different. As if I was suffering from some kind of heartache or grief. A grief so glorious it had actually changed the shape of my heart.

Outside, the birds in Leicester Square were squalling. The sound hurt, not only my ears, but my skin. I wanted somewhere quiet and dark.

'Let's go to your place right away,' I said to Beth.

'No drink!' she exclaimed. Then, sensing something in my mood, added, 'All right. Chocolate biscuits here we come.'

We walked to the car in silence.

Because of the heavy traffic it took us more than twenty minutes to get out of the West End alone. As Beth lived in Whitechapel, we took the City route home. Driving down the Strand to St Paul's, I asked, 'Did you like the film?'

'Well, the beginning made me jump,' she replied, giggling.

'I noticed.'

'And I liked the child. I thought he was beautiful. Those eyes! Didn't you think he was wonderful?'

'Yes,' I said.

A pause.

'Anything else?' I said.

'Oh, I don't know.'

'Well, did you like the film or not?' I asked. 'It's not a difficult question.'

'In a word,' she replied. 'No.'

'Why?' I snapped.

'I just didn't. I can't explain. I know *you* liked it.'

'There was nothing *not* to like.'

'Oh, I knew this was going to happen,' she said. 'Don't cause an argument. You liked it and I didn't. What does it matter?'

'It matters a lot!' I exclaimed. 'We've just sat through the greatest cinematic experience ever. If you didn't like it, I want you to explain why.'

'I can't.'

'Try.'

'Can you explain why you did?'

'Yes,' I said. 'For a start, the script was well written and beautifully structured. Second, the photography by Vilmos Zsigmond was crystal clear, with blacks like velvet. Third, Douglas Trumbull's special effects were a revelation. Fourth, the acting by Richard Dreyfuss, Teri Garr and Melinda Dillon was very moving and totally believable. And, apart from anything else, it contained some of the best set pieces I have ever seen.'

We were passing through Bank now, heading for Aldgate.

'Set pieces?' queried Beth.

'The child's toys coming to life,' I explained. 'The lights rising behind Richard Dreyfuss's truck. The spacecraft coming round the mountain. Richard Dreyfuss kissing Teri Garr and looking up at the stars.'

'All right, all right,' interrupted Beth. 'Don't carry it on.'

Turning into Whitechapel Road.

'And,' I continued, 'don't forget the best bit of all.'

'Which is?' she asked.

'The appearance of the Mother Ship,' I told her. 'The bit you fucking slept through.'

Suddenly Beth turned into a side street. The tyres screeched as the car came to a halt. Beth was crying. She turned the engine off. I listened to her sob for a while.

'I'm sorry,' I said softly.

'No, you're not,' she said breathlessly. 'You might think you are. But you're not. You think I deserve it. But … I can't stand it any more. All I wanted was a Saturday night out. But not you. Oh no. Not you. Everything's like a test with you. I feel I have to prove myself all the time.'

'Don't exaggerate.'

'I'm not exaggerating. I know what you think of me. You think I'm fucking stupid because I don't know directors' names and things like that. But you … you never ask me anything about myself. You know more about that film than you do about me. Well, I'll tell you, I might not know what set pieces are, but I know one thing. That film was about communication. That's what those aliens were trying to do. Communicate. Trying to find a way of making … making one heart speak … to another. But you … you … ' She was sobbing so hard she found it difficult to speak.

I put my arm around her.

She shrugged it off. 'I'd rather go out with one of them than you,' she said. She got a tissue and wiped the tears from her face. 'All this because I didn't like the film. It's not a crime, you know.'

'It's not a crime,' I found myself saying. 'It's a sin.'

'Oh, get out!' she yelled, pushing me. 'Get out! I don't want to see you again!'

'Don't, Beth –'

'Fuck off!'

I opened the door and got out. The night was cold and it had started to rain. The engine started and the car pulled away.

Suddenly I was chasing after it. Running as fast as I could down the Whitechapel Road. 'Beth!' I screamed. 'Stop! Stop!'

The car pulled up at some traffic lights. Beth rolled down the window. 'What?' she sobbed.

'I forgot my programme,' I said.

She grabbed the programme and flung it at me.

'Bastard!' she cried.

I walked down Vallance Road. It was raining quite heavily now. I felt a tightening in my chest that told me an asthma attack was on the way. By the time I reached Bethnal Green Road I could hardly breathe. My breath was coming in painful gasps. I had to rest after every few steps.

I was soaked by the time I got home, and so short of oxygen I felt faint. I closed the front door behind me and fell to my knees. The programme was nothing but a soggy mush in my fist.

Mum, who could tell if something was wrong just by the way I put my key in the lock, came rushing down the stairs in her night-dress. Before she even saw me she was asking, 'Where's the inhaler?'

I had too little breath to answer. Instead, I just looked at her.

'Take your time,' she coaxed. 'Relax.'

Finally, I managed 'Leather jacket.'

Mum ran upstairs, got the inhaler, and woke Dad. The two of them came down. Dad held my head while Mum tried to spray some Ventolin into my mouth. The first attempt got into my mouth, but, as I wasn't breathing in, it didn't reach my lungs. Mum asked if I could do it myself. I shook my head. My arms felt numb. Mum took aim again. This time, I inhaled the Ventolin. Breathing immediately became easier.

Dad picked me up and carried me upstairs. My brother and his girlfriend were standing on the landing, bleary-eyed and half naked.

'What's wrong?' asked my brother. 'Is he all right?'

'He's fine,' replied Dad. 'Go back to sleep.'

Dad laid me on my bed, then propped the pillows up behind me. Mum turned the electric fan on and aimed it at my face. I was now able to use the inhaler myself, and breathed in three more lungfuls of Ventolin.

'You can go,' Mum told Dad.

Dad nodded, then left.

'I told you to take the inhaler with you,' Mum said, annoyed now that the worst was over. She took what was left of the programme from my hand and threw it away. Then she got a towel from the bathroom and started to dry my hair. 'Have you had an argument with Beth?' she asked.

'Yes,' I replied.

Mum rubbed my hair harder. 'Didn't she like the film?'

'No.'

My hair dry, Mum put the towel down. 'Beth loves you,' she said. 'I could tell that by the way she spoke about you. You can't carry on like this. You expect too much from people.'

'But the film was a masterpiece,' I said. 'I don't understand how anyone could *not* like it.'

'You don't have to understand what you love,' Mum said, stroking my hair. 'Just the loving is enough. You know your trouble? You want it all. And life's not like that.'

My heart was beating very fast from the Ventolin. Mum lay her hand on my chest. 'Are you all right?' she asked.

'I don't know,' I said softly.

'Do you want anything? Tea? Chocolate biscuits?'

'No,' I replied, 'I just want ... I ... ' My voice trailed away.

'What, darling? Tell me.'

'I ... I ... ' I began, then took a deep breath and continued. 'They met at a place called Devil's Tower. They sang to each other. It was very beautiful.'

'I bet it was,' Mum said, smiling. She kissed me, turned out the light, and left.

I stared at the ceiling for a while. Then I got up and looked out of the window. It had stopped raining by now and the night was clear.

My face was reflected in the window. It stared down at me from the night sky, larger than any spacecraft. A petrified face, full of moonlight and brittle with stars.

Alien, I thought.

Philippe Rousselot

A portrait of Julia Roberts

First the two eyes, before the mouth. Two brown eyes, the roundness of the iris contrasting with the oval of what surrounds it. Then, as if there were a set path that guides the visiting of a face, one's gaze descends along two symmetrical lines tracing the high cheek-bones overlooking the sunken cheeks, which separate light from dark, the convex from the concave. Then the lips, the higher dominating the lower. After the eyes, the mouth is the second factor dominating the face. After the gaze, speech. The nose is straight and long, a little turned-up at the end, with large nostrils.

A shadow above the mouth, because of the curl of the lip. During a smile, it unfurls itself like a wave on a beach. A bluish shadow under the eyes reinforces the golden luminosity of the skin.

The face arranges itself more easily into triangles than cubes, upside-down triangles resting on their points, each triangle linked to its neighbour as if by invisible hinges, creating an ensemble of stability in movement and a coherence of functions.

Every face operates from a mechanism built upon a structure. Painters know very well that both the mechanism and the structure convey something imponderable: an 'other' who can only be made to appear by reconstructing both elements. The analysis, deconstruction and fragmentation engendered by verbal description only describe the materials with which the face is built, and miss the architecture, everything that reveals the order and disorder of a world and a being.

Studying this architecture closely, one constantly questions how these forms operate, the power they have to show what is beyond voluntary gestures (the expression, the performance of an actress), what comes before the look, what survives after it, what has always been the way of being of a face in relation to the world and to time.

It's early morning and she arrives on set, still garlanded by sleep, her hair flattened, ready for the wig. The vapours from the working lights give off a feeble illumination, fall like cold rain from the ceiling, and create incoherent shadows on her face. The face is closed up, looking back at the past, at sleep. The whole long silhouette, made clumsy by the denim dungarees, seems to want to curl around an imaginary pillow. The set is not yet ready to be looked at, but makes itself available for conversations, greetings, for the day's roll-call. For half an hour, there's the operation of starting, of launching the day.

The set is a building site. It's as if it were recovering from a disaster that had occurred the previous evening. Everyone waits to be told what to do. In the absence of costumes, make-up and certainty, the actors only pretend, and live within the mere envelope of their characters. The camera occupies notional positions, chalk-marks on the ground; the lights stay dumb on their stands. The face hides, the nose is lowered, the mouth shut, the eyes furtively seek an imaginary means of escape. The simulation of the tasks to come becomes almost a caricature, and the face refuses to take part in the act. Suddenly, it's a stampede. She is no longer in the centre of things, but swallowed up by a small group of make-up artists, hairdresser, wardrobe, who usher her through a little door. Then starts the countdown to the first shot.

Absence

During her absence, lighting means finding the face in one's memory, reinventing it, rediscovering the essential lines, the structure, the mechanism. But the memory delivers only a fixed, immobile, two-dimensional picture, the kind of image that will be reproduced on screen, an image impossible to travel around and whose expression never changes. Lighting in her absence means playing with a fixed image and knowing that her return will make a mockery of you. When she does, the image in one's memory will disintegrate, not so much because of the unlikeness, but because of its present completeness, because of its rediscovered third dimension. And this face, now moving in the light, triggers disquiet, and this disquiet will make us move, make us anxious, an anxiety contrasting with the desire to fix the movement, image after image, and to keep each one immobile in the memory. The desire to possess the other, her face, is accompanied by the knowledge that such immobilization, such appropriation is impossible: 'The face resists possession, resists my powers. In its epiphany, what is sensible – which is still catchable – transforms itself into a total resistance to being caught.' [1]

But filming a face isn't just a matter of making an addition of twenty-four frames a second. There comes a moment when one must give in and let oneself float away from a reality which is no longer controlling itself, when one must resign oneself to being less, to being just a somewhat sympathetic observer, and leave on tiptoe.

Return

The face made-up, powdered, the hair dressed, the body clothed, re-dressed,

[1] Emmanuel Levinas.

disguised, masked. The face would like to be something else, red hair tumbling over the shoulders, is looking to group itself with the Pre-Raphaelites, Burne-Jones, Rossetti most of all, and makes all kinds of shapes, characters, images, references, before immutably becoming itself again, strengthened by these brief incarnations and appearances, having absorbed them and enriched itself with them.

Concentration

Three minutes before the shot. For three seconds perhaps I look at her. She is gazing into space, a gaze which looks at nothing, but which sees, no doubt, what will be tomorrow on screen, which sees itself, which sees what it will show. A moment when the face invites one to look elsewhere, to gaze into the invisible. The presence of a third party begins to be felt, the person to come.

To film a face is to surrender to a monologue which doesn't wish to be heard, to speak to someone who is speaking to another, who is uttering a mute language which will transfer into a silent picture and which silences the person who, in the absence of a listener, has chosen to pull the switch, to 'turn over'.

Lighting

But what does light change, whether it comes from the right or the left, from above or below? It's still the same face, the infinity of images it inspires with a little less or a little more shadow. In its multiple variations, light changes nothing. It is the face in movement which moves the light and the shadows.

The repositioning of light-sources only accomplishes a labour of detail, speaks only of itself, and leaves the face indifferent. But one moves a light a little and suddenly the face disappears, not in shadow, where it would still continue to exist, but somewhere else, leaving only the appearance of an unrecognizable, indecipherable face. A disappearance giving way to abstract signs, to a form one doesn't even try to recognize any more, which no longer contains the emotion always present in a being. By excess, the light hasn't modified the face but destroyed it. In the changing light the face is always itself, completely or not at all, but it is never something else, never different.

And that is where responsibility lies, the responsibility of restoring not only the face, but also the gaze, its own gaze, which during the film will discover, question and recognize.

To film a face is to give oneself over to an encounter where all violence disappears and an infinite responsibility is born.

Knitting

Between takes, she knits amidst a coterie of knitters, a little school set up amongst the cables and the consoles, in the draught created by the cooling machines, a little symposium of which she is the centre and where she conveys the knowledge of knit and purl. She raises her eyes from her work and looks around as one would look around the place one wakes up in after a dream, when one's on holiday, reassured that one's in a friendly place. She looks around at others, and her look demands one should look at her in the same way, smiling and surprised.

Tears

She's been crying since this morning. Judging from the call-sheet, this might last three days. A cemetery, a vale of tears, wetness, the face weeps, and everyone keeps their distance as if they were respecting a real loss, a real pain, or perhaps to avoid contamination. What difference is there between a real loss, a real pain, and these images?

The mouth is dumb, the ears don't hear, but the eyes, searching for something just as untraceable, for a lost communication, never rest. They show us a pain, a fracture, an entire sensibility exposed. It puts paid to all clumsy reflections on beauty, which the shadows digging under the eyes, the red lines under the eyelids, and the tears glittering like silver in the light do not diminish.

Face

To light a face is to push a phenomenology to its extreme. It's an experience which constantly destroys itself for the benefit of an experience to come, where the aesthetic finality underpinning the phrase 'to film a face' gives way to the relationship with the other, and the infinite responsibility which that other requires.

It's an agitated, anxious contemplation. The gaze resting on the face (and the act of filming reinforces the feeling the face inspires in me) brings with it a hope rejecting all knowledge.

The work of lighting and composition leads one to an admission of what is and always has been, which makes one forget the work for the benefit of the face itself, now rediscovered.

(With thanks to Julia Roberts and Stephen Frears.)

David O. Russell

The Heartbreak Kid

When I was making *Spanking the Monkey*, I had favourite films like *The Graduate*, *The 400 Blows* and *Knife in the Water* in the back of my mind – strangely unloving families in the first two, and unpredictable, subtly-played sexual triangles in *Knife* and *The Graduate*.

Right now I'm in production on *Flirting with Disaster*, and its closest ancestor for me is probably Elaine May's *The Heartbreak Kid*, which my mother took me to on a Sunday matinée in 1972. It's probably one of the darkest things Neil Simon has ever written, and also, in my opinion, Charles Grodin's most original and disturbing performance. The movie beautifully walks the line between emotional pain and perverse comedy as Grodin's character falls in love with an icy blonde, played by Cybill Shepherd, while he's on his Miami honeymoon with his vulnerable and sincere wife (May's daughter Jeannie Berlin). The emotional brutality and black comedy of this film, and others like it in the early seventies (*Five Easy Pieces*, *Klute*, *Carnal Knowledge*), is what

The Heartbreak Kid: Charles Grodin with the wife (Jeannie Berlin) ...

interests me greatly, much more than the graphic/ironic violence of the eighties and nineties.

Grodin plays the consummate male narcissist in all his contradictions: he seems sincere, reasonable, even justified at times, as he pursues his cruel path of desire, and we cannot help rooting for him much of the time, I think, even as we cringe at the results – sort of like how we couldn't help rooting for *Bonnie and Clyde* or the gangsters in *The Godfather*. But the film consistently walks both sides of the line, finally showing us how pathetic Grodin's character is in the end, when he marries Cybill Shepherd, and how he is the same lost, unfulfilled schmuck he was at the beginning, when we'd hoped, along with him, that this amazing blonde might actually be the answer to his anguish. So much of movie culture sells sex as the answer to whatever ails us: gay sex, straight sex, the blonde or the hunk, or the homely but well-suited mate. Films that expose this lie are few and far between, and this is one of the best. I also love the spare, almost blunt, way that the film is directed.

... and the icy blonde (Cybill Shepherd).

Vincent Sherman

Bette Davis

I was having lunch at the writers' table in the Green Room at Warner Brothers studios during the last week of directing my third film, *The Man Who Talked Too Much*, a B picture with George Brent, who had been borrowed from the A department. It was a remake of an old film (*The Great Mouthpiece*) and we both disliked it, but to refuse to do it would have meant suspension (taken off salary) and incurring the wrath of Jack Warner, which we both wanted to avoid.

I was feeling depressed, when I felt a tap on my shoulder and turned to see Bette Davis standing behind me.

'Are you Vincent Sherman?' she asked.

I nodded, and quickly got to my feet.

'I'm Bette Davis,' she said.

I smiled at her modesty. She continued: 'George tells me that he has never worked as hard or enjoyed himself more.' (She and Brent were good friends, said to have been lovers at one time.)

I was overwhelmed, but recovered for long enough to reply.

'It's also a great pleasure for me working with George.'

'I was wondering,' she said. 'They want me to do a comedy as my next film. Maybe you could read the script, and if you like it I'll ask Hal Wallis' – the executive producer at WB – 'to let us do it together.'

Suddenly the sun burst through on to my clouded future. I wanted to shout Hallelujah, but controlled myself.

'It would be a great honour and privilege to work with you, Miss Davis.'

She smiled, and with a twinkle in her eye said, 'They just haven't caught up with me yet.' She returned to her table as I stood mesmerized and watched her.

Later I read the script, entitled *Affectionately Yours*, hated it, thought it would be a disaster for everyone concerned, and let it be known that I'd refuse to make it (a B picture, even with George Brent, no one would expect much from, but an A film with Bette Davis – expectations would be high). This led to a confrontation with Wallis, a formidable executive. He was appalled that a B director would turn down a chance to direct Bette Davis, and demanded that I write her a letter praising the screenplay, but excusing myself from directing it because of lack of experience. The details and aftermath of this, including Bette's strange reaction (ignoring me), are both shocking and amusing.

Old Acquaintance: Hopkins and Davis.

However, she was soon cast in a different film, and *Affectionately Yours* was made with Merle Oberon starring and Lloyd Bacon directing.

Two years later, after I had directed *All Through the Night* with Humphrey Bogart and *The Hard Way* with Ida Lupino – for which Ida won the New York Film Critics' Award – I had become an A director, and was sent the screenplay of *Old Acquaintance*, to be made with Bette Davis and Miriam Hopkins.

They had been successful with *The Old Maid*, directed by Edmund Goulding a year or two before, and the studio saw the possibility of another profitable film.

It was the Golden Age of picture-making in Hollywood. Each studio had its own roster of stars male and female, supporting players, writers, producers, directors, cameramen, scenic artists, wardrobe and make-up people, and all the facilities for production: paint shops, carpenter shops, prop shops, greeneries, exteriors, and façades of dirty tenements, New York brownstones, western streets, various foreign streets, as well as apartments, office buildings, churches, almost any locale you could desire. Also, twenty stages with a variety of interior sets, even a ranch for vast vistas.

I was happy to be making *Old Acquaintance,* and especially pleased to be directing Bette Davis, whom I had admired for a long time. She was not a great beauty in the conventional sense, but to me the most provocative, intriguing, appealing and desirable actress in Hollywood. Her energy, passion, fury, vulnerability, were incredible. She could be hard and ruthless, as in *Human Bondage* and *The Little Foxes*, soft and sympathetic as in *Now Voyager*, confused and tragic as in *Dark Victory*, saucy and arrogant as in *Jezebel*. Her emotional power was tremendous.

The conflict between Bette and Miriam Hopkins was well-known – their past relationship, the petty jealousy and plain bitchiness. Most of the time I was able to handle it tactfully, but one day, when they were sparring for favourable camera positions, I said so that everyone heard me, 'Ladies, there are times when I feel I'm not *directing* this picture but *refereeing* it!'

Bette roared with laughter, which endeared her to me, but Miriam was glum. And so it went on until Miriam was finished on the film.

A few weeks later, on a Saturday morning as I was approaching the end of the film (we worked Saturdays in those days), Jack Warner called me and requested that I try to finish the film that night, even if we had to work late. I said I was willing, if Bette would agree. She did, but asked if afterwards I would drop her off at her mother's house on Laurel Canyon (I lived on the Hollywood side of the canyon).

It was after two a.m. Sunday morning when we actually finished. On the way home, as we approached a Simon's drive-in restaurant, she said, 'I'm starving. Could we stop for a hamburger?' We stopped, gave our order to a waitress. Bette lit a cigarette. We sat quietly for a moment, then she spoke. 'Well, Mr Sherman,' she began, her voice lively and enthusiastic, 'it was fun working with you, except for a few bad moments with Miriam, but you handled her beautifully, and I love you.'

'I love you too,' I replied, thinking she merely meant friendly approval.

'You don't understand,' she said, her voice now solemn and subdued as she put her hand on mine. 'I mean I really love you!'

It was such a surprise and shock to me, I became confused and almost speechless. I finally blurted out a banal 'I'm flattered beyond words.'

For me, it was a most difficult moment. I was happily married, with a darling three-year-old daughter. It could not have been easy for Bette either. She was also married, to Arthur Farnsworth, a handsome, charming New Englander, whom I had met and talked with several times.

How things worked out, the anxiety and anguish of all concerned, the accidental death of Farnsworth, Bette's feelings of guilt, her temporary hatred of me, the conflict between us during the making of *Mr Skeffington*, which I directed, and our eventual love-affair, I have tried to tell honestly in my autobiography.[1]

1 To be published by the University of Kentucky Press.

Mr Skeffington: Davis and Richard Waring.

The end of our relationship came when she told me that Warner thought *Skeffington* was great, but I said I had reservations.

'Oh, you're too close to it,' she observed. 'Anyway, he wants us to do *Stolen Life* together.'

I hesitated, then said, 'Okay, if we can have an understanding.'

'About what?' she demanded.

I explained that during *Old Acquaintance* she had behaved beautifully, never questioned any direction I gave her, approved of everything I suggested, but on *Skeffington*, filled with guilt about her husband's death and taking it out on me (even before we had begun our affair), she had thwarted me. I was not satisfied with her performance, and did not want to go through it again: 'I want you to let me direct as I see the story.'

'Do you want me to do everything you tell me, as if I was some young starlet?'

'I have never asked you or any other actor to do anything that I could not give you a good reason for.'

She thought for a moment, suddenly tightened, and said furiously, 'Well, if that's the way you feel about it!', turned away angrily, got into her car, and drove off in a huff. It was the end of our professional relationship.

Her performance in *Old Acquaintance* was, I think, excellent, and closer to her own personality than any other role she'd ever done. And despite all the trouble we had during *Mr Skeffington*, she and Claude Rains were nominated for Academy Awards.

Her personal life was a tragic mess. She was married four times, but was never genuinely happy for long. Her relationship with her daughter was especially painful for her.

I am happy to have known her, worked with her, and held her in my arms. There will never be another like her.

David Siegel and Scott McGehee

Mirage

Mirage: Gregory Peck.

Before we realized we loved Edward Dmytryk's 1965 film *Mirage*, it was already for us an ideal example of a mid-sixties modern paranoid aesthetic. Along with John Frankenheimer's 1966 *Seconds*, Samuel Fuller's 1963 *Shock Corridor*, and a few more obscure Japanese art films and detective dramas, it was part of the package of black and white films we looked to for guidance in imagining the world of our film *Suture*. The style of this group of films is unmistakably post-*noir*, no doubt influenced by the French New Wave and other European art films, but still retaining some of the composure of classic Hollywood: modernist, empty, formalist, polished, timidly abstract. What is exciting for us about these films is the way they are able to construct a world that is at once two worlds: one is fully imagined (if somewhat austere and under-nourished) and capable of holding our interest as a site for characters and an entertaining Hollywood-style plot; simultaneously, another, more abstracted world is opened up, a site where over-nourished metaphors and subtexts can thrive – and, at times, even compete with the characters and plot for our attention. Within this class of films, *Mirage* is something of the under-achiever, and perhaps this is why we've grown so fond of it. Its two worlds are uneasily out of balance, with a ridiculously thin plot competing against sub-texts and metaphors of awesome power. In the end, even though the plot seems (unfairly) to win, the power of the repressed abstraction lingers on.

The truly saving grace of *Mirage*'s awkward story is that it centres on amne-sia, which of course has an enormous appeal right off the bat, but also allows much of the movie to progress while the more absurd aspects of the plot remain thankfully 'forgotten'. The background story, which we don't learn completely until the film's final scene, goes something like this: David Stillwell (played by Gregory Peck) is a brilliant 'physio-chemist'. He has been working for the world-peace-seeking philanthropist Charles Calvin in a lab in California for the past two years, and has discovered a way to 'neutralize nuclear radiation at the source'. Upon returning to New York with the formu-la scrawled on a nice large piece of notebook paper, he discovers that his boss/hero actually has a boss of his own, a man referred to as 'the Major', head of an evil, money-driven corporation called Unidyne, in whose building Calvin has his office. In a meeting alone with Calvin, Stillwell realizes that, if the Major gets his hands on the formula, nuclear disaster will surely ensue. At precisely this moment, the power in the building is cut (a ploy by the Major to keep Stillwell from leaving), and in the darkness of Calvin's twenty-seventh-floor office, Stillwell sets the prized formula on fire and lets it drift out the open window. Calvin panics, lunges for the burning document, and falls screaming to his death. The horror of watching his hero fall is too much for Stillwell, who instantly represses the entire incident and in an amnesia-driven blur spontaneously constructs a safe life for himself: he has been working as a Cost Accountant at an office in the Unidyne building for the last two years, living all alone in the New York apartment he left vacant when he moved to California.

It is at this time – the time of Stillwell's repression and the onset of his amne-sia – that *Mirage* actually begins. But of course we know nothing of the com-plicated details of Stillwell's story.

All we see as the film opens are the sparkling lights of a New York evening skyline as one large skyscraper goes completely dark. We then cut quickly inside to a stopped elevator, a pitch-black hallway on the twenty-seventh floor, and giddy office workers coming out of their offices holding flashlights and planning sexy 'Braille parties' in the dark ('You know, the "touch" system?'). David Stillwell emerges from one office, has a short and confusing conversation with a delightfully smarmy colleague named Josephson (Kevin McCarthy), and starts into the darkened stairwell with only his penlight, meeting a beautiful and mysterious woman (Diane Baker) who thinks she knows his voice. After twenty-seven flights of pitch-black conversation the two reach the light of the world outside, where she now recognizes his face, seems confused by his insistence on not knowing her, then flees in frustration. A confused Stillwell follows her down four more flights into the sub-basements – sub-basements that prove not to exist when he returns to the fully-lit scene a short time later. This confusion seems magnified by the fact that almost every person that Stillwell has bumped into has greeted him as if he's been away a long time. Standing in the subway (where else?) on the way home, a newspaper account of his (forgotten) boss's death causes a chain of associations that plays beautifully as a sort of 'montage of repression': Calvin falls from the twenty-seventh floor; a water-melon breaks open as it hits the ground; and finally we descend down the missing stairwell into the four (now clearly psychological) sub-basements.

Aside from being one of the most inspired film openings either of us can remember, the opening of *Mirage* sets out a rich, more or less Freudian landscape within which this drama will unfold, and turns the city itself into a kind of oversized model of pathological psychology. Shot in a very post-*noir* black and white style – lit with an open and stark harshness that seems to delineate a world under clinical examination – the disease of this landscape seems endlessly to expand, with pointed reminders of urban alienation and anxiety lurking behind every automated elevator door. Public parks, where much of the action takes place, are bisected by menacing highways filled with speeding automobiles. Familiar phone numbers are answered by recorded voices announcing disconnected lines. Refrigerators in apartments are randomly full or empty each time they are opened. The inner city is called 'the Incubator' and no one seems to know anyone's name.

Most of the disorientation of the film's opening is eventually explained away by the diagnosis of amnesia. But the real power of the opening is that we don't yet have that explanation. Something seems to be wrong: Stillwell seems to have an unsettlingly empty life as a Cost Accountant. But even as the diagnosis 'amnesia' suggests itself, the competing hypothesis that Stillwell is instead suffering from modernism, or urbanism, is equally compelling – and equally supported by the tone of the film. When he finally goes to a psychiatrist and confesses that 'For the last two years I've been completely alone – eating alone, spending my nights alone – and I've never questioned it,' the symptoms bear a haunting similarity to modern lives as we know them.

By the end of the film, of course, he has remembered the entire set of events that led to his amnesia, thus completing his cure. Sanity, the psychiatrist has told us, is simply a matter of knowing right from wrong, and Stillwell demonstrates this capacity with great facility in a big final confrontation with the Major. He eventually makes an impassioned, almost Capra-esque speech about commitment ('If you're not committed to anything, you're just taking up space', etc.) which even rallies the smarmy corporate low-life Josephson to the just cause. As the film closes, we are to understand that, in fact, Stillwell isn't a lonely and alienated modern urban man, but is instead a hero, a brave and gifted physio-chemist who has saved the world from inevitable nuclear destruction and stood up for all that is right and good. He even gets Diane Baker crawling back to him full of apologies for her past unworthiness, desperately in love.

It's a perfectly happy ending, and on one level it successfully and directly addresses the problem the film has set out to address: when our world is alienating and insane, how do we remain human? *Through commitment to ideals.* The film itself seems to demonstrate this kind of commitment.

But this answer is just too simple to accommodate *Mirage*'s vividly-imagined version of the problem. And ultimately that disparity is both the film's failure and its success. The villain of the subtext – which is none other than progress, modernity, and the city itself – finally has a presence so much more substantial than the straw-man Major and his silly Unidyne conglomerate that it undermines the trite conclusion, takes over the film, and follows us home. And in the process, we would argue, it turns an interesting movie about amnesia into something truly unforgettable.

Mirage: Diane Baker and Gregory Peck.

Steven Soderbergh

The Third Man

One of the amazing things about *The Third Man* is that it really is a great film, in spite of all the people who say it's a great film. Disillusion, betrayal, misdirected sexual longing, and the wilful inability of Americans to understand or appreciate other cultures – these are a few of my favourite things, and *The Third Man* blends them all seamlessly with an airtight plot and a location that blurs the line between beauty and decay. I'll also throw down the gauntlet and say that I think *The Third Man* represents the best work any of the principal participants ever did: Carol Reed, Graham Greene, Robert Krasker, Joseph Cotten, Orson Welles, (Alida) Valli, Trevor Howard *et al*, and if you object, I'll release a transcript of the first time you ever tried to talk someone into sleeping with you. So think about it for a minute and then agree with me – it'll be much easier on all of us.

The Third Man: the final scene.

276

James Toback

Alain Delon

Plein Soleil.

I am not, to my knowledge, a homosexual. And yet, if film is revelatory of the subliminal and the libidinous, I must be wary of such reductive simplicities. For the provocative icons of my formative cinematic years were – despite considerable excitement for women (Marlene Dietrich, Natalie Wood, Tuesday Weld, the Dorléac sisters) – fully as likely to be men: Gary Cooper, Alan Ladd, Cary Grant, James Stewart (the Stewart of the Anthony Mann westerns), James Dean. And the two strongest forces on my imagination, the two last, were both male: Warren Beatty and Alain Delon. Since Beatty has, over the years, become not only one of my closest friends but also a significant part of my own movie career, a natural process of demystification has occurred, a process which shifts the erotic component central to all cinematic hypnosis from the unconscious to the conscious, and therefore places it under one's control.

Alain Delon, for better or worse, has remained tantalizingly out of reach. When I called Truffaut in 1980 to thank him for having written about *Fingers* as one of his favourite films, I suggested that we meet. No, he said, he didn't think that would be a good idea: 'Let's continue to communicate with each other through our films.'

I don't know which of my own movies Alain Delon may have seen (let alone which, if any, found their way into his bloodstream). I do know that he has, for three decades, continued to communicate with me through his films. Eyes, hair, walk, rhythm, voice – the lover/killer with the beautiful face, sculpted body and broken heart of stone.

If he is something of a French institution (French factory might be a harsher, if equally accurate, characterization), churning out during the seventies and eighties a TV-like plethora of walk (or run)-through films, much of his work has not been great or close to good. And yet even in his American *oeuvre*, *Texas Across the River*, *The Yellow Rolls-Royce*, *William Wilson* and the less dreary – but still mediocre – *Once a Thief*, I sat riveted, rapt. His best films are masterpieces: *Le Samouraï, Plein Soleil, The Leopard*. Each induced multiple viewings and an almost fetishistic concentration on detail: the light-blue shirt, white pants, and nervous sweat of *Plein Soleil*; the red bandanna and narcissistically confident smile of *The Leopard*; the empty, interior spaces of *Le Samouraï*.

Where is all this deflected homo-eroticism leading? Surely not to sex. Perhaps to film. In 1982, when I was preparing *Exposed* (whose cinematographer, Henri Decae, I chose in large part because it was he who – through *Le Samouraï* and *Plein Soleil* – had introduced me to Delon), I made some oddly deflected overtures, with an eye to getting Delon to play opposite Nastassja Kinski. But the response was muddled, Rudolf Nureyev entered my life (and the picture), and a start date was fixed.

What this sort of personal – irrational – way of film viewing, this para-judgmental response to people on the screen, reveals is, finally, not just a particular and/or peculiar predilection for one actress or actor, and not just a part of one's self to different parts of one's self; but rather it reveals something fundamental about why movie-watching has been addictive to so many millions of people during its century. It, more than any other art form, can cut beneath the familiar and safe layers of perception about those Others Out There – those five and a half billion strangers – and for a moment, or a hundred and twenty moments, connect us to one of them perfectly, on our own terms, in absolute harmony, with none of the messy disappointments and sudden disasters that real love inevitably entails.

Michael Tolkin

Ward Bond and others

Ward Bond was a great actor. Allan Jenkins was a great actor too. So was Charlie Ruggles. Barton MacLane was a great actor. William Bendix was a great actor, but he starred in too many films, so maybe I shouldn't count him. Walter Brennan was a great actor, but Ward Bond was an especially great actor because he never got to do as much, which is what makes him so great. Bond never got as close to John Wayne as Brennan did in *Red River*. Maybe I'm wrong. This is all from memory.

Alan Hale!

If Ward Bond was ever the main attraction in a film, I've never seen it. I can't even think of that many movies outside of John Ford's westerns where Bond had much of a part, but in *My Darling Clementine* he has one of the great moments in the history of film. Henry Fonda is at one end of the bar

My Darling Clementine: Ward Bond, in the background behind Victor Mature.

with Victor Mature. Mature could shoot him, but Fonda introduces Tim Holt – Tim Holt! another angel – holding a gun, and then says, 'That good-looking one over there, that's my brother Morg.' And then brother Morgan, Ward Bond, tips his hat, with his gun I think. Unbelievable moment.

Thomas Mitchell ... what an artist! In one year he played Scarlett O'Hara's father and the drunk doctor in *Stagecoach*. Later he was replaced in the same kind of roles by Edmund O'Brien, who was also a great actor. Edmund O'Brien as the drunken newspaper publisher in *The Man Who Shot Liberty Vallance*. What a performance!

So many great actors! Brian Donlevy was a great actor. You know that scene in *The Big Combo* where Richard Conte turns off the hearing aid, and the soundtrack dies as Donlevy sees the flash of the tommy-guns that are killing him. Tell me that his acting isn't as good as anyone's, at any time.

Now the movies aren't really a puppet show any more, so the stock characters, and the stock players, can't do their work in the same restricted parts, so the acting isn't as much fun to watch; everyone is so serious, serious, serious. Everyone is showing off.

Did Charlie Ruggles ever show off? Never. Franklin Pangborn? Never. William Demarest? King Donovan? Louis Calhern? John McIntire? Frank

The Big Combo: Brian Donlevy and Richard Conte.

McHugh? Of course they showed off, they were actors, but did they mug? I never saw it.

Let's talk about Frank McHugh for a minute. Let's remember him. He was a towering artist too, don't let his name slide away. Mr Sensible Advice in a clear tenor, Mr Loyalty. So loyal that I don't think he was ever killed in a movie; what a violation for him if he'd been killed off! Cruelty, needless cruelty. Did Allen Jenkins ever die in a film? I don't think so. Why? Immortal. Angels, really. Cabalistic definition of angels: packets of divine energy with a single purpose. So, angels.

And Donald Crisp.

Heroes all. Angels all.

Did Frank McHugh ever let you down?

Never.

Vincent Ward[1]

Wrong Move

There's a series of moments in a train in Wim Wenders's film *Wrong Move* (aka *Wrong Movement*) where the protagonist sees some drops of blood on the seat across from him (obviously left there by someone). Some time later he sees a careworn, middle-aged man holding his bleeding nose in the same compartment. The man says, 'You'd like to know why my nose is bloody. It comes from remembering. Maybe I'll tell you at breakfast tomorrow. Do you know the story of St Januarius, whose blood is kept in a Neapolitan church? It becomes fluid once a year on the anniversary of his death.' The careworn man starts to cry, and we learn he was a soldier during the Second World War and that, although he saved some Jews (if they were professionally qualified), he also sent a Jewish friend to his death.

What remains with you are the drops of blood and the tremendous sense of shame and loss of the old man, which is conveyed in a more powerful way than the whole of *Schindler's List* – a film I also respect. There is an amazing economy of words and images here that somehow distils the shame of a nation in a face and a few drops of blood.

1 Vincent Ward's mother was a Jewish refugee who fled Germany in 1932.

Fred Zinnemann

I used to go to the cinema each week with my father. I must have been about five years old, because I remember people talking about the *Titanic* and looking at the sun's eclipse through pieces of glass blackened by candle-smoke. I remember the first time I went, clutching a ham sandwich. It was a silent film with Asta Nielsen. Three people played music. I still remember the piece and the man spraying the air with his spray-pump, making the place smell like a pine forest. Much later I heard the piece again – it was the *larghetto* from Beethoven's Second Symphony. It was like meeting an old friend.

Among the films which made the greatest impression on me in the formative years were *Intolerance* and *Battleship Potemkin*. I was shocked by the injustice, but not in a direct political sense. It was more a matter of man's cruelty to his fellow men. For some reason, during most of my life I kept turning to films about how war twists people's innermost souls. This happened for forty years from *The Seventh Cross* (1943), *Act of Violence* (1948), *The Search* (1948), *The Men* (1950), *Teresa* (1951), *From Here to Eternity* (1953), *A Hatful of Rain* (1957) and *Julia* (1976) and on to the unrealized project about the repatriation of the Cossacks to Stalin after the Second World War.

Another film that formed my character was Dreyer's *Passion of Joan of Arc*. If anything, conscience has been a theme in my films: the Marshal in *High Noon*, Prewitt in *From Here to Eternity*, Thomas More and Julia among others.

Perhaps the problem with films today is that there is no longer a shared system of belief. Most often, the people in the audience go out as empty as they were when they entered the cinema. Perhaps it is because there is no longer a feeling of Good or Bad, or of Retribution, in most pictures; like ships without a compass, many films wallow in heavy seas without knowing where they are going or why. But in this, we the film-makers are as always reflecting the spirit of the times.

It is not for film-makers to provide the answer, but without a doubt we must insist on asking the questions again and again.

After all these years, it still seems to me that if the best of cinema is about anything, it is about saying Yes to the human spirit.

(From a conversation with Walter Donohue.)

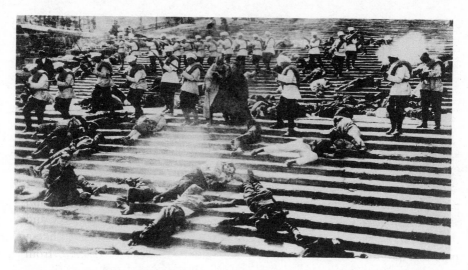

Eisenstein's *Battleship Potemkin.*

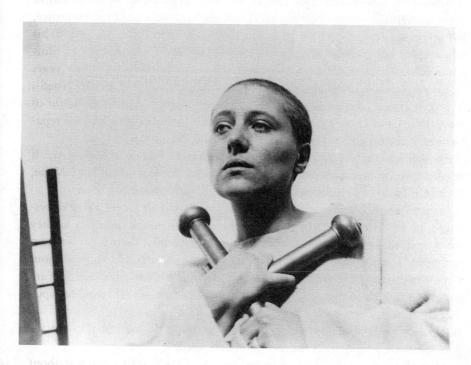

Dreyer's *Passion of Joan of Arc.*

Buster Keaton:
The D.W. Griffith of Comedy

Kevin Brownlow

The D.W. Griffith of Comedy

My devotion to Buster Keaton goes back more than thirty years, to the first showings of *The General* and *The Navigator* at London's National Film Theatre. When, by a series of unlikely circumstances, I found myself in Hollywood, in 1964, one of the first people I set out to see was Keaton.

I expected a star to live in one of those huge mock-Tudor or Castilian buildings in Beverly Hills. Confronted by a simple wooden bungalow in the San Fernando Valley, I thought I'd come to the wrong house. But you couldn't argue with the name: 'The Keatons'.

I expected Buster Keaton to be a morose, bitter man. I expected to find him sitting glumly in a corner, talking in monosyllables about the people who had ruined his career. I was prepared for a difficult encounter and was already making allowances for 'great artist ... hard life'. The reality could scarcely have been more different.

Mrs Keaton opened the door, and before I could enter, the gap was filled by a colossal St Bernard. Grinning, Mrs Keaton tried to keep the door open, drag the dog in and shake hands, all at once. From the next room came thundering hoofs and gunshots from a television set. 'Buster!' called Mrs Keaton. The noise stopped abruptly. 'The studio put Buster on standby today,' she explained. 'If I'd had some place to call you, I'd have cancelled the visit. But they aren't shooting today after all.'

Buster Keaton emerged from the next room. He was short and stocky, and he looked younger in actuality than the photographs one saw of him – and he laughed. That was the last thing I expected from the deadpan comedian. But several times during the interview, a suddenly-remembered incident would be accompanied by a spontaneous, infectious laugh. As for his voice, it sounded like a chain anchor going out.

The St Bernard – Elmer – nuzzled him hopefully. 'This dog sits on the couch to watch television,' he said. Aware that a demonstration was required, the dog trundled over to a couch, and heaved his back legs on to the seat, leaving his front paws on the ground. He then stared, deadpan, at the Keatons' Christmas tree, substituting that for the TV set. Keaton grinned. 'Come on,' he said. 'We can talk better next door.' The dog raced us inside, and, as I set up my tape recorder, it panted noisily into the microphone.

On a lower level than the rest of the house, the room was decorated with photographs, certificates and awards. A billiard table occupied one side;

Keaton's 'saloon' was on the other. It had swinging bar doors, and the best beer in town, but was only the size of a telephone kiosk. Two cowboy hats, one presented by the Cattlemen's Association of Fort Worth, Texas the other, from Oklahoma, hung in the far corner of the room, next to a fireman's hat, signifying that Keaton had been made a member of the Fire Department of Buffalo, New York. An Oscar stood on a table – 'to Buster Keaton for his unique talents which brought immortal comedies to the screen' – next to a 'George', one of the Eastman House awards, which Keaton seemed especially proud of. I was taken aback by the smiling photograph of Roscoe Arbuckle which dominated one wall – I was affected by the propaganda that still surrounded the Arbuckle case, and which made one think him guilty. An original lithograph of *The General* dominated the other. Underneath was a hilarious shot of three Busters sitting in the pose of the three wise monkeys. There was a still of his father, Joe Keaton, with the locomotive he drove in *Our Hospitality* and, surprisingly, one of Natalie Talmadge, Keaton's first wife, with their two children. A more recent photograph showed Buster Keaton with Harold Lloyd and Jacques Tati. A stunt cheque for $7.50 commemorated a stunt Keaton did for Lew Cody in 1928 for *Baby Cyclone*.

I have just listened again to the tape I recorded on this occasion, and while I am embarrassed by my wide-eyed naïveté, it did have the effect of engaging Keaton's interest. I got many of the standard answers – which have become familiar from other interviews – but I also got a lot that was fresh. He was full of enthusiasm and charm, and Eleanor chimed in occasionally with additional information. The most touching moment occurred when Mrs Keaton prompted him to tell a story about a lion on *Sherlock Junior*:

Keaton chuckled. 'I'm in the cage out at Universal, where they had all the animals at that time. It's a big round cage, about 60 to 80 feet in diameter, full of tropical foliage. With a whip and a chair and a gun, the trainer gets the two lions in position and I go to mine. My cameraman is outside the cage, shooting through a hole. The trainer says, "Don't run, don't make a fast move and don't go in a corner." Well, there is no corner in a round cage!' Buster laughed, pushed the table out of the way and began to demonstrate. It was a perfect recreation of the scene in *Sherlock Junior* with Keaton doing his wonderful walk across the room, whistling nonchalantly. I was so accustomed to seeing him in silent films that I was astonished to hear the whistle.

'I start to walk away from one lion – and lookit, there's another one, there! I got about this far and I glanced back and both of them were *that* far behind me, walking with me!' Keaton was helpless with laughter. 'And I don't know these lions personally, see. They're both strangers to me. Then the cameraman says, "We've got to do the shot again for the foreign negative." I said,

"Europe ain't gonna see this scene!" More laughter and Keaton returned to his seat.

'Years later, Will Rogers used that gag – Europe ain't gonna see this scene. We made a dupe negative out of *that* baby. I've worked with lions since, and some nice ones.'

At the end of the interview, I reluctantly took my leave. Keaton called out to Eleanor: 'Mademoiselle!'

'You didn't feed the girls,' she called back.

'Yeah, I did it a minute ago,' he said. 'I was about forty-five minutes feeding my chickens out in back,' he explained. 'And they were all standing at the gate like this.' And Keaton became a chicken, staring glumly at the sky and tapping his foot with impatience.

It was the only time I met Buster Keaton. He died just over a year later, in February 1966. I printed the interview in my first book, *The Parade's Gone By* (1968). In 1986, David Gill and I were able to make a three-part documentary for Thames Television which we called *Buster Keaton – A Hard Act to Follow*. Unlike our 1983 documentary *Unknown Chaplin*, which consisted of outtakes and home movies which had never been shown before, the Keaton film had little in the way of rushes or shots of Keaton at work. However, a generous collector from America, Harold Casselton, sent us a precious fragment – a little film of Buster at work on *The General* in Oregon. He had discovered it in an otherwise unrewarding roll of home movies, into which it had been spliced upside down. He had instantly recognized the locomotive, even the wrong way up.

We decided that the best way of handling *The General* was to go back to the location and try and find as many people as possible who had worked on it.

The epic scale of *The General* had been made possible by the success of Keaton's previous picture, *Battling Butler*. This had grossed nearly three-quarters of a million dollars (domestic) and it encouraged Keaton's mentor, Joe Schenck, to bring Keaton into United Artists, of which he was President and which had been founded by Chaplin, Mary Pickford, Douglas Fairbanks and D. W. Griffith.

We learned so much which we couldn't squeeze into the documentaries that I put it all into a book. At one time, I seriously considered a volume about the three greatest comedians – Chaplin, Keaton and Lloyd – but soon realized that however well they may work on their own, they don't fit together. Here, to help celebrate Keaton's centenary, is the chapter on the making of *The General*.

*

Keaton made his finest comedy, *The General*, in Oregon in the summer of 1926, and it was to Oregon that we flew precisely sixty years later. At Cottage Grove, near Eugene, we met a retired lumber mill proprietor called John Wilson who had worked on the original film. He drove us to the Culp Creek location, on the Row River, where the battle scenes had been filmed. Our

The Cottage Grove Sentinel.

researcher, Linda Phillips, arranged for half a dozen other veterans to be interviewed – all of them remembered the film as a high point of their lives.

John Wilson also dug out for us a full range of Cottage Grove and Eugene newspapers, which between them contained a remarkably full account of the making of *The General*. In California, we were able to interview the leading lady, Marion Mack, and a girl called Gene Woodward, who was being groomed for stardom with Keaton and who came out to the location to learn something about film-making.

We were able to put together the case history of one of Keaton's films in detail – fortunately, it proved to be Keaton's most important film. When Donald O'Connor, who starred in *The Buster Keaton Story* saw this picture, he pronounced Keaton 'the D. W. Griffith of comedy'.

When Keaton was growing up, the war between the States was the most recent dramatic event in the life of the nation. How often he must have listened to men, only slightly older than his father, tell stories of those remarkable days. And how often must he have gazed at the photographs by Matthew Brady which gave credence to those stories.

Before the making of *Battling Butler*, probably during *Go West*, Clyde Bruckman had drawn Keaton's attention to William Pittenger's account of the Andrews' Raiders. It described how in 1862 a group of nineteen Northern raiders hijacked a train – the General – in the hope of destroying track, burning bridges and cutting telegraph lines. Southern railroads were in so bad a state that trains were restricted to 18 mph. The pursuers, led by the heroic conductor, M. Z. L. Fuller , used three locomotives. One was facing the wrong way; Fuller drove it backwards. The chase became so desperate that they hit speeds of 60 mph. Pittenger describes it as like breaking the sound barrier – 'the iron wheels were rimmed with fire'. Far from crippling communication lines, the raiders achieved nothing. Every man was captured, several hanged. The survivors received the first Congressional Medals of Honor from President Lincoln.

Despite, or perhaps because of, their bungling, the raiders passed into legend along with the General, and little attention was paid to the heroic feats of Fuller. Keaton was fascinated by the story. Pittenger told it from the Northern point of view; Keaton switched it to the Southern. He avoided real characters; he played the Fuller role, but called himself Johnny Gray. Andrews he called Anderson, but he gave the role to an ex-soldier with a career almost as colourful as Andrews himself, Glen Cavender.

In 1926, the General locomotive was on display at Chattanooga's Union Station. It had last been used in a film in 1914 – a dramatic version of the same events – and Keaton enquired if he could use it again. The North Carolina and St Louis Railway (successor to the W A & P) agreed to co-operate and Keaton and Fred Gabourie travelled around the country, visiting

Keaton switched the story to the Southern point of view.

Chattanooga, Tennessee and Marietta, Georgia. They were not entirely impressed. The scenery lining the railroads lacked the splendour Keaton had envisaged. The railroads were too crowded and too modern.

Curiously enough, even though Keaton's name was synonymous with comedy, nobody imagined that he would fail to give the story the drama and gravity it deserved. However, when the news spread that he intended to make a comedy, descendants of the original participants protested and the railroad company withdrew its co-operation.

In interviews, Keaton always maintained that he needed narrow-gauge railroads and that was why he went to Oregon. For a railroad enthusiast to make such an error is odd – perhaps Keaton was muddling the trains in this film with that of *Our Hospitality*. For neither Civil War railroads nor the lumber lines in Oregon were narrow-gauge.

Keaton had sent his location manager, Bert Jackson, to look at Oregon, because the state was networked with railroads belonging to lumber companies. And Jackson sent a telegram saying that he had found exactly what was wanted. Not only did Oregon offer locomotives, track and rolling stock in profusion, it also had breathtaking scenery – it looked more like the Tennessee of the 1860s than Tennessee itself.

The advance guard of the company of sixty pulled into Cottage Grove, with eighteen carloads of equipment, on 28 May 1926. A wave of excitement swept through the town. Residents talked of Cottage Grove as a new Hollywood. And merchants dreamt of the huge sums of money that would be spent in the area. Two boys set up as bootleggers, and the barber hired extra help and installed new chairs – only to find everyone growing their hair to Civil War length.

The following day, Buster Keaton, his wife, Natalie, and their two sons arrived by car, as did other members of the company including Clyde

Cottage Grove, 1926: The company stayed at the Bartell Hotel.

A location at Cottage Grove.

Bruckman, due to help Keaton with the direction, and first cameraman J. Devereaux Jennings. Dev Jennings's background as a railroad man and civil engineer would prove valuable on this location.

Headquarters was established at the Bartell Hotel and it was here that leading lady Marion Mack[1] lived: 'Buster let everyone take their wives or husbands,' she said. 'I took my husband, Louis Lewyn, who was a producer. Buster took Natalie, and Mr Bruckman took his wife Lola with him. They were sort of cliquey. When I came on the scene, I didn't know them so they sort of gave me the brush, you know – a little air. Then all the wives and husbands got into arguments, and immediately I became the friend of everybody, so I had a real good time. The next time we went up – we went up twice – Buster didn't take any wives or husbands. He said, "No one gets to go." '

The first weekend was spent by Keaton, production manager Fred Gabourie, Jackson and business manager W. G. Gilmour, inspecting locations. The rest of the company picnicked by the Row River. On Monday 31 May – the Keatons' fifth wedding anniversary – construction began on the town of Marietta, Georgia.

Although Fred Gabourie was production manager on this film, there was no union demarcation. He was also art director, trouble shooter and Keaton's right-hand man. Because so many sets were needed, they had brought along a

1 Marion Mack died at the age of eighty-seven in May 1990.

construction man, Frank Barnes, who had put up sets for De Mille's *Ten Commandments* (1923) and had worked on *Go West*. He was twenty-eight, and handsome enough to be an actor, so Keaton cast him as Marion Mack's brother. Barnes and his crew built the town of Marietta using engravings in the Pittenger book as their only blueprints. The buildings were flats; when high winds toppled one, they just pushed it back into place.

The Oregon, Pacific and Eastern railroad was owned by the Anderson-Middleton Lumber Company, who were very helpful to the film. From them an old logging engine, Old Four-Spot, was purchased and taken to a locomotive works to be converted into the General. (It was a Cooke engine, like the original.) Another old locomotive became the Columbia, hauling a troop train. A third engine was brought in from the Mount Hood railroad – their original Number One. It bore the name-plate Yonah. By coincidence, a locomotive of the same name was used in the original chase. The Yonah was remodelled into the Texas, to be wrecked in the big scene. Passenger cars of Civil War vintage were built on flat cars. To both set constructors and locomotive builders alike, Keaton said there were to be no short cuts. 'It's got to be so authentic, it hurts.'

Shooting began on 8 June 1926 at Marietta. The editor of the Eugene *Guard* visited Cottage Grove and was enchanted by Keaton's people – 'The most courteous folk to be found anywhere. Even the most trivial of questions meets with a willing answer.'

Keaton's patience, even when townspeople wandered into shot, impressed the editor. Onlookers could stay all day, so long as they stayed behind the cameras and kept an eye on their shadows. During the long waits, Keaton often performed intricate juggling tricks to entertain the bystanders. His skill as a baseball player was quickly appreciated. The movie people organized 'Keaton's Hollywood Stars', and played local teams, to the delight of the neighbourhood boys.

'Anyone who thinks a movie star like Keaton lives a life of ease ought to see him out on a job,' reported the Cottage Grove *Sentinel*. 'Union hours don't go. He is either working on his picture, about his picture, thinking about something for the picture, directing what is to be done or out on a fishing trip or playing baseball. And the hours that go for Keaton go for the others. Keaton fishes and plays ball with the same energy that he puts into the making of a picture, and even when he is enjoying these diversions he appears to be planning some humorous situation or the correct setting for some part of his film.

'Although Keaton lives in a world of make-believe, he doesn't want that make-believe when outside that make-believe world. Someone suggested that he have his picture taken with a 14-inch trout that someone else had caught. "Nope, when my picture is taken with a 14-inch trout, I'll catch it myself."

'A movie star is a monarch in the world which is his company, especially when he is his own director, as is Keaton, who is a kindly monarch. As he

Keaton astride ...

under ...

alongside ...

and in front of ... The General.

Marion Mack with Keaton.

answered the reporter's questions, he gave directions for the ball game to start within a few minutes, directed the purchase of balls, gave an order for the entire company to be in the lobby by 7 o' clock the next morning, answered half a hundred questions by his production manager (Fred Gabourie) about this and that, described the making of a picture, visited briefly with a stranger who had known him in his childhood and gave the address at which other members of his family could be located, ordered his car, sent for members of his ball team, told the story of the present picture and a few other things, frequently smiling at something humorous, which was at variance with his immobile face when being filmed.'

Construction kept pace with the shooting. The Kingston depot was nearing completion, but the site for the bridge for the climactic crash had still not been decided upon. There was an excellent bridge across Culp Creek, owned by Anderson-Middleton, but for some curious reason the lumber company didn't want it wrecked. Above Wildwood, the Keaton company converted a deep cut in the main line into a convincing tunnel, using timber and black building paper. Fifteen hundred vehicles arrived to watch the filming and roads were blocked. But the scene was never used.

The scene where Marion Mack is pulled through a small opening in a box car was filmed from an automobile travelling on the highway alongside the

300

Keaton and Mack on the footplate of The General.

track. A road scraper had smoothed the surface and Westinghouse shock absorbers were fitted to the vehicle. Travelling shots were also achieved, as the home movie we used in the programme revealed, by running a camera train on a second track.

'To get to location, I had to get up at six in the morning,' said Marion Mack. 'We rode in the caboose, and Buster took his cook along, which was very good. I liked to eat. And we would have lunch on location. I had to be made up all ready for work, whether I worked or not. So then we wouldn't get back till after sundown, so it was kinda hard. Sometimes they'd take two or three hours to think about how it should be, and set up what they were going to make, so they weren't working every minute.

'Clyde Bruckman was the director, but Buster directed most of the scenes. Clyde would line up the shots, and the long shots and things like that. As far as directing me, I sort of directed myself. I mean, they tell you your scene, but none of the directors hardly ever act it for you. If you don't know how to act, then you shouldn't be there.

'The first scene I had in the picture, I was supposed to look over and see Buster, who hadn't enlisted, and I was kind of ashamed of him, and then I look at my brother. The way they gave you direction, they'd say, "Now you see Buster, and you're mad at him, so then you look at your brother and you're proud of him and you pat his medal, and you look back." They tell you that much and then you do it.

'Buster had two gag men, Al Boasberg and Charles Smith (who played the role of the father). In the evening they used to talk over the gags, and Buster would give his opinion. Buster was really good on thinking up these gags. We didn't have a regular shooting script but they made notes, you know, of what they were going to do. If they thought of something out on the set that would be funny, they would add to it.

'There was only one scene that I was responsible for, and that is the little scene where I pick up the little stick and I show it to Buster and he grabs me and kisses me. I wrote that gag. I didn't sit down and write it – I told them the gag and they did it.

'They made one scene with me that I didn't know they were going to make. It was a scene with a water tank and they didn't tell me that the water spout was aimed at me and that when the train stopped they would let me have it. So the scene you see in the movie, where the water knocks me down, that was quite a surprise. I was pretty mad about it – I had sort of a fiery temper, being Irish. I think Buster got a kick out of my reaction.'

The production was fraught with minor accidents. Assistant director Harry Barnes was accidentally shot in the face with a blank cartridge. His face was burned, but he carried on – he left his shirt-tails outside his trousers, he said, in case he had to leap out of his clothes again. The blast from the shell of Buster's railway cannon – a charge buried in the track and fired electrically by explosives man Jack Little – proved far too powerful and knocked the raiders off their feet. Keaton himself was knocked unconscious when he stood too close to the cannon as it fired.

Gene Woodward, a young actress who was being groomed for future Keaton productions, recalled that sparks from the engine caused havoc. 'Oh, the sparks! When Buster used the General on location, the sparks were flying. The farmers had their haystacks out along the tracks, ready to be picked up. The sparks would set off these haystacks. And so coming back, the crew was met by the farmers and they paid them $25 for each stack that caught fire. And that was a ritual. Going up they'd start the fire and coming back they had to pay for it.'

Keaton, Gabourie and Jackson searched western Oregon for a suitable bridge for the crash – to no avail. They began to consider the possibility of building their own trestle. In the story, the raiders set loose a boxcar, which rattles along in front of Buster. While he attends to something in his cab, the box car hits a tie and crashes over a bank. When Buster looks out again, the track is clear and he blinks in disbelief.

'The stunt called for quick action of the derailing switch, hidden from the camera, in order to make the wreck certain. The locomotive sped down the track not more than 20 feet behind the boxcar, and had the switch not been thrown at the right instant, the engine would have plunged over with the car. Those who were watching the stunt fully expected that very thing to happen, but it didn't.

'The first time the scene was tried, the engineer slowed up a bit just before he came to the switch. Buster was disgusted. The whole thing had to be done over again, with another freight car. They took the property car, and loaded the props on a flatcar. Now the two wrecked boxcars lie together in the gully.'

Crowds lined the river for an even more exciting scene: the locomotives racing through a burning covered bridge. In the film, the bridge is set on fire by the raiders. When it was shot, Keaton drove his General into the bridge, set the fire going and sped on his way.

'The Texas following him, found the bridge a veritable furnace. People who were watching gasped when the kerosene-soaked bridge became a solid mass of flames and no one expected the engineers (Jimmy Bryant and Al Handon) to really go through. They did, though, and came out safely the other side.

'Just as the locomotive cleared the bridge, one end was dropped. The props were pulled by the movie men. It gave the appearance of a natural collapse from the fire. It took fire fighters some time to quench the flames. Four hose lines were working full force from a pump on the river bed, and eventually the conflagration was checked.

'The two scenes were all that were filmed yesterday, but they were enough for any picture in a single day.'

The search for a suitable trestle proved fruitless, so the decision was made to erect a bridge at Culp Creek. The big factor that influenced the decision was the cost of moving equipment to a distant location. The level of the river was too low, so a dam had to be built, adding another hefty sum to the budget. A 400-yard spur had to be provided from the main line across the trestle.

George E. Potter, owner of the Culp Creek store, was engaged to cut the timber, and the Keaton company carpenters constructed the bridge. On 9 July 1926 more actors arrived from Hollywood, including Frederick Vroom, playing the Southern general, who was old enough to remember the Civil War; Mike Donlin (Northern major), one of the most popular of all baseball stars, who captained the New York Giants for years and was also a stage veteran; Edwin Foster (Captain of the supply train); another ballplayer, James Farley (Northern General) and Thomas Nawn (Lieutenant Colonel, Union army), who did a famous vaudeville Irish act.

Rumours spread that *The General* might cost as much as $1 million – an inconceivable amount for a comedy. The company had been in Oregon for six of the scheduled eight weeks – and six more were planned.

The covered bridge was rebuilt and burnt again for a retake. In the rushes of the first attempt, the walls burnt too rapidly. But now the engine followed the supply train too closely and collided with the rear cars. The collapsing section was supposed to fall on the engine, but it fell just after it went through. The bridge was to be rebuilt, the scene had to be retaken – adding thousands more to the already unwieldy budget.

Forest fires were now raging across the Umpqua forest reserve – fifty-five of them, one burning out of control near the old Bohemia mine, not far from Culp Creek. Some were caused by the wood-burning locomotives of the Keaton company, although whenever they realized they'd started one, they dropped everything, rushed back and put it out. The atmosphere was becoming smoky, which hampered photography.

The newspapers reported that Fred Lowry, employed as a brakeman on one of the Keaton trains, sued the company for $2,900 for an injured foot. The drawhead of a car buckled as he was trying to couple two cars together, and as he tried to scramble clear, a wheel went over his foot. He complained that in converting the trains to Civil War vintage, safety had not been taken into account. The papers reported no more, so presumably the amount was paid and added to the soaring budget.

Incredibly, it only took ten days to put up the trestle bridge. The bridge was 213 feet from bank to bank, the main span was 74 feet long, and it rose 34 feet above water level. The ground was cleared for 1,000 yards on the far side of the river, where a small mountain had been made of rock, timber and concrete. High on a scaffold was a platform made to resemble a bluff for cameras to capture a bird's-eye view of the battle.

At 2 p.m. on 22 July, a special train left from Corvallis and picked up the Eugene contingent. They were uniformed and equipped at Cottage Grove and, together with the Cottage Grove Coast Artillery Co., were taken to location. Several young men joined the National Guard for a two-week period just for the chance to work in the movie.

The Keaton company had arranged with the Southern Pacific to bring in sixteen sleeping cars to the Culp Creek siding. To these were added five carloads of cavalry and artillery horses. Powder man Jack Little, who had been in charge of battle effects for *The Big Parade,* had prepared 900 'shots'. These grenade-like objects could either be set off on the battlefield, via electric cable, or hurled into the air, to explode like shrapnel.

On Friday, the day scheduled for the big scene, Cottage Grove closed down. Many had left on Thursday night, camping at Culp Creek to make sure of a good view. During the morning, cars arrived from all over the state and special trains had been laid on. Between 3,000 and 4,000 people stood patiently in the hot sun, waiting. The crash through the trestle had been scheduled for 11 a.m., but again and again it was delayed. Keaton spoke his orders into a telephone with a loudspeaker attachment.

Cameras were positioned, and then Keaton changed his mind and they were set up elsewhere. The doomed locomotive made several runs across the bridge for the benefit of cameramen and those setting the explosives. It was not a simple shot; the flames on the bridge had to be the right height. The timbers at the base of the bridge had to be sawn through to precisely the right degree. The troops had to move forward at exactly the right moment ...

Of course, the inevitable happened. The locomotive pulled back to its start position, the supports were sawn, the fire was started – and two soldiers mistook a signal and charged into the water far too early. Luckily, the locomotive had not started, but the fire had to be put out and the whole thing was delayed. When the signal was finally given, some time after 3 p.m., the light was much better. Six cameras were in position. The engineer started the Texas then leapt from the footplate, leaving a dummy aboard.

Among the onlookers was Grace Matteson, whose father, a carpenter, had helped to build both Marietta and the trestle bridge: 'I was twelve and I had the measles at the time and I wasn't allowed out. But this was such a spectacular thing that my father said, "You can't miss it. It's just a one-shot deal." And so my mother decided to take me, spots and all. And I wasn't the only one with spots there, either. There was quite an epidemic going around.

'They had to use dynamite and there was an awful lot of apprehension about it. I can remember my father and some of them being afraid of using too much. They had to be sure, otherwise they would blow up the train instead of just the bridge going down. And they had to know that the saws had sawed through the logs enough to let it go down at the right time; I remember them going back and sawing it just a little bit more.

'We were all on edge, just not knowing when it was going to happen. Two women I remember sat with the camera crew knitting all the time, just waiting. There was quite a crowd there. Whole families were sitting on the rocks.

'There was a rumour that one of the engineers was offered a hundred dollars if he'd ride across, because they used a dummy in there – it had a white shirt as well, as I remember, and a vest and an engineer's cap. As the train went down, the people screamed – I suppose we all screamed, because it was such a tense moment, and one of the ladies fainted because this dummy leant forward and we all thought it looked like a real person in there. And when the train went down, it had a whistle on it, a very shrill whistle. Even after it went into the water this whistle kept going. It was a kind of mournful thing and everybody felt like something dreadful had happened.'

This shot had been budgeted at $5,000. A miniature might have cost $500. It proved to be the most expensive single shot of the entire silent era – $42,000. 'After the engine had taken its pretty spill,' said the Cottage Grove *Sentinel*, 'the taut nerves of those handling the production were greatly relieved and Buster himself was as happy as a kid.'

Actually, no one could afford to relax, for right on top of this stupendous

The exploding bridge ...

shot – enough of a climax for any ordinary picture – came the battle scene: troops wading into the river, cannon opening up from the opposite bank, shells bursting overhead, shattering trees and panicking the horses.

'It was very exciting,' said Keith Fennell, 'and a little bit alarming, because there were shells going off and they blew parts of trees to pieces and horses had riders on them that weren't the greatest riders in the world and some of them were falling off and, well, it was kind of scary as far as I was concerned, but it was very realistic.'

Another soldier of the Oregon National Guard – Ronald Gilstrap – was advancing down the hill. 'I happened to be a little bit in the rear, and they had put stakes out where they had bombs or explosives. I've forgotten how they designated who would die and who wouldn't, but somebody would fall by a stake and he'd look at the stake and he'd crawl like a devil to get away from it!'

The troops had been told, once they reached the river, that the water was wadeable.

'They said the water was only knee-deep, and hip-deep was the deepest,' said Harold Terry. 'I was the first one to step out into the water. Well, the water wasn't just knee-deep, it went clear over my head. They said it was 18 to 20 feet deep, the hole I stepped into. And I swam, oh, not quite halfway

... and the aftermath.

across. They said we'd have to pay for any part of our uniform that we lost. If we lost the rifle, it'd cost us $25 and that was pretty good size money in those days. And when I got into the water, I tried to hold my rifle out of the water with my left hand, and incidentally I had had my arm broke and it was weak and I dropped my rifle down between my legs and clamped my legs around it and I swam with both hands. And I swam right back out into the big hole and that's where I went down. And I went down three times.'

'I don't know how many of them almost drowned in there,' said Ronald Gilstrap. 'We kept pulling them out every ten minutes, I guess.'

'There was a pontoon bridge that was sunk under water,' said Ivan Currin, an officer in the National Guard. 'That's how about 90 per cent of the troops got across the river. But some fell off. I was standing near to this stunt man named Fisher. And all of a sudden I saw a man and his gun go down and I could see that he was in trouble. I turned to say something to Fisher – and Fisher wasn't there. He was already diving into the water, going after this man. I helped him bring him up on the rock and then we took him back over to the medics and they took him down to the field hospital. But they never stopped the battle.'

When Harold Terry came to, at the field hospital (a nearby house) he was being given the treatment for drowning. 'Something was holding my tongue out and I had a block of wood under my stomach and they was twisting each arm and leg. I suppose they was trying to pump the water out of me. Then they put me in a bed and they said, "Well, you know what the other side's like, 'cause you was there. You was drowned. We never expected to bring you out of it."'

The next day, Saturday 24 July, saw a continuation of the battle scenes. But early in the afternoon, word reached Keaton that a fire had broken out, and that one of his trains had started it. Keaton turned out his entire force of film crew and National Guardsmen, nearly 600 men. Cameras turned on the unusual sight of Confederate and Union troops fighting side by side. Lacking adequate fire-fighting equipment, many of the men had brought their blankets, and were beating the flames with those. Keaton told them to use their uniform jackets instead. He was not wearing a jacket, so to set a good example he took off his trousers and fought the flames in his BVDs.

'He was running around in long shorts with the back down,' said Keith Fennell. 'And he had a pitchfork and he was sneaking up on a little puff of smoke and putting it out. And of course everybody thought it was just hilarious.'

Natalie Talmadge served refreshments to the fire fighters, who planned to stay on guard all night. 'That evening,' said Harold Terry, 'Buster Keaton and his leading lady (Marion Mack) came in and she held my hand. They were really nice folks to talk to. Buster Keaton then told me about the fire and she had quite a laugh about it because he'd taken his trousers off and used them to fight the fire with. He must have wanted me to stay in the hospital. He said "Just you make this your home here for the rest of the time, 'cause you don't have to work any longer." He said I didn't have to worry about the outfit or the rifle. "No," I said, "I want to get back to the boys." I was only fifteen and I didn't want my parents to know so I gave the newspapers a different name.

'A boy was brought into the hospital and they said that he fell off a horse and he rolled over where one of these charges was and it went off and it just peppered him. And then he remembered the tree (marked for explosion) and the top of the tree blew off. And when he got up from there somebody was running with a rifle and they shot him in the back of the neck. Well, they got him into the hospital and he was a nervous wreck. It was just as though he'd been through a real war.'

The damage to uniforms from the fire-fighting was considerable, and it looked as if there might be a delay as fresh uniforms were sent up from Los Angeles. But the culmination of the battle was the northern retreat and so the company managed to disguise the damage, since everyone was on the move, shot from the rear and scorch marks after a battle wouldn't matter. The bill from the Western Costume Company, and the loss of a camera, put the cost of the fire up to $40,000 or $50,000.

By Sunday evening, Culp Creek was once more a deserted lumber camp. Keaton made the decision to repair part of the bridge so that he could shoot a scene to explain the presence of flames on the bridge. A few days later, the company went to the McKenzie River, where scenes of the raiders struggling in the rapids were filmed. This was to follow the scene of the dam being blown up by a stray shot from Keaton's cannon. For this, they returned to Culp Creek. Keaton was dismayed to find a pall of smoke from all the forest fires hanging over the area. When they set up to shoot the dam blowing up, the dam collapsed of its own accord. It did this twice. And when the cameras were turning, and the explosion went off, the crew were showered with rock. Yet the onrush of water was not powerful enough to sweep the soldiers off the rocks. Keaton decided he would have to shoot it at the beach at Santa Monica, with a breaker sweeping away the soldiers.

The McKenzie River scenes were dropped and a final gag was inserted to round off the battle, a gag shot at the Keaton studio against a painted backing. (The standard bearer falls; Buster grabs the flag and stands proudly with it on what he thinks is a rock, but turns out to be a crouching officer.)

Keaton made one last use of his National Guardsmen for the final scene in the picture. Earlier, rejected by his girl, Keaton's character had wandered back to his engine, and perched miserably on the coupling rods. It was a hazardous shot.

'I asked the engineer whether he could do it. He said: "There's only one danger. A fraction too much steam with these old fashioned engines and the wheel spins. And if it spins it will kill you right then and there." We tried it out four or five times, and in the end the engineer was satisfied that he could handle it. So we went ahead and did it. I wanted a fade-out laugh for that sequence; although it's not a big gag it's cute and funny enough to get me a nice laugh.'

Keaton was afraid to risk Marion Mack in the same way, otherwise he would have repeated the gag for the final shot. As it stands, Buster and Marion sit on the rods of the static locomotive. In his new officer's uniform, Buster looks dashing and romantic, but he has to salute the passing soldiers and this gets in the way of his kissing Marion. He tires of saluting with his left so he exchanges places with Marion and salutes mechanically with his right hand while his lips stay glued to Marion's.

The smoke from the forest fires was so thick that Keaton could no longer film at Culp Creek and some of the other locations were affected. It wouldn't be so bad for scenes after the battle, but it was hopeless for scenes before it. Waiting for the atmosphere to clear was too costly and so the decision was made to return to Hollywood. Studio scenes would be filmed until the smoke cleared. Business manager Gilmour would stay at Cottage Grove.

For a short while, it looked as though the fame of Cottage Grove as a production centre had caught on, for another movie company arrived. They behaved a trifle oddly, for none of them would associate with the Keaton people. Streets were graded, property rented and hotel rooms were booked – but it all turned out to be a stunt by prohibition agents to nail the two boys who had been selling liquor.

Keaton returned to Cottage Grove on 29 August 1926, as soon as he had been informed of the recent rains. A smaller company came up – and this time they left behind their wives – and were billeted once more at the Bartell Hotel.

Keaton shot the scene in which he and Marion Mack set the bridge alight on the repaired trestle. No long shots could be taken because, with the dam gone, the wrecked Texas was revealed, lying half out of the water on the bank.

Shooting took less than a fortnight, and then the sets were dismantled, the engines were sold to J. H. Chambers, a lumber man, who also planned to salvage the engine in the creek. This evidently proved too costly, for the locomotive remained there until 1941, when the demands of the war led to part of it being hauled out for scrap.

'There was a big party at the end,' said John Wilson. 'A celebration to finish it. They got out and just had like a Fourth of July. The only thing was they didn't shoot the fireworks in the air. They put 'em down in the streets and it was about a quarter of a mile to the end of the main street and these sky rockets

The General: a scene cut from the film (Snitz Edwards, Gene Woodward and Keaton).

310

would go clear to the church. They never set the church afire, but they'd go with a pretty bang when they hit the church at the end. We had just one policeman and he had quite a time keeping the party under control.'

The General was first shown on 31 December 1926 at two cinemas in Tokyo. When it opened in New York in February 1927 the reaction was distinctly cool. Louise Brooks, a friend and admirer of Keaton, offered a possible reason: 'It was the title, The General. We thought Buster was playing a general, a Southern general. Not funny. The Civil War killed thousands of Americans fighting against their own families, almost wrecking our country. Nobody connected The General with the name of the engine. Many people stayed away. Those who saw The General were puzzled.'

Variety was savage. It reported that the Capitol, where Flesh and the Devil had done four weeks of record-breaking business, 'looks as though it were virtually going to starve to death this week'. Audiences were low in the first three days, for the simple reason that The General was far from funny. 'You cannot continue a chase for an hour and expect results. Especially when the action is in the hands of its star. It was his story, he directed, and he acted. The result is a flop.'

Variety acknowledged some corking gags, but 'there isn't a single bit in the picture that brings a real howl. There is a succession of mild titters and that's about all ... The General is a weak entry for the deluxe houses.'

Mordaunt Hall of the New York Times thought that Keaton had bitten off more than he could chew. 'This is by no means as good as Mr Keaton's previous efforts.' Picture Play called it 'a long dull comedy'. An admirer of Keaton's, Robert Sherwood, complained in Life of the 'vaulting ambition' of Keaton in trying to enter the epic class. 'That he fails to get across is due to the scantiness of his material as compared with the length of his film. He has also displayed woefully bad judgement in deciding just where and when to stop.' He objected to the sight of men being killed in action. 'Many of the gags at the end of the picture are in such gruesomely bad taste that the sympathetic spectator is inclined to look the other way.'

Schenck rounded up his top stars and gave the Los Angeles première, on 11 March 1927, the full Hollywood treatment with Klieg lights and sun arcs. Keaton's sisters-in-law, Norma and Constance Talmadge, attended with John Barrymore and Estelle Taylor.

The picture did not do well partly because United Artists had a less efficient distribution network than Metro. The film grossed only $474,264 in the USA – over $300,000 less than Battling Butler and not enough to cover its costs ($415,232).

Part of the problem lay with the projection. The General was cranked close to the speed of sound. At David Gill's and my revival at the London Palladium, we ran it at 24 fps, and it looked perfect, except for the shots of troops hurrying into battle. There is an absurd claim that it was shown at 32 fps. Undoubtedly, some of the theatres ran it too slow. (Some film societies today run it at 16 fps.) Reviewers seeing it cold, at the wrong speed, with no music, would be unlikely to review it well. The critic of the Brooklyn *Daily Eagle*, a perceptive writer called Martin Dickstein, thought it a work of genius. But his paper didn't sell tickets across the nation, unlike *Photoplay* or the other fan magazines. And even he felt Keaton had perhaps made a financial *faux pas*.

He certainly had. Joseph Schenck, himself reeling from a whole series of failures, insisted that Keaton have a proper director on his next picture, and a new business manager. W. G. Gilmour was replaced by publicity man Harry Brand. Furthermore, Schenck required that Keaton's next picture be simpler and more commercial.

Seventy years later, *The General* has been accepted as one of the greatest of all film comedies. In Ten Best polls, even when few other silent films are mentioned, *The General* invariably appears high on the list. For our staging of the 'live cinema' presentation at the London Palladium, with a new score by Carl Davis, we were privileged to be able to show a print made direct from the camera negative. The reaction was ecstatic.

Terrible things have been done to *The General*. It has been chopped down to four reels and reissued with sound effects, it has been transferred to video at 16 fps instead of the 24 fps stipulated by Keaton, because the video people thought it 'looked' better[1] – but seen in anything approaching its original state, it succeeds triumphantly.

Keaton chose *The General* to launch his revival, which was masterminded by Raymond Rohauer. Keaton felt that if the public was going to accept him at all, they would accept him in that film. 'The opening night,' said Rohauer, 'was in Munich in 1962. I was there, Buster was there with his wife Eleanor and we stood in front of the theatre, and on the marquee was "'Buster Keaton in *Der General*". We could hear the laughter of the people out in the street and Buster said, "What are they laughing at?" I said, "Your picture." He couldn't believe it. I said, "Did you ever believe that you would see your name on a marquee as a star again?" "No," he said. "I never thought it would happen." '

1 The Connoisseur video edition of *The General* was made from the same print we showed at the Palladium, with the Carl Davis score. Connoisseur also have our documentary, *Buster Keaton – A Hard Act to Follow*, which contains many of the interviews quoted in this account.